PRAISE FOR *RED PLATOON*

'I read the first half of *Red Platoon* in one sitting and that night had such intense combat dreams that I actually thought twice about picking the book up again. In addition to being a superb soldier, Romesha is an utterly irresistible writer. I'm completely overwhelmed by what he has done with this book. The assault on Camp Keating is a vitally important story that needs to be understood by the public, and I cannot imagine an account that does it better justice that Romesha's'. – Sebastian Junger

'Rendered hour-by-hour and sometimes second by second, here is battle narrative the way it's supposed to be written. Gritty, plangent, and unflinching, *Red Platoon* is sure to become a classic of the genre. Through his courageous and no doubt painful act of remembrance, Romesha has done his comrades, indeed all of us, a great service – leaving an epitaph that will live through the ages.' – Hampton Sides, author of *Ghost Soldiers* and *In the Kingdom of Ice*

Red Platoon is riveting. Like many who were in either Iraq, Afghanistan, or both, I often read books about the wars reluctantly, because it is hard to capture the essence of the experience. In my view *Red Platoon* is a brilliant book. Had Clint Romesha depicted the soldiers at Keating as a collection of steely-eyed warriors, their feat would have been impressive. Because he captures the reality of a collection of personalities as diverse as America itself, their courage is truly inspiring. – General Stanley McChrystal, U.S. Army, Retired

Red Platoon celebrates the most crucial aspect of military operations: the team. Clinton Romesha and the men of Black Knight Troop faced harrowing conditions and a determined enemy during the Battle for COP Keating, and in the process discovered exactly who they are. This account is an important tribute to everyone who fought, and especially to the eight Americans who on that day made the ultimate sacrifice for their country. – Mark Owen, author of *No Easy Day*

A visceral, heart-pounding account of men in close-quarter combat that is simply impossible to put down. Astonishingly intimate and beautifully written. A word of advice: don't start this book if you're planning on doing anything else for the next few hours. – Scott Anderson, author of *Lawrence in Arabia*

The men of Red Platoon and their actions at COP Keating deserve to be known. Clint Romesha's story takes hold from page one and makes you feel every ⬛⬛⬛⬛⬛⬛⬛⬛⬛⬛⬛ that will stick with ⬛⬛⬛⬛⬛⬛⬛⬛⬛⬛⬛ Afghan war. – Kev

D0273760

RED PLATOON

12 Hours in Hell.

The True Story of a Heroic Last Stand

★ ★ ★

CLINTON ROMESHA

MEDAL OF HONOR RECIPIENT

arrow books

1 3 5 7 9 10 8 6 4 2

Arrow Books
20 Vauxhall Bridge Road
London SW1V 2SA

Arrow Books is part of the Penguin Random House group of companies
whose addresses can be found at global.penguinrandomhouse.com.

Penguin
Random House
UK

First published in Great Britain by Preface Publishing in 2016
First published in paperback by Arrow Books in 2016

www.penguin.co.uk

A CIP catalogue record for this book is available from the British Library.

ISBN 9781784751814

Book design by Amy Hill

Map © 2016 by David Cain

Printed and bound by Clays Ltd, St Ives Plc

Penguin Random House is committed to a sustainable future
for our business, our readers and our planet. This book is made
from Forest Stewardship Council® certified paper.

MIX
Paper from
responsible sources
FSC® C018179

To my fallen comrades and their families,
and to all of the soldiers of 3-61
who served with us in Afghanistan

Of comfort no man speak:
Let's talk of graves, of worms, and epitaphs

—Shakespeare, *Richard II*

RED PLATOON

1st Platoon

B Troop 3-61 Cavalry,
4th Brigade Combat Team,
4th Infantry Division

Alpha Section

1st Lt. Andrew Bundermann
Staff Sgt. Clinton Romesha

Sgt. Joshua Hardt
Sgt. Bradley Larson

Spc. Nicholas Davidson
Spc. Justin Gregory
Spc. Zachary Koppes
Spc. Timothy Kuegler

Pfc. Josh Dannelley

Bravo Section

Sgt. 1st Cl. Frank Guerrero
Staff Sgt. James Stanley

Sgt. Justin Gallegos
Sgt. Joshua Kirk

Spc. Kyle Knight
Spc. Stephan Mace
Spc. Thomas Rasmussen
Spc. Ryan Willson

Pfc. Christopher Jones

Attachments

Sgt. Armando Avalos Jr., forward observer
Spc. Allen Cutcher, medic

BLACK KNIGHT TROOP

COP KEATING

HQ Platoon

Cpt. Stoney Portis
1st Sgt. Ron Burton

Red Platoon

1st Lt. Andrew Bundermann
Sgt. 1st Cl. Frank Guerrero

White Platoon

1st Lt. Jordan Bellamy
Sgt. 1st Cl. Jeff Jacops

Blue Platoon

1st Lt. Ben Salentine
Sgt. 1st Cl. Jonathan Hill

★ ★ ★

INTERNATIONAL SECURITY ASSISTANCE FORCE (ISAF)

AFGHANISTAN
May–October 2009

Bagram Airfield, Kabul

Gen. Stanley McChrystal, Commander, ISAF
Gen. David McKiernan, Commander, ISAF

FOB Fenty, Jalalabad Airfield, Nangarhar Province

Col. Randy George, Commander, 4th Brigade Combat Team

FOB Bostick, Kunar Province

Lt. Col. Robert Brown, Squadron Commander, 3-61 Cavalry

COP Keating, Nuristan Province

Cpt. Melvin Porter, Commander (outgoing), Black Knight Troop
Cpt. Stoney Portis, Commander (incoming), Black Knight Troop
Lt. Robert Hull, Executive Officer, Black Knight Troop

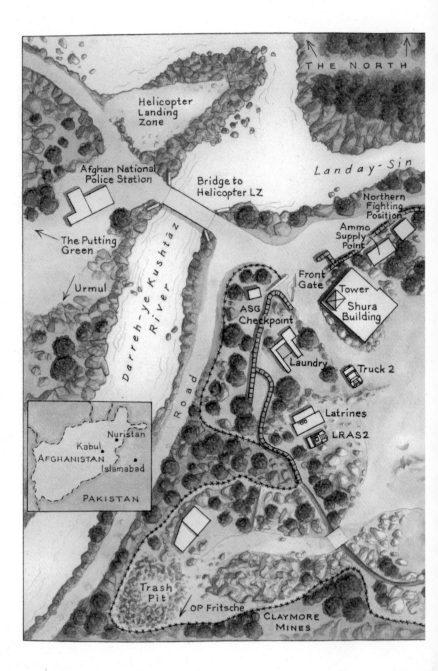

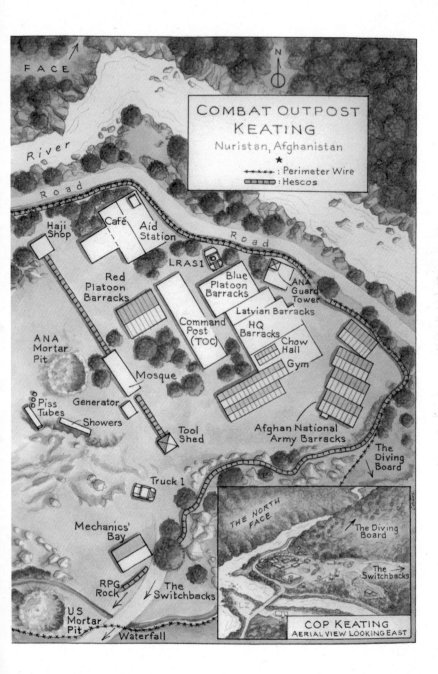

CONTENTS

RED PLATOON

It Doesn't Get Better

5:45 a.m., Red Platoon barracks
Combat Outpost Keating
Nuristan Province, Afghanistan

ZACH KOPPES lay in his bunk, half-awake with an ear tuned to the radio in the next hooch, a few feet down the hallway. In the predawn darkness, he was anticipating "the call," the deeply unwelcome summons that usually arrived just a few minutes before he was slated to pull early-morning guard duty.

Sure enough, like clockwork, there it was:

"Hey, uh . . . could somebody tell my relief to get on out here?" came the static-charged voice over the combat network. "I *really* need to take a shit."

Koppes sighed.

Every morning, it was the same deal. Josh Hardt, one of Red Platoon's four team leaders—and therefore a man who outranked Koppes by a full grade and nearly five years of service—could never quite make it to the end of his early-morning shift without needing to ease the volcanic surge in his bowels. Hence the request, which was really more of an order, for whoever was relieving him to get up early and hoof it out to the armored Humvee known as LRAS1 on the eastern side of the outpost so that Hardt could make a dash for the latrines, which lay a hundred yards to the west.

1

Somehow, it seemed to Koppes, it was invariably him and never anyone else who was on the receiving end of that call. But as he reminded himself while he levered out of his bunk and threw on his kit, this day was different for a number of important reasons, one of which was lying right there on the bed beside him.

When he finished with his gear, he reached over and grabbed the newly arrived magazine that he was planning to read from the turret of the Humvee, rolled it up as tightly as possible, and prepared to shove the thing into a place where nobody would spot it.

Needless to say, a dude couldn't just cruise out to the guard post swinging a magazine in his fist. That was the kind of infraction that would win you a full-on ass-chewing from our first sergeant, Ron Burton, who was a raging stickler when it came to even the smallest rules. But Koppes had a little hidey-hole, which he called his "go-to zone," in his body armor, the ceramic plates we wore to protect our necks and torsos.

We hated those plates for their weight and for how hot they were, even though they had a couple of advantages—the chief one being their ability to prevent an AK-47 bullet from turning the contents of your chest into wet dog food. But in addition to that, right there in the front of the armor was a small pocket of dead space into which, Koppes had discovered, you could stuff a magazine to see you through to the end of your guard-duty shift.

This system had worked well enough that during our five months in-country, Koppes had taken to semiregularly bringing old *Playboy*s with him when he went out to the Humvee. His buddy Chris Jones had a respectable stash that his older brother had been sending him in care packages. They featured women like Carmen Electra and Bo Derek and Madonna, which Jones and some of the other lower-ranking enlisted guys, after much discussion, had agreed offered up some compelling evidence that centerfold chicks from the unimaginably distant era of the 1980s were actually kind of hot.

On the morning of October 3, though, Koppes had something even better than vintage soft-core porn riding under his armor. The previous afternoon one of the Chinooks had made a supply drop-off, and by some miracle, we'd actually gotten our mail. Included was an almost-current issue of *SportsPro* with Peyton Manning on the cover, which offered a comprehensive rundown of the top one hundred NFL players for the 2009 fall season.

True, we were nearly seven thousand miles from the nearest sports bar. And yes, we'd be stuck here long past the end of the play-offs and the Super Bowl. But Koppes knew, like the rest of us did, that when he was finally allowed to go home he might be making that trip inside a metal coffin draped with an American flag. So the prospect of paging through the player stats and the team rankings, and thereby permitting his mind to travel far beyond the black walls of the Hindu Kush, which framed our world and restricted our movements and offered a perfect vantage for our enemies to smoke us—the mere idea of making an imaginary trip like that, no matter how brief—was enough to put him in an exceptionally positive frame of mind. Which is why, as he jammed the magazine inside his vest and trundled out to the Humvee—a journey of no more than fifty steps—Koppes muttered a phrase that we all liked to invoke in such moments. A mantra whose succinctness and sagacity summed up the many double-bladed paradoxes that dominated the thoughts of every American soldier who found himself stuck inside the most remote, precarious, and tactically screwed combat outpost in all of Afghanistan.

It doesn't get better.

UP IN THE RAFTERS of our platoon's plywood barracks just three cubicles down from Koppes's bunk, there was a plank on which one of the previous tenants, a soldier who was part of the unit that had been deployed here before we arrived, had scrawled a little message to himself, a reminder about how life worked in Afghanistan.

Me and the rest of the guys in Red liked what was written on that board so much that by the end of our first week on station, we had adopted the thing as our informal motto. It epitomized precisely how we felt about having been shoved up the wrong end of a country so absurdly remote, so rabidly inhospitable to our presence, that some of the generals and politicians who were responsible for having stuck us there were referring to the place as the dark side of the moon.

Those words were so cogent that whenever something went off the rails—whenever we learned, say, that we were heading into yet another week without any hot chow because the generator had taken another RPG hit, or that last month's stateside mail still hadn't been delivered because the Chinook pilots were refusing to risk the enemy's guns for anything but the most critical supplies—whenever news arrived of the latest thing to go wrong, we'd give one another a little half-joking smile, cock an eyebrow, and repeat:

"It doesn't get better."

To us, that phrase nailed one of the essential truths, maybe even *the* essential truth, about being stuck at an outpost whose strategic and tactical vulnerabilities were so glaringly obvious to every soldier who had ever set foot in that place that the name itself—*Keating*—had become a kind of backhanded joke. A byword for the army's peculiar flair for stacking the odds against itself in a way that was almost guaranteed to blow up in some spectacular fashion, and then refusing to walk away from the table.

We took Keating's flaws in stride, of course, because as soldiers we had no business asking questions so far above our pay grade—much less harboring opinions about the bigger picture: why we were there, and what we were supposed to be accomplishing. Our main job had a stark and binary simplicity to it: keep one another alive, and keep the enemy on the other side of the wire. But every now and then, one of my guys would find himself unable to resist the urge to ponder the larger mission and to ask what in God's name the point was of holding down a firebase that so flagrantly violated the most basic and timeless principles of warfare.

Typically enough, the sharpest and most defiant response to those queries would come from Josh Kirk, one of the other sergeants and probably the biggest badass in the entire platoon. Kirk had grown up on a remote homestead in rural Idaho not far from Ruby Ridge, and he never backed down from any kind of confrontation, no matter how big or how small it might be.

4

"You wanna know why we're here?" he'd asked us one evening as he was peeling back the plastic wrapping on his chow ration—a veggie omelet MRE, which was everyone's least favorite item on the menu, because it looked like a brick fashioned from compressed vomit.

"Our mission at Keating," he declared, "is to turn these MREs into shit."

The real beauty of *It doesn't get better*, however, was that it had a two-sided quality that enabled it to work like a coin. On its face, the phrase not only expressed but somehow managed to celebrate what Kirk was getting at, which was that Keating's awfulness was both magnified and under-scored by its pointlessness and futility—and that to a man who was pre-pared to adopt the necessary frame of mind, being stuck in such a place could instill a perverse but ferocious kind of pride.

On the other hand, if you took that phrase and flipped it around in your mind, you'd see that it could mean something completely different, and that this new meaning hinged on the fierce sense of purpose that young men sometimes embrace—especially young men who are permitted to carry extremely heavy weaponry—when they find themselves drop-kicked into a situation that is totally and incurably fucked up.

The main reason why life wouldn't get any better at Keating, of course, was that it was so irremediably impossible to begin with. But in one of those odd little twists—the kind of irony that only a group of guys who pull time in a frontline infantry unit can truly appreciate—we were con-vinced that we would all look back on our tour there, assuming we man-aged to survive the damn thing, as one of the most memorable times of our lives.

It stood as a point of considerable irritation among my guys that in Red Platoon, First Sergeant Burton, the highest-ranking enlisted man in our troop at Keating, wasn't willing to try to wrap his head around any of this. Burton, who was a big admirer of formal military protocols that tend to work in a stateside garrison but make absolutely no sense in a free-fire zone, decided that our little slogan was an expression of "poor morale." So whenever he heard one of us repeating those words, he'd make a point of going up to that guy and telling him to shut the hell up.

Inside Red Platoon barracks

What Burton never understood, however, was that it was categorically impossible to lay down a decree like that in a place like Keating. By the end of our first week on station, the outpost had already implanted *It doesn't get better* deep within us, down in the dark, fertile layers of the mind where words take root and then sprout into conviction and belief. Weeding it out of us would have been like trying to weed the Taliban from the slopes and ridgelines that ringed every side of the outpost. And that would have been like trying to yank up every thornbush and poisonous little flower that had anchored itself to the flanks of the Hindu Kush.

As far as we were concerned, Keating not only wouldn't get better, it *couldn't* get better, because we were already doing our damnedest to make it, by sheer force of will, into the best thing going.

That was something we all grooved on, and a good example of how it worked was exactly what Koppes was doing as he strolled out to the gun truck with his magazine to relieve Hardt.

THE ARMORED HUMVEE where Koppes was headed was one of five such vehicles positioned along the perimeter of the outpost that served as part of our primary defense. It featured a steel turret mounted directly above the cab that was armed with a Mark 19, which is basically a machine gun that shoots 40-mm grenades instead of bullets. When fully engaged, the gun is capable of pumping out almost three hundred rounds per minute, an astonishing level of firepower. In less than three minutes, a Mark 19 is supposed to be capable of reducing a two-story building to a pile of rubble.

Koppes had never actually witnessed such a thing with his own eyes. But that little factoid afforded a certain measure comfort each time he clambered into the Humvee and was forced to ponder the truck's many glaring vulnerabilities, starting with the fact that when he hunkered down behind the Mark 19, his legs, arms, and torso were shielded, but his head and shoulders were totally exposed. Equally disconcerting, the turret rotated along an arc of only 110 degrees, which made it impossible for him to return fire at anyone who was trying to shoot him in the back.

Like almost everything else at Keating, this was decidedly not ideal, which was why we'd been planning to replace the gun truck with a properly reinforced guard tower. But those plans had recently been put on hold when we'd been told to prepare to dismantle the outpost, pack it up, and get the hell out of this part of Nuristan. That operation was actually scheduled to start within seventy-two hours, although most of the lower enlisted guys at Koppes's level hadn't been told about this yet.

By the time Koppes reached the side of the truck, Hardt had already climbed down from the turret with the aim of getting over to the latrines as quickly as possible. He paused just long enough to update Koppes on the latest intel.

According to the small network of Afghan informants who were supposed to keep Keating's officers abreast of any developments in the surrounding area, a group of Taliban had been mustering in the village of Urmul, a tiny hamlet that lay less than a hundred yards to the west of the outpost on the far side of the Darreh-ye Kushtāz River.

This hardly qualified as news. Since our arrival four months earlier, it seemed as if we'd received a warning along these lines every three or four days. Each time, the pattern was the same. The report would state that fifty or seventy-five enemy fighters were massing for a major attack. But when the attack finally arrived, it would turn out to involve four or five insurgents—or even more frequently, just one or two gunmen. Eventually, we'd started taking these warnings with a grain of salt.

Which is not to say that we didn't expect to get nailed. Throughout the summer and into the fall, we'd been getting hit, on average, at least four times a week. But for the men on guard duty, word of a massive impending assault was no longer capable of setting off alarm bells. And so when Hardt passed along the report, Koppes simply nodded and settled himself into the turret while concentrating on more immediate matters.

For a soldier of Koppes's rank and stature, the pleasures afforded by life at Keating were few and far between, so it was vital to savor any diversion, regardless of how small it might be. The new issue of *SportsPro* certainly qualified as one of those. Indeed, the magazine all by itself would have been more than enough to make Koppes's entire morning. But there was an added bonus, because today was Saturday, which meant that every one of the fifty American soldiers at Keating was scheduled to get not one but two hot meals, an event whose importance was almost impossible to overstate.

Ever since we first arrived at the outpost, we'd been receiving about one hot meal a *week*, and surviving for the rest of the time on MREs, liberally supplemented by Pop-Tarts and chocolate pudding that was so long past its expiration date it made you wonder if maybe the army wasn't trying to give the Taliban an assist.

Under these circumstances, two hot meals in the same day was almost beyond Koppes's ability to imagine, especially considering that breakfast was supposed to be eggs and grits. What's more, if Thomas, our cook, was in a generous mood, maybe there would be some bacon too. But even that wasn't the whole story.

The best thing about all of this, in Koppes's mind, was that if you were on guard duty when Thomas started slinging breakfast at the chow hall, the guy you had just relieved was required to go up there and get your food, then bring it out to the truck and actually *serve* the stuff to you.

To Koppes—whose name, fittingly, was pronounced just like the word "copacetic"—the confluence of these events was like the greatest thing on earth. He not only had his top-100-football-players magazine, but a hot breakfast was about to be hand-delivered as if he'd pulled the Humvee into a Sonic drive-in.

It was true, of course, that this grub would be forked over by a guy who had just taken his morning dump. But did that matter? To a man like Koppes—a man who, thanks in part to the motto we all had adopted, was able to embrace the brighter side of pretty much anything, no matter how shitty it might be—the answer was an emphatic *no*, this did not matter one bit.

You know what, Hardt? he told himself as he got behind the Mark 19 and his sergeant dashed off toward the latrines. *You head on up to the shitter and do your thing.*

Everything here is absolutely cool.

AS KOPPES WAS SETTLING into position on the guard truck, another soldier, a private by the name of Stephan Mace, was counting down the final minutes of his own four-hour guard shift in one of our other gun trucks, which was positioned on the opposite end of camp, about 120 yards to the west. Known as LRAS2, that Humvee was the most remote and exposed guard position on the entire outpost. It sat just forty yards from the Darreh-ye Kushtāz River and faced directly toward the cluster of some three dozen mud-walled buildings that comprised the village of Urmul.

Mace, who was Koppes's best friend, was waiting to be relieved by a sergeant named Brad Larson, who happened to be *my* best friend. And just like Koppes and Hardt, Mace and Larson had a little ritual that they enacted on most mornings when they were trading off guard duty.

Although Mace was one of the lowest-ranking soldiers at Keating, he was also one of the most entertaining characters inside the wire. Armed with razor-sharp wits and a wickedly inappropriate sense of humor, he

9

generated a continuous stream of off-the-cuff jokes and smart-aleck remarks that could always take your mind off the surrounding miseries, even if it was just for a second or two. In short, Mace was the kind of guy who everybody enjoyed having around, and a measure of that enjoyment was that even Larson—a laconic and self-contained Nebraskan who rarely had more than two words to share with anyone, including me—would *voluntarily* get up a few minutes early and trundle out to the guard position just so that he could sit in the front seat of the Humvee and listen to Mace's bullshit.

What those two guys talked about spanned a wide spectrum. It could run the gamut, from heated debates about which animal you'd most want to shoot during a big-game hunting safari in Africa to minutely detailed descriptions of hot teachers they'd had back in grade school. But the substance of their conversations probably mattered less than the fact that they liked each other's company enough that sometimes they'd simply sit in the cab of the gun truck, staring out the windshield in silence while Mace pulled on one of his Marlboro Lights and Larson took a dip from his can of chewing tobacco.

On this particular morning, however, they'd skipped over their usual routine because Larson had some business to take care of first. Instead of climbing directly into the Humvee, he strode past the driver's door toward the front of the truck, set his helmet and his gun on the hood, then spread his legs, unzipped his fly, and stood there, bareheaded and facing west, taking a long and much-needed wake-up piss.

Technically speaking, Larson should have taken care of this back at the piss tubes, the row of four-inch-diameter pipes made of PVC that were sunk more than three feet into the ground just outside our shower trailer. The path out to the gun truck had taken him right by them, and normally he would have stopped there. But the tubes reeked worse than almost anything else in camp, and for whatever reason he'd decided that the odor of stale urine wasn't something he was keen to inhale just then.

Meanwhile, when Mace saw what Larson was up to, he climbed down from the gun truck and headed east across the outpost toward the barracks building, where the rest of our platoon was still fast asleep in our bunks.

It was 5:50 a.m. and dawn had just broken as Larson went about his business while staring up at the scene before him. The first rays of the morning sun were painting the mud walls of Urmul with a golden pinkish light, and his gaze was pulled toward the tallest structure in the village, which was its mosque.

Unlike the *masjids* that graced the larger and more prosperous towns and cities of Afghanistan, Urmul's mosque boasted neither a delicately tapered spire nor an onion-shaped dome. It was a square-sided tower, coarse and humble, that reflected not only the harshness and the austerity but also the humbleness of this impossibly distant and cut-off corner of Afghanistan.

Closer at hand, Larson could see the river, frothy and bright as it churned beneath the single-span concrete bridge leading out to the small island that doubled as a landing zone for the massive, anvil-shaped Chinooks that served as Keating's lifeline to the outside world, ferrying in everything from diesel fuel and ammunition to crates of Dr Pepper and plastic bottles filled with drinking water.

On the far side of that river, a dense green wall of vegetation concealed the monkeys, the birds, and the other wild creatures that populated the sides of the impossibly narrow valley in which Keating was nestled. And soaring above all of that, Larson could see the features that dominated and defined our lives in that place, which were the mountains.

Their cliffs rose up out of the river valley, straight-sided and steep, and high above those cliffs and far in the distance, he could see the snow-covered peaks that were now glittering with the orange tint of dawn against the backdrop of a sky that had taken on the deep and impenetrable color of cobalt.

In another place, at another time, a view like the one laid out before Larson would have been nothing short of glorious. But here you could never allow a thing like glory to seduce you into forgetting that we were at war and that the men we'd been sent here to fight, the soldiers whose deepest desire was to kill as many of us as possible, lay concealed within that beauty.

• • •

LOOKING BACK on that moment now, I've tried to imagine the scene from the perspective of the three hundred Taliban fighters who had moved into position overnight, forced the civilians in the area to leave their homes, set up firing positions in the buildings and across the hillsides along all four cardinal points of the compass, and who were now counting down the final seconds to launching a coordinated attack on us from all sides with RPGs, mortars, machine guns, small arms, and recoilless rifle fire.

The force they'd assembled outnumbered us by six to one, and the onslaught they were about to unleash would qualify as the largest, fiercest, and most sophisticated assault ever seen in the portion of Afghanistan that US high command referred to as Sector East.

As impressive as all of that may sound, however, what is perhaps even more remarkable is the depth of our collective ignorance in that instant.

Brad Larson had no clue, as he stood there with his dingus on display, absentmindedly registering the sound of splashing in the dirt just beyond the toes of his boots, that his head was framed in the crosshairs of at least ten snipers, each armed with a Russian Dragunov rifle and intent on putting a 7.62 cartridge through the front of his face.

Zach Koppes had no idea that there would be no delivery of a hot breakfast, that his magazine would never be opened, and that within seconds he would be cut off inside his Humvee and squaring up against dozens of insurgents while more than three dozen Afghan Army soldiers who were supposed to be our allies and partners abandoned their positions and fled, allowing Keating's eastern defensive perimeter to completely collapse.

Josh Hardt didn't have the faintest notion that within the hour, those insurgents would breach our wire, seize our ammunition depot, set fire to most of our buildings, and eventually be pointing an RPG at him with the aim of blowing his brains through the back of his head.

As for me, as those final seconds ticked down before the Taliban's hellfire was unleashed, I was racked out in my bunk, fast asleep and oblivious to the fact that within thirty minutes everyone inside our besieged outpost who was still alive would be falling back into what would later be called "the Alamo position" and preparing to make a final stand in the only two buildings that weren't on fire, while ten of our comrades were stranded outside the line.

Which brings me back to our little motto, the phrase that sustained us: *It doesn't get better.*

There were fifty Americans inside the wire at Keating that morning, including the men who were part of Red Platoon. Partly thanks to those words, we not only understood but also accepted, with total clarity, just how bad things were: how untenable our lines were, how impossible it would be to effectively defend our perimeter, how far we were from the nearest help. But in reality, not a single one of us had the faintest inkling of the sheer fury that was about to rain down on our heads.

WHAT FOLLOWS is not the story of one man, but of an entire platoon. It is a story that has the hair and the dirt still clinging to it: a saga whose characters, in ways both large and small, are less heroic than one might wish and yet far more human than the citations to the medals that this battle yielded might suggest.

The men of Red Platoon were no pack of choirboys. Nor were we the sort of iron-willed, steely-eyed superheroes who seem to populate so many of the narratives that have emerged during the last decade of war. We were quite unlike the squadron of special forces hard men who had ridden across the plains of northern Afghanistan on horseback to capture the city of Mazar-i-Sharif in the weeks following 9/11. And we had almost nothing in common with the four-man team of American spec-ops assassins whose ordeal in the summer of 2005, just a few miles south of Keating, would later be chronicled in the book and the movie called *Lone Survivor.*

If we qualified as heroes, then the heroism we displayed that day in the autumn of 2009 was cut from a more ragged grade of cloth—a fabric whose folds conceal the shortcomings and the failings of exceptionally ordinary men who were put to an extraordinary test. Men who were plagued by fears and doubts. Men who had bickered endlessly and indulged in all manner of pettiness. Men who had succumbed to—and in some cases, were still running from—a litany of weaknesses that included depression and addiction, apathy and aimlessness, dishonesty and rage.

If we were a band of brothers bound together by combat, then it's important to note that our brethren included a private who had once tried to commit suicide by drinking carpet cleaner, a soldier who was caught smoking hashish in a free-fire zone while standing guard duty, and me: a man so keen to go to war that he never even bothered to consult his wife before volunteering to be deployed to Iraq—and then later lied to her, declaring that he'd had no choice in the matter.

But if all of that is true, what is also true is that we were soldiers who loved one another with a fierceness and a purity that has no analog in the civilian world.

To fully understand how that worked, you need to know a bit about how my platoon came together, and the path that drew us to Afghanistan.

PART I

★ ★ ★

The Road to Nuristan

CHAPTER ONE

Loss

I COME FROM an old Nevada ranching family with military traditions that date back to my grandfather Aury Smith, who took his brother's place in the draft during the summer of 1943 and eventually wound up getting sent into Normandy as a combat engineer just a couple of days after D-day. Six months later, Aury got himself stuck inside the besieged perimeter of Bastogne with the 101st Airborne Division during the Battle of the Bulge. Somehow he made it through, then finished out his time in Europe helping to put on USO shows as a bareback rodeo rider.

Almost thirty years later, my dad was sent to Vietnam. And although he never said a single word about either of the two tours that he pulled up near the Cambodian border with the 4th Infantry Division, which was known to have taken some horrendous casualties during that time, his silence carried enough weight that all three of his sons enlisted in the military.

My oldest brother, Travis, enlisted in the army right after high school, participated in the invasion of Haiti, then later transferred to the air force. Next in line was Preston, who hitched up with the marines. By the time I was a senior in Lake City, California, a town so tiny that our high school graduating class numbered only fifteen, my brothers assumed that I would join up too, despite my father's hopes that I might break the mold and follow the path he'd laid out by enrolling me in the Mormon seminary I had been attending since ninth grade.

My brothers were right. I joined the army in September of 1999, and was assigned to Black Knight Troop, a mechanized armor unit whose sixty-five men were spread across three platoons: Red, White, and Blue.

In military jargon, Black Knight belonged to the four-thousand-man 4th Brigade Combat Team, which itself was part of the twenty-thousand-man 4th Infantry Division. In laymen's terms, what that boiled down to was that I was a tiny cog nestled deep inside the world's largest and most sophisticated war machine. It also meant that I was part of the very same infantry division in which my dad had served.

My first deployment was to Kosovo, where we performed peacekeeping duties and saw very little action. But following the attacks on the World Trade Center in 2001, I volunteered to go to Iraq. After a fifteen-month detour through Korea, I found myself commanding an M1A1 armored tank in Habbaniyah, an area about fifty miles west of Baghdad that sits directly between Ramadi and Fallujah. There we spent the better part of 2004 battling hard-core Al Qaeda fighters who specialized in improvised explosives. We took an average of roughly one IED strike per day.

At the end of that first Iraq deployment, we were sent back to Colorado and the entire unit was reclassified from heavy armor to light reconnaissance so that we could start preparing for the type of fighting we'd eventually be facing in Afghanistan. As part of that transition, I was shipped off to school to learn how to be a cavalry scout. Eleven months later, in June of 2006, we were back in Iraq, this time in a place called Salman Pak, about twenty miles south of Baghdad along a broad bend of the Tigris River and not far from a notorious military installation rumored to serve as a keystone of Saddam Hussein's biological and chemical weapons program. It was also a hotbed of extremist militia, and they did their best to make our lives as miserable as possible.

This was where my new training really began to kick in.

A cavalry scout is generally thought to function as the eyes and ears of a commander during battle. But in fact, a scout's role extends quite a bit further. We refer to ourselves as "jacks-of-all-trades, masters of none," and we are trained to have a working familiarity with—quite literally—every job in the army. We are experts in reconnaissance, countersurveillance, and navigation, but we're also extremely comfortable with all aspects of radio and satellite communications. We know how to assemble and deploy three-man hunter/killer teams. We're pretty good at blowing things up using mines and high explosives. We can function as medics, vehicle mechanics, and combat engineers. And we have a thorough understanding of every single weapons system, from a 9-mm handgun to a 120-mm howitzer.

Many soldiers find it challenging to master such an eclectic skill set. So it was odd that it all came so easily to me. Prior to the military, I found school to be quite difficult, especially when it came to abstract ideas. But these new disciplines came to me so instinctively that it was almost disturbing. Regardless of whether it was small-unit tactics or maneuvering an entire company's worth of armor, the logic seemed inherently obvious. What's more, I loved every aspect of being a scout—although I had a particular knack for something called "react-to-contact" drills, which involved coming up with a combat plan on the spur of the moment as the shit was hitting the fan.

There were two things, however, that didn't come easily at all.

The first had to do with the position in which we found ourselves in Iraq, where we were consigned to a reactive role, and where we found ourselves bound by strict rules of engagement, or ROEs, that prevented us from shooting first—which meant that we were usually able to return fire only when attacked.

I found this intolerable not only from a tactical standpoint but also at a psychological level. And to compensate, I developed an unorthodox style of leadership that hinged on provoking a reaction from the enemy. When I was leading an armored convoy, for example, I would often order my tank driver to abruptly switch lanes, taking the entire column down a city street directly against the flow of traffic, forcing oncoming vehicles to get out of the way or risk head-on collision. At the extreme end of things, I would even use myself as a decoy. To ferret out snipers, for example, I would climb onto the sponson box, a big rectangular storage compartment on the turret of our lead tank, pretend it was a surfboard, and balance myself out there as we clattered through the streets of Habbaniyah, daring any Iraqi marksmen to take a shot at me and expose their positions.

Often these tactics worked well, although they never fully relieved my frustration with the rules of engagement. But as impossible as I found the ROEs, this challenge was dwarfed by a second problem, one that arose as an inevitable consequence of serving in a leadership position in a war zone.

What I found harder than anything else, by far, was witnessing one of my guys get killed. The first time this happened to me was just outside of Sadr City, and it involved one of the finest soldiers I've ever known.

THE SUMMER AND FALL of 2007 was a bad time for all three frontline platoons in Black Knight Troop. By this point we were several months into a new strategy in which the administration of George W. Bush attempted to stabilize Iraq by sending in five additional brigades while extending the tour of almost every soldier who was already on deployment. While the surge did lead to a drop in overall violence, for reasons that remained mysterious (and which may simply have resulted from bad luck), our troop started getting hit harder and more often. In September, one of White Platoon's team leaders got shot in the back, and although he survived, the bullet severed his spine and paralyzed him from the chest down. Not long after that, White lost two other men to a roadside bomb. And then, in September, Snell got hit.

Eric Snell was a thirty-four-year-old scout when I first met him in Iraq, but even as a newly enlisted private he'd managed to stand out as something extraordinary. He had been drafted as an outfielder for the Cleveland Indians straight out of high school in Trenton, New Jersey, but he had decided to forgo a career in the major leagues and instead focus on academics. He got a degree in political science, then moved to South Africa to work as a project manager for AT&T. He could speak French and he'd lived in Italy. He was also good-looking enough that he'd been recruited as a male model, appearing in magazines like *Mademoiselle*, *Modern Bride*, and *Vibe*.

Eric Snell

Snell had the entire package, and he brought all of it to the task of being the type of soldier that did everything *perfectly*. You never had to give him an order or an instruction twice. He learned fast and he learned well. He showed initiative and he demonstrated leadership. In fact, that only thing that seemed even remotely off about the guy was the confusion he provoked among the rest of us over why he had signed on as an ordinary soldier in the first place.

"For Chrissake, Snell, you got all this education and all these credentials," we'd say to him. "Why the fuck did you come into the army as enlisted?"

"Well, yeah, I'm gonna go and be an officer one day," was his response. "But first I want to know what it's like to be a soldier."

That impressed us too.

He was promoted to sergeant two years after he enlisted, far ahead of his peers. Just over two weeks later, on September 18, 2007, me and him and two other guys were ordered to perform overwatch just outside of Sadr City on a group of Iraqi soldiers who were setting up concrete barriers to block suicide bombers. White Platoon had been on duty for most of that morning and our captain had ordered Red to relieve them—an idea that me and my platoon sergeant deemed unwise, because if there were any snipers in the area, they now knew our pattern of movement.

Our objections were overruled, so me and Snell started setting up our perimeter security. I was leaning inside the Humvee, coordinating on the radio with another platoon on the other side of the battle space, and Snell was standing right beside me in back of the vehicle with just his head exposed, when a sniper from across the way got him. The bullet came in just beneath the lip of his helmet, went through his right eye, and blew out the back of his head. As soon as I looked down and saw him lying on the ground, I knew he was dead.

It was the first time I'd seen one of my own guys get killed.

Up to that point, I'd been convinced that there was some sort of connection between how good you were and what happened to you in the theater of battle. But after watching Snell get assassinated like that, I realized that one of the fundamental truths about war is that horrible things can—and often will—happen to anybody, even to a soldier who has everything dialed to perfection.

In the days that followed, I found myself wrestling with the implications of this. While you could strive to be your best, and while you could demand that everyone under you adhered to those standards, the reality was that in the end, none of this might make a rat's ass of difference—even for an ace like Snell.

When you lose a man like that, it can fuel a sense of resignation that can be totally debilitating. If there is no causal link between merit and destiny— if everything on the battlefield boils down to nothing more than a lottery— what's the point of bothering to hone your skills or cultivate excellence?

The loss can create a practical problem too. When a soldier as good as Snell gets drilled through the brain, even if you want to try to replace him, how could you ever find someone to fill his shoes?

As it turned out, however, the rotten luck of losing Snell wound up having a silver lining to it because it triggered the arrival of a soldier who was destined to become my right-hand man in Afghanistan. A man who would provide the foundation of what Red Platoon was to become, and what it would later accomplish during its trial by fire in Afghanistan.

ABOUT A MONTH after Snell died, a batch of new replacements arrived in Iraq from Fort Carson, just outside of Colorado Springs, to fill the ranks of our dead.

Whenever a surge of soldiers arrived, the sergeants from all three platoons would size up the new guys and then haggle over how to divvy them up. These assessment-and-bargaining sessions were often intense because the outcome would have a big impact on the quality of each platoon. And the criteria on which everything hinged basically boiled down to our greatest pastime: platoon-on-platoon football.

Ray Didinger, a sportswriter who covered the NFL for more than twenty-five years, once said that football is the "truest" team game because nothing happens if all the players aren't performing their roles to perfection. "Everyone has to contribute on every single play," he argued. "You could have the guys up front all do everything exactly the way they're supposed to; but if one guy breaks down—if he doesn't get the play right or goes in the wrong direction—then the whole play falls apart."

That's not a bad summary of small-unit military tactics either—especially when you consider that football is all about assaulting another team's territory, then holding that ground against a series of counterassaults. Plus, and this is Didinger again, "football is also a violent game and the guys who play it have to accept that fact." Maybe that's why we bonded so deeply with the game—especially in Red Platoon, where we took it with such hyperseriousness that we literally went for years without losing a single platoon-on-platoon matchup.

Brad Larson was a recruit from Chambers, Nebraska, a town whose population (288) was almost as tiny as the miniscule spot where I'd come from. He had jug-handle ears that kicked out from the sides of his head,

Brad Larson

cartoonishly thick eyebrows, and almost nothing to suggest that he possessed the sort of athletic prowess we were looking for in Red Platoon. So when we wound up getting stuck with him, I initially made a point of ignoring the guy and saying as little to him as possible, despite the fact that he was serving as the driver of my Humvee. Aside from "go left" and "turn right," I don't think I directed a single word to him for more than two weeks.

As it turned out, Larson had played free safety at the junior college he'd attended in Nebraska before joining the army. But as we discovered after finally condescending to allow him on the field during one of our platoon-on-platoon games, he could play just about anywhere because he was so astonishingly fast. Even more impressive was his uncanny sense of *vision*. Whenever the quarterback drew back his arm to throw, Larson knew exactly where the ball was heading. Except for one guy who had a weird sidearm throw that was almost impossible to read, Larson could figure out where the ball was headed just by looking at the quarterback's eyes and the angle of his forearm. And then, thanks to his ferocious speed, he was able to make a beeline for that spot and destroy whoever was the target.

That made me sit up and take notice of him. It also served as the basis of the relationship that swiftly developed between us, because it didn't take long for me to realize that when we were practicing combat maneuvers, Larson was taking the skills he exhibited on the football field and applying them to me.

He was also unbelievably quick to adapt—so quick that I almost never had to sit down and explain anything to him. Instead, he would simply look at me as I was doing something and, just by the fact that he was concentrating so hard and that he was so fricking *on it*, he would absorb the lesson.

As soon as I realized what was up, I started integrating him into the role that Snell had previously filled as my team leader. Like Snell, Larson did everything with ferocious precision and attention to detail. But what I valued even more was the way we connected.

Within a few months, the two of us had built the kind of rapport where if we were out doing a platoon exercise—assaulting an objective, say, or trying to find a weapons cache—I would give my team the commander's brief, sketch out the mission, and announce, "Larson, you're on point." Then we'd start walking on patrol: Larson in front, me in the rear, with two or three guys between us.

As we came up on a place where we had to make a tactical pause and decide what to do next—whether to transition from high ground to low ground, or how we'd pass by an obstacle of some sort—Larson would turn around and look at me. We both had radios, but we wouldn't need to use them. Our eyes would lock, I'd give him a nod, and whatever I was thinking, he would know *exactly* what to do. It was almost like each of us was an extra pair of eyes and a second set of hands for the other.

In addition to that, our strengths and weaknesses overlapped in a way that complemented each other, so that together we were more than twice as good as we were alone. For example, I'm sort of an idiot when it comes to numbers and math, but this was something that came naturally to Larson. Whenever we were on patrol and I was in charge, I would often be deluged with information and struggle to write things down with a marker on either my gloves or on the window of my Humvee, which served as my notepads. If I couldn't keep up, I'd lean over to Larson and say, "Hey, they're calling up a target grid at 4S M6J 180 2245. Remember that."

Twenty minutes later when I'd ask him to give me the grid, he'd spit it right back from memory.

Up to that point, I'd never experienced anything quite like this in the military. We synced. We *clicked*. And in doing all of those things, each of us made the other better.

If there's a term for this sort of connection, I've never come across it— perhaps because the mechanism is so hard to pin down that it resists encapsulation. I don't know how we meshed, I just know that we did, and there was really no way of explaining it, except to acknowledge that it worked. In fact, it worked so well that it was soon obvious to the rest of the platoon too, where it provoked enough curiosity that our lieutenant finally pulled us aside and asked what was up.

At a loss for a better answer, Larson and me fell back on the only explanation that made sense to us.

"It's kinda the same way that a Posi-Traction clutch works on the rear end of a Ford Mustang," I said.

"And how's that?" asked the lieutenant.

"One way to explain it," I replied, "is that it's a limited-slip differential gear that allows for some variance in the angular velocity of the output shaft."

"But the *better* way of explaining it," Larson chimed in, "is to say that it just boils down to PFM."

"Okay, I'll take the bait," said the lieutenant. "What the hell is 'PFM'?"

"PFM is technology so advanced that it can't be explained to the layperson as anything other than sorcery or witchcraft," I replied. "It's pure fucking magic."

"So there you go," said Larson. "PFM."

LIKE PFM, the intensity of combat can create a level of trust that you don't get anywhere else. Which in turn can create some serious obligations—and that brings me back to the insight I drew from the manner in which we'd lost Eric Snell.

Snell's death forced me to acknowledge and accept that the dynamics of combat are impervious to human control. But in the wake of that revelation, I decided that there were at least two things worth concentrating on that I *could* control.

The first involved stacking the odds in the favor of my men and me by being very, very good. Snell and Larson embodied that principle.

The second thing involved, for lack of a better way of putting it, the paramount importance of cultivating a sense of defiance about how we ended things.

I may not have been able to control what happened during combat. But I had a lot to say about what happened after it. And given that, I decided that the follow-through and the finish mattered. Hugely.

After we'd picked Snell up off the street, we had to get him back to our base—the first leg of a journey that would take him through the Dover Air Force Base in Delaware, home of the largest military mortuary in the United States, where the remains of those killed overseas are traditionally brought, and from there to Trenton, New Jersey, where he was buried. In a situation like this, the normal procedure was to place the body on the hood of your Humvee, but I didn't want Snell riding out there and exposed for everyone to see. Because he was so incredibly tall, however, we couldn't shut the rear door on the passenger side of the Humvee, even when we placed Snell across the two dismount seats in the back and bent his legs to get his knees up.

Keeping a door open on an armored Humvee was a serious security violation, but I couldn't have cared less. I sat in the commander's seat with my right arm extended back and holding the strap on that four-hundred-pound door. And that's how we rolled through the middle of Baghdad, taking turns as fast as we could without flipping the gun truck.

This was the sort of gesture that may well sound pointless and perhaps even a little absurd. At the time, however, it seemed to me that the manner in which we brought Snell home was terribly important.

Looking back on it now, I've never changed my mind.

CHAPTER TWO

Stacked

DURING OUR TIME IN IRAQ, Black Knight Troop lost three men, including Snell. A half-dozen others were wounded, several of them horribly. But by the time we wrapped up the deployment and returned home to Colorado in March of 2008, our numbers had been whittled down even further by an attrition of a different sort.

Thanks to a spate of transfers, retirements, and disciplinary relocations during the weeks immediately following our return, Red Platoon was quickly reduced to a faint shadow of its former self. Of the twenty men we'd had in Iraq, only three remained: myself, a guy who would soon get injured when a trailer fell on his hands, and the jug-eared Nebraskan with immense black eyebrows. Everybody else was gone.

This meant that in addition to spending time with our families, as well as all the other things that we'd dreamed of doing back when we were choking on the heat and the dust of Iraq, we were going to have to rebuild ourselves from the ground up.

That would entail quite a bit more than simply snatching up good guys by any means we could. We would also have to find a way of forging those newcomers into a cohesive unit. A band of men who could work well together, trust one another, and keep one another alive during our next deployment. And in the context of larger events that were unfolding around us, that was going to be one hell of a challenge.

In the aftermath of 9/11, when America had committed itself to fighting two extended wars overseas, one in Iraq and the other in Afghanistan, it consigned a relatively small group of young soldiers to something relatively new, which was to send them abroad repeatedly and throw them into combat again and again and again.

These overseas combat deployments were not restricted to one or two tours for each soldier, as was often the case during World War II, Korea, and Vietnam. Nor was the burden of those deployments shared across an entire generation. The brunt of our fighting during this time was performed by less than one percent of our population, and many of the folks who wound up on the front lines—especially the ground-pounders in the infantry—were guys just like me, men who joined up straight out of high school and had three or four deployments under their belts by the time their peers were finishing college. Some of us, especially those who became medics or aviators, or joined the special forces, had seven or eight combat hauls under their belts. By the late winter of 2008, almost a full decade into the Iraq and Afghanistan wars, the toll that those multiple deployments had taken on the army were really starting to show.

One of the clearest signs of the problem was the alarmingly high rate of PTSD, especially among enlisted soldiers. This wasn't always easy to detect, at least not directly. But you could discern it in the rising incidents of suicide and drug abuse. Within a month or two, the brigade found itself wrestling with substance-abuse problems ranging from marijuana to cocaine and meth, as well as incidents of depression that would contribute to three suicides. At the same time, Fort Carson was also saddled with some of the highest crime rates of any military base in the country, including domestic violence, armed robbery, and assault, as well as rape and murder.

Over the course of that year, six of our brigade's soldiers would be charged with killing other soldiers or civilians. The most notorious of these was a specialist from Michigan named Robert Marko, who was part of Black Knight Troop. Marko suffered from the psychological delusion that he belonged to a species of alien dinosaur-like creatures known as the Black Raptor Tribe. Several months after we returned from Iraq, he was charged with raping and murdering a nineteen-year-old developmentally disabled woman he had met online. After confessing to the police that he had taken the woman into the mountains overlooking Colorado Springs, where he'd blindfolded her and slit her throat, he pleaded not guilty by reason of insanity. (In February 2011, he was convicted of first-degree murder and is currently serving a life prison sentence, with no possibility of parole.)

That was enough to make national news.

In some ways, it may be unfair to mention Marko, because he was such an extreme aberration. But if Marko was an exception to the rule, he offered stark evidence of the unsettling fact that not all of the men who were being pulled into the army at this point represented the cream of the crop—and that the problems Marko brought with him, like everybody's, were exacerbated by multiple combat deployments.

Marko also provides an indication of what me and Larson were up against as we set about rebuilding the platoon with the best material we could find, a process known as "stacking."

As the longest-serving member of Red, I was afforded quite a bit of leverage when it came to selecting new personnel, and I knew exactly what I was looking for. But I had no influence whatsoever over one of the most important elements of all—because he would set the tone for the entire unit—which was who our new leader would be.

ANDREW BUNDERMANN WAS a history major from the University of Minnesota who'd made a serious (and extremely successful) effort to amass the absolute minimum number of credits necessary to graduate so that he could spend the rest of his college tenure "cocktailing," which basically meant drinking and hanging out with his bros. In the midst of those pursuits, he also fulfilled his ROTC requirements with the goal of flying jets off of aircraft carriers, a dream that was deep-sixed when the navy flat-out turned him down. Which is how, in May of 2007, Bundermann came to find himself enrolled as a junior-grade lieutenant in the United States Army.

He was sent through the usual officer's tour of induction duty: first to Oklahoma for some basic training at Fort Sill that involved, among many other things, teaching him to assemble and take apart a .50-caliber machine gun in under ten minutes without embarrassing himself. That was followed by a stint in Kentucky at Fort Knox, where he got to cruise around in tanks and Bradley fighting vehicles blowing stuff up, which he thoroughly enjoyed.

This progressive escalation of training and seriousness was partly designed to impart a baseline of military how-to knowledge. But its primary purpose was to expose Bundermann to the men upon whom he would most closely rely in combat: the first sergeants, staff sergeants, and line sergeants who would serve as his noncommissioned officers (NCOs) and who would bridge the gap between the orders that Bundermann passed down from his superiors and the enlisted grunts whose job it would be to make shit happen. And it was during this period that Bundermann began absorbing the first lesson for a newly minted officer who is *not* a ring-knocker from West Point—a lesson that not every lieutenant in Bundermann's position chose to absorb—which is to listen to your NCOs and allow them, in a certain sense, to mold you into their leader.

As it turns out, this was more complicated than Bundermann initially realized because the main message that his NCOs wanted to impart was *always trust your NCOs*. That advice was generally good; but as Bundermann soon discovered, it wasn't *always* good. Sure, it was important for a young lieutenant to take his sergeants' opinions seriously and make an effort to understand where they were coming from. But this didn't mean that he should literally do everything they told him to do. In fact, doing that would get him screwed incredibly fast.

Although a platoon's sergeants often know far more than their lieutenant, at least from a technical standpoint, they don't tend to think strategically. Instead, what they're mostly doing is trying to make sure that things roll smoothly for them and the guys in their squads. And thus one of the key lessons that a lieutenant needs to absorb boils down to this: listen to the people who you're leading so that they feel like they have a voice, even if they don't actually have a voice, but never lose sight of the fact that your primary concern is not the men but the *mission*.

Lieutenant Andrew Bundermann

Sometimes it's the case that the mission's best interest aligns with that of the men. Sometimes it isn't. Regardless, an officer's primary concern starts and ends with the mission. So while it's important to listen to your men, you're not there to make friends, because you don't always have their best interests front of mind.

I was well versed in this mind-set when I was summoned into Black Knight's office building in the early fall of 2008 to meet the man who would lead Red Platoon through its next deployment, so I had a decent grasp of the ideas that had been drummed into the new lieutenant's head. But I didn't know the first thing about the man himself.

The gangly-looking dude sitting before me in a metal chair was as thin as a beanpole, at the top of which someone had affixed a thatch of blondish-brown hair and a face framed by some exceptionally geekish wire-rim glasses.

"All right, here's the deal," Bundermann announced by way of introduction. "I like to chew tobacco, I like to drink beer, and I don't like to work very hard."

That was enough to get my attention.

"You're an NCO, which means you're smarter than me and you have more experience than me," he continued. "I will trust you one hundred percent to do whatever you think is necessary, and if you fuck up, I'll take care of the paperwork and I'll make sure that you have your shit straight."

Now he really had me.

"All I ask in return is that you don't make me look like an asshole, okay?"

That was a surprise. It told me that the man I was talking to wasn't your typical officer, and that if me and the other guys treated him right, we might have a good thing going.

By this point, I'd already had a bunch of platoon leaders, but none who I truly liked. When I stepped out of that cubicle, I didn't know if I liked Bundermann either. But I knew that I liked what he said—and it would soon become clear that the other NCOs felt the same.

From that day forward, we had an unspoken quid pro quo deal with the lieutenant. On our side, we would take care of him by making sure that he always had an ample supply of chewing tobacco and beer, and we'd do our best to make him look like a rock star in the eyes of his superiors.

In return, we understood that he'd leave us alone to do our jobs— especially our most important job at that moment, which was stacking the platoon by encouraging Black Knight's first sergeant and the squadron's sergeant major to take the strongest of the incoming soldiers who were being sent to beef up the troop, and steer them to us.

A TYPICAL PLATOON consists of sixteen frontline soldiers who are divided into two sections, designated "Alpha" and "Bravo." Each of those sections has two squads composed of four men who are under the command of a sergeant known as a "team leader." Justin Gallegos was a densely built Hispanic team leader from Tucson who I knew from back in 2005, when

Justin Gallegos

we'd both been sent to scout school in Fort Knox, Kentucky. Gallegos's most obvious asset was his size. He wasn't exceptionally tall—no more than five ten—but he weighed around 230 pounds and every ounce of it was muscle. He boasted so much bulk and brute strength that the lower enlisted guys called him "Taco Truck," although that was something they would only do behind his back and never to his face because otherwise they knew they probably wouldn't survive the beating he'd hand out.

The quality that truly defined Gallegos, however, had nothing to do with size and everything to do with a high-voltage aggression he could flip on and off like a light switch. That had worked to his advantage when he was a young man moving through the gang scene in Tucson, and it had played an important role when he joined the army in the hopes of avoiding the fate that befell two of his older brothers (both of whom were rumored to have been killed in gang fights). When he arrived at Carson, he'd just finished pulling the second of his two Iraq deployments, and we scooped him up immediately, knowing that we were lucky to have a team leader who was thoroughly battle tested.

Gallegos would spend the next couple of weeks in cruise-control mode, often showing up for our morning physical-training sessions with a Gatorade bottle laced with vodka. But we marked that kind of behavior down to his need to blow off some steam after returning from Baghdad. The bottom line was that he had his duties down cold.

In addition to mastering every aspect of his job, Gallegos made sure that the men who were part of his squad in Bravo section knew their stuff too. He was an exceptionally competent team leader—and his strengths were augmented in a serious way when, just before Christmas, we managed to snag another sergeant named Josh Kirk, who would become Gallegos's counterpart and companion in Bravo.

Having recently returned home from his first Afghanistan deployment, where he had seen some significant combat in Kunar Province and been recommended for a medal of valor, Kirk was eligible to spend three or four months in the United States before he could be deployed again. Instead, he'd waived that privilege and put in a special request to be sent back overseas as soon as possible—a highly unusual move, as well as a blunt statement about his love for combat.

Kirk brought a level of fervor and courage to the platoon that was so far off the charts it was almost crazy. He was *all about* getting them before they got us, and his energy was nothing short of demonic—attributes that were further magnified by his size and strength. He was taller than Gallegos, weighed at least 210 pounds, and had such powerful hands—they looked like shovel blades—that once, when he lost his temper during a wrestling match, he almost snapped all of his opponent's fingers. But what put Kirk in a class by himself was his ardor for the tools of war.

In pretty much any given combat situation, the men who serve in a cavalry platoon have an insane amount of firepower at their fingertips. Given the range of options available, most guys will tend to gravitate to their favorite piece of hardware. Some swear by Mark 19 grenade launchers, while others prefer to lay down the law behind .50-caliber machine guns. But Kirk could never restrict himself to just one weapons system, because he coveted and cherished them all.

According to some of the men with whom he'd served in Afghanistan, Kirk had been like a kid in an arcade over there. At the start of a firefight, they told us, he'd grab hold of an AT4 rocket launcher and let loose, then jump on the .50-cal for a couple of long and deeply satisfying bursts before switching over to the Mark 19. It wasn't unusual for him to finish out by having another go with the AT4. He so loved the shooting and the adrenaline rush it inevitably triggered that sometimes his commanders needed to reel the dude back in.

"We're not looking to pick a fight today," they'd tell him, "so let's calm down a bit."

Like Gallegos, Kirk was utterly fearless, although he preferred to allow his responses during battle to be driven by emotion rather than analysis, whereas Gallegos was more methodical and deliberate. In this way, they balanced each other out, and their combined fury made us considerably more formidable than we otherwise would have been.

These were all things that Bundermann appreciated and valued, which enabled our lieutenant to overlook both men's drawbacks: Gallegos's drinking and volatile moods; Kirk's arrogance and refusal to shut the hell up, along with the pleasure that he took in committing minor infractions like not keeping his hair cut or wearing a nonregulation special forces neck scarf under his uniform, which would drive our sergeant major nuts.

In Bundermann's estimation, Kirk's and Gallegos's skills and personalities dovetailed in a way that provided a rock-solid foundation for Bravo section. They knew what they were supposed to do, they took care of the people under them, and they were in absolute top-notch physical condition. (That last item may not sound super important, but it was a *huge* deal in Bundermann's book because nothing brought more grief down on his head than a major or a captain strolling past the platoon and catching sight of some guy who appeared flabby or weak.)

In short, Kirk and Gallegos reinforced a sense that our unit was in tune and humming—an impression that offered an effective counterweight

Josh Kirk

when we found ourselves taking on a couple of new characters who were slightly less hard-core.

ZACH KOPPES had grown up in the middle of Amish country in Ohio and attended a Mennonite school until he was booted for stealing the key to a test and trying to sell the answers to his fellow students. That was the beginning of a long slide that took Koppes through an ungodly amount of pot smoking, a dead-end gig at an Auntie Anne's pretzel stand in Colorado, and a trip to a Petco store—where he was hoping to apply for a job— that was waylaid when he passed by an army recruiter's office, spotted a sign promising a twenty-thousand-dollar signing bonus, and decided that working with animals didn't sound nearly as exciting as shooting people.

At the end of that road, which ushered him through basic training and a stint in Korea, was our platoon. And there, shortly after arriving in June,

Zach Koppes

he struck up a friendship with another new arrival: a guy who shared Koppes's penchant for combining idiocy and humor with a wild streak that was spectacularly and uniquely his own.

Stephan Mace was from rural Virginia, and when he was growing up, he was so deeply into firearms that he'd apprenticed himself to a gunsmith in high school, fashioned a rifle from scratch, and given it to his dad for Christmas. He also had a taste for the kind of irreverence that involved stunts like pulling down his pants while riding in the passenger seat of his mom's car in order to moon his football coach as they drove past.

When Mace got to the army, that mischievousness started coming out in ways that were both maddening and endearing, often at the same time. If he was bored by what you were saying, he'd close his eyes and tilt his head to the side, then slump down in his chair and start snoring loudly, pretending that you'd put him to sleep. On the other hand, if he happened

Stephan Mace

to walk by your bunk while *you* were asleep, he'd insistently tap you on the shoulder until you woke up and asked what was going on.

"Oh, I was just making sure you were sleeping," he'd say innocently before walking away.

In between gambits like these, he'd brag to the rest of the platoon about the "awesome" results he was getting with ExtenZe, a penis-enlargement supplement that he'd discovered on the Internet. Then he'd earnestly suggest that some of the other guys might want to think about giving it a try because it was clear that they needed help in that department even more than he did.

Pulling crap like this could be dangerous, especially when it was directed at no-nonsense dudes like Larson, Kirk, and Gallegos. But whenever one of those guys was provoked to the point where he was ready to stick Mace's head down a toilet, he was often forced to hold off because he found himself laughing too hard.

Which, of course, encouraged Mace even more.

Koppes had some of that same energy going for him, and this was probably a big part of why he and Mace quickly became inseparable. But the main thing that welded them together, I think, had more to do with Mace's deepest and most appealing attribute, which was his willingness to go to any length in order to support a friend.

When Mace realized that Koppes was constitutionally incapable of waking up and getting himself out of bed each morning at five thirty for first formation and physical training, he developed a routine that involved coming down the hallway of their barracks and pounding on the door until Koppes opened up. Then Mace would stand there smoking a cigarette until Koppes got dressed and was ready to go.

He did that every morning without fail.

Later that spring, Koppes was brutally dumped by a woman he'd been dating. One night, when he tried to call the woman with the aim of begging her to get back together, Mace interrupted the call with a time-out sign.

"I know how upset you are," he said gently. "Give me the phone and I'll talk to her for you."

"LISTEN, BITCH," screamed Mace when Koppes handed him the phone, "STAY THE *FUCK* AWAY FROM MY FRIEND!"

Shortly after that incident, Koppes tore some ligaments in his ankle during a platoon-on-platoon basketball game. Mace immediately seized on this as opportunity to recruit a replacement girlfriend for Koppes by dragging him off to a party, where Mace started feeding every available woman a different lie about Koppes's injury.

"Hey, would you mind going over and saying hi to my buddy?" he'd ask, pointing to Koppes. "He just got back from Afghanistan, where he got nailed by an IED, and he could really use some support."

If that didn't pan out, he'd move on to another woman.

"So, yeah: my friend over there hurt his ankle doing some training that involved jumping out of helicopters at night," he'd say. "He's kinda bummed out because he's an awesome dancer, but maybe you could just go talk to him for a minute?"

By the end of the summer, Mace was orchestrating a nonstop campaign to either find Koppes a permanent girlfriend or, barring that, ensure that his friend got laid as often as possible before we deployed. In pursuit of these twin goals, they spent most of their free time that autumn running around Colorado Springs in mullet wigs, which they were convinced—despite overwhelming evidence to the contrary—made them irresistible to the women they were chasing.

Mace's loyalty and generosity to Koppes weren't especially unusual in the army, where friendships often take on an intensity that can be difficult to find in the civilian world. But what made Mace so singular was that his bond with Koppes didn't prevent him from reaching out and forging new connections with other incoming recruits—including guys whom no one else would even talk to, like Jonesie.

WHEN CHRIS JONES was nine years old, his dad bought a small farm in the southwestern part of Virginia, right next to the Tennessee border, where he intended to make a go of raising chickens until Tyson backed out of a contract that they'd drawn up with the old man, leaving the family high and dry. From that point on, Jones had been not just poor, but dirt-poor. By the time he graduated from high school, joining the army looked like not only his best option but the only one.

After completing basic training at Fort Benning, he got transferred out of infantry in February of 2009 and was sent out to Fort Carson, where he was ordered to join our cavalry brigade, a move that left him totally mystified.

"Hey, what the fuck is cavalry?" he asked, turning in confusion to the only other guy from Benning who had been dispatched to Carson with him.

The answer he got was succinct and accurate:

"Cav basically does the same thing that we did in infantry," came the reply. "They just do it with less fucking people."

Well, all right, Jones muttered to himself. *This keeps getting better and better.*

Chris Jones

Thanks to his infantry background, none of us would even look at Jones when he got to Red Platoon—except, of course, Mace. On Jones's very first day there, Mace bought a Monster energy drink and gave it to Jones, a gesture that was intended to welcome him to the platoon and make him feel a little bit at home. Then, to let him know that the rest of what followed wasn't going to be easy, he hauled off and punched Jones directly in the balls.

That was a pretty decent preview of what awaited him.

During his second week, Jones showed up late for morning formation, and to make matters even worse, he arrived wearing a black fleece that had just been issued to him, but that was a *different* kind of black fleece—a jacket rather than a pullover—from what the rest of us were wearing.

Needless to say, both infractions caught the attention of Kirk.

"Jones," barked Kirk, shaking his head in disgust, "you show up fucking fifteen minutes late, and when you get here, you have the fucking wrong clothes on." Then Kirk stepped outside.

This ain't gonna be good, Jones thought to himself.

When Kirk returned, he was carrying a long yellow stick. The stick was heavy, and at the very top Kirk had affixed a sign emblazoned with the words LATE STICK.

"See this stick?" said Kirk, handing the thing to Jones. "From now on, you will carry this with you everywhere you go."

With that, we all headed off on a fifteen-mile training run.

For the next week, Jones obediently hauled the late stick with him no matter where he went: to PT, to the chow hall, to the bathroom. In addition to being exhausting, it also made him look ridiculous. Several times a day, some bemused NCO or officer would stop him and ask, "Why you got that stick, soldier?"

"This is my late stick, sir!" Jones would declare, reciting what he'd been told to say by Kirk while standing stiffly at attention. "I carry this stick with me everywhere I go!"

At the end of the week, Kirk came into Jones's room, took the stick away, and mumbled something about how Jones hadn't been a bitch or whined about his punishment. It wasn't exactly a thank-you, but it was Kirk's way of letting Jones know that he was doing okay.

From then on, Jones was one of us.

Kirk may or may not have known it at the time, and even if he did it's hard to imagine that he would have cared, but this was exactly the right way to handle a guy like Jones. It earned Kirk a level of loyalty from Jones that was as fierce and pure as Tennessee moonshine. A loyalty that was matched only by Jones's affection for Mace—the one guy in the platoon who had deigned to speak to him back when nobody else could give a fuck.

Although Koppes, Mace, and Jones weren't necessarily cut from the same mold as the platoon's hard men, they added something important to the mix, starting with the fact that all three of them were good dudes and that they always made the rest of us laugh. Sure, they often poured more effort into thinking about what their next prank was going to be than on doing their jobs. But they were eager to succeed. They would do anything they were ordered to do in a heartbeat. And what mattered even more, they would do what they were told with a cheerfulness that made it clear they would not allow their spirits to be broken by the sort of drudgery that is part of life at the bottom of the enlisted ranks.

In addition to all of that, they were incredibly earnest and genuine, a quality that came through in their eagerness to learn. What they absolutely *loved* more than anything else was when their team leaders—guys like Larson, Gallegos, and Kirk, who were only a couple of years older than them but who wielded heavy authority because of their previous combat experience—would sit them down and teach them things they would need to know when we got overseas, like how to clean a .240 machine gun so that it wouldn't jam, or how to break down a Mark 19 grenade launcher.

With proper mentoring and discipline, it was clear to me and the rest of the NCOs that these three young guys had the potential to become excellent soldiers.

Plus, we liked them enormously—which helped buttress our sense of unity as the last members of our team showed up.

JOSH HARDT was a bit of an outsider from the get-go. After spending 2007 with a completely different infantry division in Iraq, where he'd formed some tight connections with the guys in his platoon, he was sent to Fort Carson and ordered to join Black Knight. In addition to missing his buddies from his old unit, he was also newly married, which meant that he tended to spend most of his downtime with his wife. But even so, we snatched him up at the first opportunity because we liked what we saw.

In the same way that Kirk meshed well with Gallegos, we saw Hardt as a ferociously aggressive-minded sergeant with the potential to form an effective partnership with Larson. Hardt had a fierce work ethic, which would help Larson reinforce the leadership of the platoon's Alpha section. Also, he was something of a hotshot when it came to sports—particularly football. Finally, Bundermann was encouraged by the fact that Hardt chewed tobacco, which meant that he would always have someone to bum

Josh Hardt

some Copenhagen off of (although Bundermann would eventually discover, to his intense annoyance, that most of the bumming went in the other direction).

In all of these ways, Hardt offered a striking contrast to the guy who showed up shortly after him: a man who, perhaps more than anyone else, would eventually come to represent the soul of Red Platoon because he embodied so many different aspects of each of us—which is to say, both our best and our worst qualities—while combining those elements together in a manner that was totally original.

When Thom Rasmussen was transferred to us in February, he'd just broken his wrist after plunging into a bar fight (something that happened quite frequently), and then later that same evening and outside the same bar, getting jumped by a bunch of Hispanic dudes, one of whom had beat him into the street with an expandable metal baton known as an asp. To avoid punishment, Rasmussen had concocted an elaborate story that involved getting drunk and punching out a window. From the way he successfully sold that lie to the sergeant major (who was normally nobody's fool), it was evident that Rasmussen possessed a gift for projecting a rock-solid conviction that the course he'd chosen would yield exactly the result he was looking for, while at the same time making it clear that if things went totally south, he truly didn't give a fuck—an attitude that would later make him someone in whom I had no hesitation about placing my trust in combat.

Raz, as we came to call him, was a hulking six-foot-five Minnesotan who had arms that looked like they were milled from bitternut hickory trunks, and whose no-bullshit forthrightness could be as rough as tree bark. If you asked him how he got into the army, he'd look you straight in the face and declare:

"I joined up because I never graduated from high school, was living in people's basements, and used to be a fucking meth addict—that's why."

Because Raz was so huge, we initially assumed that he'd be really good at sports. As it turned out, he wasn't—although he could be entertaining on the field, especially when he did something like borrow Mace's mullet wig and wear it during softball games. But there was something about Raz that struck all of us as decent and cool, and perhaps that's the reason why so many of the younger guys instantly took to him in a way that set up an interesting dynamic with Larson.

To those younger guys, Larson and Raz were like big brothers, but each in a different way. Larson was the stern older sibling who would show up in Koppes's room on a Sunday night and drink fifteen beers while watching episodes of *The Unit*—thereby leading Koppes to assume that our physical training the next morning was going to be a cakewalk. Then he'd reappear at six a.m. and announce that even though we'd won our last football game against Blue Platoon, we hadn't won by enough points, so everyone was going to do a twenty-mile warm-up run and spend the rest of the morning doing uphill wind sprints until at least half of us puked.

Larson was also a no-nonsense big brother in the sense that he was

47

Thom Rasmussen

always teaching us stuff. Often, he'd come in the barracks and look around to see if he could spot somebody who wasn't doing anything.

"Grab that .240 and meet me out back," he'd say. Next thing that guy would know, he'd be in the middle of a three-hour machine-gun tutorial.

Raz, on the other hand, was the let's-smooth-things-over big brother. If, say, you'd been dumped by your girlfriend—or if you'd just gotten done puking after Larson had smoked the entire platoon—Raz was the guy who would come up and give you a bear hug just to make you feel better. He was also the guy you would call when you wanted to get drunk, as well as the guy you called when you were trying to extract yourself from trouble after having gotten drunk. And he was the guy you'd turn to for the sort of favor that you'd never ask Larson for—like, say a ride to the airport when you were heading home on Thanksgiving—even though you knew that Raz might pick you up two hours late because he was, of course, drunk.

The bottom line was that Raz liked to drink almost as much as he liked to fight, but what he enjoyed even more than both of those things combined was being on good terms with almost everybody in the platoon. In the context of his tumultuous upbringing and the lost years that had preceded his time in the army, Red Platoon may have been the closest he'd ever come to having something that felt like a home and a family.

THROUGHOUT THE LATE WINTER of 2008, as the last of our new arrivals trickled in and everyone slowly found his place, the platoon started to gel. To be sure, there were a few weak links in our chain. Three of our recruits were too lazy to whip themselves into shape and constantly dragged their feet on the ruck marching that we were doing in the mountains outside of Colorado Springs. Another newcomer, a guy by the name of Josh Dannelley, developed a bad habit of dumping out the contents of his med pouch—the bandages and drugs that your buddies would use to save your life if you got hit—and filling the thing up with cheese and crackers so that he'd have something to munch on while he was pulling guard duty. And Ryan Willson was such a mess—not just on a symbolic level, but also literally—that one afternoon Kirk ordered him to pack up the entire contents of his barracks room, set everything up outside, and then stand there for several hours holding a poster that demonstrated how a clean and properly organized room should look.

Those examples may seem innocuous, but they illustrate a key point. Civilians often harbor the impression that a platoon consists of a "band of brothers," but that's almost never the case. Any time that you throw nineteen or twenty young men together, not all of them are going get along. And in the army, that tendency is further torqued by the fact that not everyone is a badass. The upshot is that you tend to wind up with a tight nucleus of insiders who like and trust one another, orbited by a scattered cluster of loners who never seem to fit in.

Nevertheless, by the following spring, I was starting to believe that we had built up a crack unit, a platoon that was cohesive and capable enough to qualify as *stacked*.

Across the spectrum and as a team, we had an extremely aggressive mind-set, whether it was playing football or going out and running a patrol. We didn't wait on anything, ever. We weren't afraid to pull the trigger on any aspect of life, and we were unconcerned with the consequences, both good and bad, of going with what we thought was the right call.

Needless to say, those qualities don't always work well in normal life. But Bundermann was nevertheless pleased with what he was seeing because on the battlefield, this type of mind-set is essential. What's more, as we prepared to deploy overseas, it seemed like there was something about us that made us stand apart. And oddly enough, part of the proof—at least in my view—lay in our reluctance to fully participate in the kind of swagger that the army tends to foster at the platoon level, where virtually every unit is completely convinced that it's God's gift to the US military.

By this point, the guys in White Platoon, whose barracks were right next door to ours, had adopted "Warlords" as their call sign. Meanwhile, the guys over in Blue, one building down, were insisting on being referred to as the "Bastards." Under different circumstances, we might have selected a comparable handle for ourselves. But somehow that didn't strike us as classy.

We preferred to keep things simple. So instead of coming up with a jazzy moniker to trumpet what total badasses we were, we decided that we'd let our actions speak for us. We were just Red, and nothing more. But if you wanted something done, regardless of how messy or unpleasant it might be, all you needed to do was to call us up, and it would get handled.

If that offers a decent summary of how we rolled, it shouldn't be taken to mean that we were always happy with our lot—a fact that is perhaps best illustrated by Kirk's response when we finally got the news about where, exactly, we were headed in Afghanistan.

He was familiar with the spot, having been posted close enough not only to hear the rumors but also to talk directly to guys who had been there and seen it firsthand.

"That place," he announced, "is a fucking death trap."

CHAPTER THREE

Keating

THE PROVINCE OF NURISTAN is so isolated and poor that US soldiers who have logged time there often refer to it as the Appalachia of Afghanistan. Like Appalachia, this region on the southern side of the Hindu Kush is home to a population of fiercely independent people who have a reputation for insularity and backwardness, and who take a dim view of outsiders. They also know how to fight.

These are the direct descendants of tribes that went up against the armies of invading emperors like Tamerlane and Babur and even Alexander the Great. More recently, their fathers and grandfathers were the first Mojahedin guerrilla fighters to rise up against the Soviet invasion of Afghanistan in 1979. The revolt they kicked off inspired other parts of the country to join the rebellion, which bled the Russians for the better part of a decade until the last Red Army units finally limped back across the northern border in the winter of 1989. Within a few months a series of revolutions in Eastern Europe, triggered in part by the disaster that the Russians had endured in Afghanistan, would culminate in the fall of the Berlin Wall and, soon thereafter, the collapse of the Soviet Union itself.

If you're not from this part of the world, you should think very carefully before you decide to fuck with the people of Nuristan.

When the US government decided to fling itself into Afghanistan following the attacks of 9/11, it encountered a problem in the eastern part of the country that would have made every Russian commander who had served time in the region back in the 1970s nod in recognition. By the summer of 2005, American forces and their NATO allies found themselves confronting a sharp increase in insurgent activity along the Pakistan border, right where Nuristan sits.

Here, in a forbidding sector of impossibly steep mountains pierced by rushing rivers of snowmelt, Al Qaeda and Taliban fighters were employing a network of secluded valleys as transportation corridors to move fighters and weapons between the two countries. (There were rumors that this corridor system may have also been used to smuggle Osama bin Laden out of Afghanistan sometime after US forces drove him from his fortress of caves in the mountains of Tora Bora.) If you sat down in front of a map and plotted out those routes, they looked exactly like the supply lines that the Afghan Mojahedin had used to funnel men and arms against the Soviets back in the eighties.

In the summer of 2006, the American military decided to tackle this problem by making a firm push into Nuristan and Kunar, the province directly to the south, with the aim of establishing a string of forward bases deep inside both provinces. The idea was that these bases would enable us to disrupt the enemy's supply lines while simultaneously winning over suspicious local villagers by providing them with things they lacked. New roads. Clean drinking water. Schools.

The initial phase of this thrust was known as Operation Mountain Lion, and most of the donkey work was performed by units from the army's 10th Mountain Division. The operation took roughly three months, and by the end of this period, they had established almost a dozen outposts, including a handful of very small bases along an extremely narrow road that winds next to the Kunar River and one of its main tributaries.

Each of those outposts seemed more remote and inaccessible than the last. But the final one, which would eventually come to be called Keating, was in a class all by itself.

"WARS," observed the writer Sebastian Junger during a year that he spent with a small unit of American soldiers in Kunar Province, "are fought with very heavy machinery that works best on top of the biggest hill in the area and used against men who are lower down. That, in a nutshell, is military tactics."

In two sentences, Junger nailed the most elementary principle of small-arms combat, a concept that dates back to when the cutting edge of military technology was catapults and war elephants. In the face of that truth—which represents a distillation of roughly four thousand years of martial wisdom—it's not unreasonable to ask why, when they sat down to draw up the plans for Keating in the summer of 2006, the intelligence analysts at the 10th Mountain Division thought that this principle could be tossed out the window.

In one form or another, that question continues to haunt every soldier who later served there.

The location the analysts selected was unacceptable by almost any yardstick you'd care to measure it with. Positioned only fourteen miles from the Pakistan border, the site was ensconced in the deepest valley of Nuristan's Kamdesh District at a spot that resembled the bowl of a toilet. It was surrounded by steep mountains whose summits went as high as twelve thousand feet and whose ridgelines would enable an enemy to pour fire down on the outpost while remaining concealed behind a thick scrim of trees and boulders. To mount an attack, the Taliban needed only to scramble along its ratlines—the foot trails lining the backsides of the ridges that the enemy used to bring in supplies and ammunition—set up, and start shooting directly into the compound.

In military parlance, this is known as "plunging fire" and it is extremely difficult to suppress, because whenever the defenders started returning fire in earnest, the enemy had only to disappear down the far side of the ridges. The moment the defense let up, the enemy was free to return and resume work. This pattern of strike and dodge would continue until the Americans called in their attack helicopters from Jalalabad (eighty miles away), its fighter jets and Spectre gunships from Bagram Airfield just outside of Kabul (two hundred miles), or, when things really got bad, the long-range B-1 bombers in Qatar, more than thirteen hundred miles away.

View of the North Face from COP Keating

View down into COP Keating from the North Face

The village of Urmul

This enormous tactical disadvantage was obvious to anybody inside the base who took the trouble to tilt his head and look up. But that was only the start of Keating's liabilities.

In addition to the fact that it was ringed by mountains, it was flanked by rivers: the Darreh-ye Kushtāz on the west, which separated the outpost from its helicopter landing zone, and the Landay-Sin to the north. It also sat adjacent to Urmul, home to about twenty families whose mud-brick homes—and in particular, their mosque—offered additional cover for enemy fighters. And as a final grace note, the closest US base, which was located in the little village of Naray and would eventually come to be known as Bostick, was a six-hour drive along the only road in, which was barely thirteen feet wide and often skirted the edge of impossibly steep cliffs.

In short, the site was remote, isolated, virtually impossible to supply, and so breathtakingly open to plunging fire that massive amounts of artillery and airpower would be required to defend it. Those flaws were so glaringly evident that that the young specialist who was ordered to draw up the initial plans dubbed it "Custer."

If you wanted to find an illustration of the worst possible place to build a firebase, a site that violated every morsel of wisdom that had been pounded into the heads of the soldiers who would be ordered to defend COP Keating, it would be hard to come up with a better example than this. And yet that's exactly what the army did in the summer of 2006.

The problems started surfacing almost immediately.

WITHIN THREE WEEKS of the first troopers' arrival, the camp was assaulted in force—not once, but twice. The second time involved a three-pronged attack that demonstrated how exposed the soldiers inside the new location were to enemy surveillance and fire.

Meanwhile, the overland supply line turned out to be unusable. Armed convoys met heavy resistance on the narrow mountain road from Bostick, and the resulting firefights also prevented Afghan construction workers from improving the road. To further terrorize the locals, insurgents set up fake checkpoints, then began cutting off the ears and noses of Afghan truck drivers who worked for the Americans.

The perils of that road, which by now everyone was calling "Ambush Alley," were demonstrated most graphically that autumn when a young American soldier, a bright and energetic lieutenant from Maine, attempted to drive a massive armored supply truck—one that never should have been taken up the road to begin with—back to Bostick. When the berm collapsed under the weight of the nine-ton vehicle, the truck was sent plummeting over a three-hundred-foot cliff toward the Landay-Sin River. The officer was flung from the cab, and when his comrades climbed down to him, they found him broken in so many places they barely knew where to begin. His legs had multiple open fractures. Both of his feet appeared to have been almost severed at the ankles. His back was broken and he was bleeding profusely from the head, abdomen, and groin.

After applying tourniquets and splints, his rescuers placed him on a stretcher and began pulling him back toward the road. Halfway up, his pulse disappeared. By the time he reached the top, he was obviously dead. Still, they flew him to Bostick by helicopter, where the doctors spent forty minutes attempting to resuscitate him with open cardiac massage.

His name was Ben Keating, and in addition to ending the use of the road, his death gave the outpost its official name.

That was November of 2006. During the next two years, the regular drumbeat of attacks took an increasing toll on each succeeding unit of soldiers until, in October of 2008, a targeted assassination attempt was made on Keating's then commander, Captain Robert Yllescas, who later died from his wounds. This meant that two of the outpost's four American commanders had now been killed.

By this point, it was obvious to everyone that Keating was simply too isolated to defend. And so, plans were finally set in motion to shut the base down—a decision that actually compromised Keating's security even further, because now no additional effort or resources would be invested into improving the fortifications.

This didn't bode well for Keating's final group of soldiers, the unlucky cavalry troopers who would be tasked with one of the most unenviable missions one can imagine. Because the only thing worse than being ordered to defend an outpost that never should have been built is having to dismantle the thing and take it down.

That, in a nutshell, is what me and the rest of Black Knight Troop were told to prepare for as we boarded the first of a series of flights that would take us from the airstrip at Fort Carson through Germany, Kyrgyzstan, and eventually to Jalalabad Airfield, where we spent several days on the tarmac awaiting the final set of helicopter rides that would drop us into Bostick, Keating's main source of support and supplies, as well as the final jumping-off point in the journey to our new home.

IN THE HINDU KUSH, pilots often say that the weather is "valley-to-valley." What that means is that on any given morning, especially in the fall, one drainage can be bright and clear while its neighboring sector just a few miles away can be shrouded in storm. Depending on the wind, the temperature, and a host of other variables, you might be able to fly up and down the entire Kunar Valley without a second thought while the Kamdesh Valley is buttoned down tight enough to make even the shortest flight unthinkable.

For military aviators, especially those who pilot the low-flying helicopters that were responsible for providing transportation and close air support to American ground troops in the spring of 2009, this made for one of the most challenging flying environments on earth.

The helicopter pilots of the 7th Squadron, 17th Cavalry Regiment, 159th Combat Aviation Brigade of the 101st Airborne Division were the bread-and-butter backbone of the war effort in those mountains, and one of the machines they flew, the CH-47 Chinook, served as flying delivery trucks that hauled everything imaginable, from hand grenades and claymore mines to Pop-Tarts, air conditioners, and incoming groups of soldiers like us.

By this point, things had gotten so bad that the Chinook pilots from Jalalabad were wary of flying into Keating for anything other than to deliver diesel fuel, food, and ammo. Even then, they would make their runs only during "low illume," the portion of the month when there was little or no moonlight to paint a chopper into a fat target for the Taliban gunners. So it wasn't until May 27 that we had a night dark enough for them to bring in our advance party, a group that included me, Bundermann, and First Sergeant Burton, plus two of our medics and half a dozen other guys.

By the time we hit the landing zone, it was well after midnight. We could barely see a thing as we helped shove crates out the back of the double-bladed bird. Then we were ushered up to the chow hall for a quick bite to eat.

It was confusing in the dark, and despite our night-vision goggles, we couldn't see much. Every major feature of what was about to become our home—the twenty-odd small buildings clustered haphazardly inside an area the size of a football field—was shrouded in shadow. As for the terrain beyond the wire, it was completely invisible.

The soldiers who would be turning the place over to us didn't show us much that first night before we hit our racks and bedded down—mainly just the piss tubes and the latrines. And then, very first thing the next morning, we were under attack.

We hadn't even awoken when the Taliban started blasting us with small-arms fire from places in the surrounding slopes whose names would soon become way too familiar. The North Face. The Putting Green. The Diving Board. The Switchbacks. They also punched us with a couple of 84-mm explosive rounds from a B-10 recoilless rifle, rounds that came in with a whoosh and a roar that left us stunned.

In the middle of this attack, a soldier who belonged to the unit we would be relieving ducked into the barracks and told us that one of their sergeants had just taken a nasty shot to the head. To prevent additional casualties, he said, it would probably be best if us new guys refrained from running around and instead stayed put inside the barracks. As he left, we all agreed that we were being offered an extremely useful gut check: the sort of reminder that drove home not only how dangerous this place was, but also how vulnerable we would be.

A few minutes later, when the incoming fire died down, we stepped outside to take stock of our surroundings. That was when we got our *real* gut check.

I LEANED BACK and gasped in amazement as I gazed up at the mountains and ridgelines shooting into the sky in every direction—steep-sided escarpments studded with exposed granite and blanketed with trees that made the trails running through them completely invisible.

"Man," I said to myself, "I'm gonna build some strong neck muscles in this place over the next year."

That was followed by a more sobering realization.

The placement of the outpost not only made no sense—anyone could shoot into the perimeter from almost any position you'd care to imagine—but it violated everything I'd ever been taught. Almost without realizing it, I started running through a checklist of broken rules:

A large, diffuse perimeter too big for defenders to man a sufficient number of guard posts?

Check.

Nowhere to hide, aside from a few low-slung buildings and a couple of armored Humvees?

Yep.

A helicopter landing zone on the far side of a river?

Roger that.

"This is like being in a fishbowl," I muttered. "Those fuckers can see everything we do."

My final thought that morning was of Kirk and his warnings about what a terrible position this was.

Kirk really liked to embellish things, so most of us, me included, had brushed him off. But now that I was here, I could see that for once, he hadn't been blowing smoke up our butts.

"Kirk, you bastard, you were right," I said. "This place is a total shithole."

THAT VERY FIRST DAY, those of us in the advance party spent most of our time walking around the outpost in an effort to get a sense of how the place was laid out.

The primary structures at Keating were fashioned from stone and wood, and most of them had plywood roofs reinforced with sandbags. The walls of the command post and those of the barracks for each platoon were more than a foot thick. The roofs of these structures were also reinforced with up to five inches of concrete, plus a layer of sandbags on top, which meant that they were capable of sustaining direct hits from rockets or mortars.

The other location that enjoyed heavy protection was the mortar pit, a small niche tucked beneath an overhanging rock on the southwestern corner of the outpost. This is where the 120-mm and 60-mm mortars were located, along with a concrete barracks for the four-man crew who served those guns. But most of the other buildings inside the wire, including the latrines, the showers, and the chow hall, were much more vulnerable. Slapped together with plywood and two-by-sixes, they had no protection whatsoever from direct or indirect fire.

Some of the structures at Keating

The buildings were also arranged haphazardly, with little or no sense of a larger plan. There were narrow alleyways running between some of them, while others were connected by shallow trenches. A handful of them simply sat out in the open with nothing to shield or protect them other than some camo netting and a few trees.

There were also a total of 577 Hescos—five-foot-high, seven-foot-wide wire-mesh containers filled with dirt, which offered an effective shield against explosions and small-arms fire. The Hescos were strung together to form Keating's outer walls on the east, north, and west sides of camp, plus one major wall that ran directly through the center of the outpost on a north-to-south axis.

The southern perimeter was protected only by triple-strand concertina wire.

To supplement those barriers, the camp maintained five main battle

Hescos forming the perimeter of the COP

positions from which we could lay down heavy defensive fire and hopefully stop an attack. Four of these were armored Humvees, each of which featured a gun turret on top of the cab. The fifth position was a tower built into a building that overlooked the front gate on the northwest side of camp. The weapons systems on the gun trucks and the tower included three .50-caliber machine guns, a pair of Mark 19 grenade launchers, and two M240 heavy machine guns.

The tower and two of those trucks were also equipped with sophisticated but highly finicky electronic sensors that, in theory, would enable us to detect any enemy movements within the vicinity, and lay target grids over them. Known as LRAS (which stood for "long-range advanced scout surveillance system"), these devices were rarely operative and therefore all but useless. To really get a sense of what surrounded the outpost, you had to actually get outside the wire on patrol. When we did that on our second

**An armored Humvee mounted with a Mark 19,
which composed the battle position known as Truck 2**

day, I was able to start familiarizing myself with the geographic features that would dominate life at Keating.

Keating was nestled on the south side of the Darreh-ye Kushtāz River and situated at the base of two mountains. On the southwestern side—at the rear of the outpost and directly behind you if you were facing the river—a huge escarpment rose more than a thousand feet. A zigzagging trail, known as the Switchbacks, ascended that escarpment from our outer perimeter all the way up to the ridge, which stretched in an unbroken line to the southeast, where a massive rock, which was known as the Diving Board, protruded into the sky. The flanks of this massif were approximately sixty degrees steep, and the ridgeline afforded superb cover for enemy gunners to look—and shoot—directly into camp.

On the opposite side of the river—which was spanned by a small footbridge that marked the spot where Captain Yllescas, Keating's former

The Switchbacks leading down to Keating

View of the Diving Board, as seen from the armored Humvee
known as battle position LRAS1

commander, was assassinated—an even larger hulk directly faced the outpost. This feature, which was known as the North Face, was so steep that in places it approached dead vertical—which is why one of the previous units had placed ropes along it. The only way to reach the top was by old-school Batman-style moves, going hand over hand directly up the cliff. In the most vulnerable spots, a single slip or gunshot could send you straight to the bottom, fifteen hundred feet below.

In addition to the northern and southern walls, there was a third significant feature. Directly to the west and looming over the little village of Urmul was a massive fifteen-hundred-foot-high spur known as the Putting Green. Like the northern and southern walls, this terrain was steep, heavily vegetated with thick trees and shrubs, and boasted numerous crevices and rocky outcroppings.

Together, these walls and ridgelines virtually ringed the outpost while providing superb cover and concealment for the forces that were watching over us.

All of this would have been disturbing enough by itself. But what truly rattled me, Bundermann, and the rest of our advance party was the placement of our observation post.

Most firebases like Keating are protected by a small, heavily fortified encampment that is separate from the main outpost. Known as an observation post, or "OP," it is typically perched on the highest ground and has a direct line of sight to the main base so that the tiny group of soldiers who are stationed inside it can provide defensive cover with their machine guns and mortars.

Thanks to the surrounding mountains, however, the highest ground at Keating sat back *beyond* the ridgelines running across the top of the Switchbacks. This meant that our observation post, which was known as Fritsche (pronounced "Fritch-ee") and was manned by a single platoon of roughly twenty-five men, had no direct line of sight linking it to Keating.

Fritsche was crucial to Keating's security because the OP was armed with 60- and 120-mm mortars that were capable of bringing some serious hurt down on any enemy position for which we could provide ten-digit

**View of the Putting Green, as seen from the armored Humvee
known as battle position LRAS2**

grid coordinates. So as long as we had radio contact—and as long as
Fritsche's guns were operational—the chances of the fifty Americans inside the wire down at Keating surviving an all-out assault were significantly
increased. But there was also a zone of dead space between Fritsche and
Keating, inside of which we simply could not see a damn thing. Within
this blind spot, which was immense, the enemy could move anywhere they
wanted, any time they wanted, without our knowledge. It was yet another
tactical weakness that the enemy understood perfectly and knew exactly
how to exploit.

To say that this terrain was disorienting would be an understatement.
Even Larson, who was one of the best scouts I've ever known, never felt as
if he truly had a firm grasp on direction and was continuously confusing
east and west. As absurd as it may sound, there was something about being

View of Keating from the Putting Green; our helicopter landing zone is visible in the lower left corner outside the perimeter of the COP across the river

at the bottom rather than the top of those mountains that made it exceptionally difficult for us to keep our compass points straight. Eventually, most of us would orient ourselves off of the North Face and use it as a kind of running cheat sheet because the direction was embedded in the name itself.

In addition to all of this, there was also the tactical and strategic pièce de résistance on the Keating smorgasbord, which was our helicopter landing zone, or LZ.

One of the details that we'd missed when the Chinook dropped us down in the middle of the night was that the LZ, which was nothing more than a flat stretch of dirt about the size of a basketball court, was located at the end of a concrete bridge on the far side of the Darreh-ye Kushtāz River, which ran along the western side of the outpost *outside* our wire.

This meant that every time a helicopter was preparing to touch down, we would be required, in effect, to retake our own LZ.

This posed an enormous security risk while making our logistics challenges immensely harder. Everything that came into that LZ would need to be carried by us across the bridge and through our front gate while exposed to enemy gunners. Even worse, if we found ourselves under siege and unable to secure the landing zone, it would be impossible for a helicopter to bring in supplies or ammunition, or evacuate our wounded.

We didn't know it at the time, but this would emerge as a critical issue during the battle that awaited us, imposing limitations that would ultimately prevent us from helping one of our wounded in a way that would haunt Keating's survivors for the rest of our lives.

But that is getting ahead of the story.

KEATING'S LIABILITIES were glaring enough that we were able to spot most of them within the very first day. But there was one more vulnerability that wasn't quite so obvious, at least not at first glance.

The main entry point to the outpost consisted of a swing-leaf gate, which was located at the point where the road that ran along the bottom of the river valley passed by the northwest corner of the outpost. The flimsy protection afforded by that metal gate arm, which you were supposed to raise to allow vehicles to pass into the camp, was further compromised by the fact that its hinges had long since broken off. Fortunately, the entire entryway lay directly beneath the armored guard tower and a machine gun that was manned night and day, which meant that it would be difficult for the enemy to storm the gate.

Keating's back door, however, was an entirely different matter.

The center of camp was defined by a cluster of buildings that included, among other structures, our command post, barracks, aid station, and dining hall, plus small pieces of infrastructure like our tool shed and electric generators, as well as a mosque. Directly to the east of this area and extending all the way to the perimeter was a cluster of small shacks that housed our allies from the Afghan National Army, or ANA, who were supposed to provide additional manpower.

These men were a real problem. They hailed from the 6th Kandak, a battalion-sized unit that had perhaps the worst reputation and performance record in the entire Afghan Army. Created just one year earlier, the unit was poorly disciplined and badly led, and in addition to that, they refused to allow themselves to be integrated into our command structure. Although they were supposed to number around forty men, it was impossible to know how many Afghan soldiers were inside Keating at any given time, because they tended to disappear on unauthorized leave whenever they felt the need to go home, especially during the month of Ramadan at the end of the summer.

These men had almost no interest in training with us and they often refused to join us on patrol, preferring instead to huddle within their living area taking naps and smoking hashish. We viewed them as lazy and incompetent, but what made them truly dangerous was that they refused to use the main latrines, which would have entailed walking an extra fifty yards to the west. Instead, they trampled down the concertina wire on the east side of Keating's perimeter, enabling them to duck into and out of camp whenever they needed to relieve themselves. So in addition to the front gate, which featured security procedures and ID checks beneath the watchful eye of whoever was on the heavy machine gun in the guard tower, the camp also had a rear entry through which anyone could come and go any time he pleased.

As bad as the Afghan Army soldiers were, at least they had one thing going for them, which was a pair of highly experienced NATO soldiers from Latvia who had been assigned to train and keep tabs on them. The Latvians were competent, resilient, and did everything they could to boost the Afghans' discipline and skills. This meant that despite their many faults, the ANA were marginally better than two other groups of locals: a small contingent of Afghan Security Guards (ASG) who were supposed to help guard the front gate, and a team of Afghan National Police (ANP) who maintained a tiny checkpoint on the road just outside of it. These two groups could not be counted on for anything whatsoever, aside from falling asleep at their posts in the middle of the day.

The ANA, the ASG, the ANP: we never really understood how this confusing array of groups was supposed to link into our larger mission. And a giant part of that confusion stemmed from the fact that the larger mission was itself something of a mystery, at least to us.

If I had to explain why we'd been sent to Keating and what we were supposed to accomplish there, what it apparently boiled down to was that we were helping the Afghan government beef up security just enough to kick-start commerce in the region. This would enable local people to start making money, which they could then use to buy a bunch of DVD players and toasters and other sweet stuff for themselves and their families, thereby magically transforming Nuristan into a hub of vibrant economic development. At this point, the government could hold elections, which would enable folks to race off to the ballot box and vote to shut down the Taliban—whereupon everybody could kick back in front of their new TV sets, break out some cocktails, and enjoy themselves.

Needless to say, this is a poor representation of the US military's strategy at the time, which was to use Keating and other remote combat outposts to tie up the insurgents' resources in the hopes of preventing them from attacking larger towns and cities to the south. But, this is what we *thought* we were being asked to do as the remaining members of Black Knight Troop were shuttled into the landing zone over the next week.

It's also probably worth noting that we didn't spend a lot of time and energy thinking about the bigger picture, because we were focused on smaller but far more urgent challenges, the main one being to figure out how the hell we were going to survive until it came time to shut this place down.

That was pretty much the first question that ran through the minds of the new arrivals over the next several days as they stepped out of the Chinook. You could see the dismay playing across their faces during those initial moments when they took it all in and realized just how stuck we were.

By the end of that week, the last members of Red Platoon arrived in a group that included Jones and Koppes. When they landed it was so dark that they had to hold on to each other and blindly feel their way through the little maze around the barracks.

The next morning, when I took them on a field trip to introduce them to the outpost, Jones summed up their reaction with his usual eloquence.

"Oh yeah, absolutely," he muttered to himself while hitting Koppes with a knowing look. "We are *so* fucked."

CHAPTER FOUR

Inside the Fishbowl

WHEN WE FINALLY COMPLETED our handoff with the unit we were replacing, Black Knight had three frontline platoons at Keating: Blue, White, and Red. We also had a Headquarters Platoon on station that included our commanding officers, medics, forward observers, and radio operators, along with our mortar crew, plus a cluster of mechanics, cooks, and other support personnel.

The plan was that HQ Platoon would stay inside the perimeter while each of the three frontline platoons rotated through Fritsche for stints of about a month at a time, providing overwatch for the rest of us down inside the perimeter. These tours at Fritsche were highly coveted because there was so little supervision at the observation post. Once a platoon was up there, they pretty much got to run their own show. Blue was lucky enough to get the first stint, and Red would have loved to have been ordered to replace them when they came down. The job was given to White, however, because Captain Melvin Porter, Keating's commander, didn't really trust me and my guys in Red.

This was understandable because we were the most arrogant and unruly platoon in the entire troop, and therefore the biggest pain in the ass. As Captain Porter grudgingly admitted, however, we also qualified, by a significant margin, as the best trained and the most aggressive soldiers under his command. That mind-set was reflected in the eagerness with which we flung ourselves into the self-appointed mission of correcting

Keating's many security vulnerabilities—an effort to which Porter did not respond well at all.

By the end of our first two weeks, we had drawn up a long list of improvements that we wanted to make. This included everything from repairing the front gate to replacing the claymore mines buried just outside the concertina wire on the southern perimeter. Porter responded by issuing denials on almost every one of our requests. That was frustrating, but what we found even harder to swallow was his refusal to go on the offensive. He continuously berated us for using up too much ammunition when we were attacked, and he gave the go-ahead for our mortar pit to fire rounds so infrequently that we started calling him "No-Mortar Porter."

Porter's behavior, which amounted in our view to a failure to grasp the severity of our situation, struck many of us as outrageous—and on some levels, I suppose it was. But it's worth mentioning that, as in most combat situations, the picture was far more complicated than it may seem from the outside. Porter was balancing directives from his superiors that we didn't even know about—directives that included orders to avoid devoting too many resources to an outpost that was slated to be dismantled, and not to antagonize the local Afghan population by saturating the sector with overly aggressive patrols or unnecessary gunfire.

On top of those demands, Porter himself was now on his third deployment and burned out far beyond his limits. In retrospect, although I found him a poor commander, I must acknowledge that many of the decisions he was forced to make during our time in Nuristan probably stemmed from far larger problems, including an army that was depleted and exhausted by two wars, multiple deployments, and inadequate resources.

Nevertheless, we still had to deal with the fact that we were stuck inside a poorly placed outpost surrounded by an enemy bent on killing us—a situation that me and my guys counteracted by the only means at our disposal. At the slightest hint of provocation, we would burn through entire cases of ammo, unleashing the heavy machine guns and grenade launchers for longer and more sustained bursts than all the other platoons combined until we finally received a direct order from Porter to cease fire.

In the end, however, that didn't stop the Taliban from doing pretty much exactly what they wanted.

FROM JUNE THROUGH SEPTEMBER, the enemy attacked relentlessly, nailing us at least every other day, sometimes for multiple sessions in the same day. At the time, it seemed as if their main purpose behind these strikes was simply to screw with us. Occasionally, for example, they'd hit us early in the morning with no more than a single burst of small-arms fire—the kind of "spray and pray" that appeared devoid of any tactical or strategic purpose other than harassment. More often than not, however, these attacks were serious: a sustained barrage from the boulder looming over our mortar pit that we had dubbed RPG Rock; or a well-placed round from their Russian B-10 recoilless rifle, which was hidden somewhere high in the slopes off to the east in a place that we couldn't ever seem to pinpoint.

That B-10 was a crude piece of junk: a two-wheeled, Soviet-era cannon with an explosive shell whose design had barely changed since World War II. It said something about the Taliban, though, that they were able to get results from it. When they fired the thing off it sounded like a freight train was dropping down on top of us, and the damage it could inflict was fearsome.

Just a few days after we arrived, Jeff Jacobs—the platoon sergeant, and therefore the senior enlisted soldier in White Platoon—caught a couple of pieces of shrapnel in the face. It broke his jaw, shattered most of his teeth, and got him a plane ticket to Walter Reed, where the doctors had to patch up the hole in his right cheek with a metal plate. (It said something about us, I suppose, that before the end of that year, Jacobs would be back in Afghanistan.)

Eventually, we would come to understand that the Taliban's primary aim with these attacks was to suck up information. Each time they provoked a response from us, they were able to refine their analysis by observing our patterns of movement and teasing out our weaknesses.

Sometimes their small-arms fire or a single round from B-10 recoilless rifle would be concentrated in the east; then all of a sudden, a bunch of

RPGs would erupt from the Switchbacks, to the west. Each attack gave them a better understanding of our defensive capabilities on the perimeter, and helped them determine where they could put down the most effective fire when they finally decided to throw the kitchen sink at us.

DURING THE LULLS between those attacks, life at Keating was still no picnic. The two frontline platoons at the main outpost were responsible for force protection, which was a fancy term for standing guard, and they traded this duty back and forth every seven days. During the week when your platoon was on guard, you and your guys were responsible for manning all five main battle positions (the front gates and our quartet of heavily armed Humvees) for two-hour stretches, twenty-four hours a day, without any letup. When we came under attack, the number of battle positions that needed to be manned would double.

This would have been difficult enough on its own. But our security challenges were made considerably more complicated by the number of local Afghans who were inside the post.

Odd as it may sound, a kind of symbiosis had evolved between us and the local people who lived in a handful of small villages that lay within a half day's walk of Keating, despite the fact that almost all of those villages were also supplying fighters to the Taliban. Many of the residents were sympathetic to the insurgents, even if they were not actually Taliban themselves. At the same time, they were desperately poor and we provided a much-needed source of income, which is why lots of these folks were only too happy to take on construction work and other tasks that we needed help with. This gave rise to a rather bizarre arrangement. Each morning, a parade of Afghans filed into the outpost through our broken front gate. Every night just before dusk, they filed back out again and returned to their homes.

This meant that on most days Keating's interior played host to a colorful population of locals. Most of them hung out in what we called the Haji Shop, a closet-sized building wedged into one of the Hesco walls just a few steps from our ammunition depot. The shop was run by a thin man with a hardened look about him, whom we called John Deere because of the baseball cap he always wore. He kept the place stocked with terrible cigarettes, cheap T-shirts emblazoned with the Afghanistan flag and the words AFGHAN COMMANDO (which all the ANA soldiers wore), and Boom Booms, a knockoff energy drink that tasted like Smarties, and that a lot of my guys thought was actually pretty good. John Deere, who was also in charge of the Afghan Security Guards who manned the checkpoint at the front gate, lived inside the store, which he had accessorized with a couch and a television set.

On any given morning, the Haji Shop would draw a crowd of Afghan regulars who gathered to guzzle tea, banter, and hang out. Many of these men were distinctive enough that we assigned them nicknames like Sugar Man, the Snitch, and the Midget. There was an uncharacteristically aggressive Afghan National Army soldier who wanted to kill the Taliban so badly that sometimes he would get up and fire his rockets at night. We dubbed him RPG Guy. Another Afghan soldier preferred to park himself at the front gate, where he would laugh and chuckle all day long. He was so genuinely nice that most of my soldiers didn't have the heart to deny him permission to sit inside our guard truck, even though his eyes were perpetually bloodshot and he reeked of cannabis, which grew all around the outpost. We called him Bong Water. And finally, there was Ron Jeremy, a short, pudgy Afghan with exceptionally hairy features who bore a remarkable resemblance to the hedgehog-like porn star. He was supposed to be our main interpreter, but we were rarely able to use him effectively because although he was fluent in Pashto, he didn't speak a word of Nuristani.

In some ways, these characters provided a much-needed diversion from the drudgery of our routine. In other ways, they were a source of constant irritation and concern.

Jones, who often pulled guard duty in the tower that loomed above the front gate, couldn't stand most of the Afghan Army soldiers, because they were so undisciplined and apathetic. Another thing that bothered him was the way that John Deere's security guards, who ran their checkpoint in the shadow of his machine gun, would allow women in burkas to waltz blithely through the gate without ever bothering to question them.

"Hey, search that lady—she's got some of the hairiest damn feet I've ever seen in my life!" Jones would yell down from the tower as a figure in a blue-and-black burka floated past. "Will somebody *please* ask that bitch a *question*?!"

This would draw no response whatsoever. As the guards placidly took another hit of cannabis or folded their arms and resumed their naps, Jones would throw his arms up in disgust and wave.

"Well, there goes the Taliban!" he'd call out plaintively. "See you later—thanks for dropping by!"

CEASELESS VIGILANCE in the face of such cartoonish apathy from our Afghan allies, combined with never being able to sleep for more than two hours at a time, was brutally draining on the men. Within the first month, things had gotten so bad that me and the rest of Red's leadership quietly started breaking the rules and allowing our guys four hours of sleep during the weeks when we were pulling security. But even the seven-day breaks when we traded off with Blue or White Platoon didn't afford much relief. If we weren't on guard duty we were sending patrols out beyond the wire almost every day in order to perform recon and to try to spot infiltration.

During these ventures, which we referred to as "nature walks," each man hauled more than sixty pounds of gear, plus his weapons and ammo. The physical demands of moving up and down steep terrain with that much weight were intensely unpleasant. But if nothing else, these outings did expose us to the beauty of our surroundings.

Even though Nuristan was wedged inside a country ravaged by thirty years of uninterrupted war and was home to God only knew how many millions of unexploded land mines, not to mention a traumatized population, it was about as close to paradise as any of us had ever seen. At almost every turn, we were greeted with another exquisite view. High above, the mountains with their caps of snow glistened in the sunlight against the hard, blue sky. Far below, the streams tumbled along the valley floor, laden with bluish glacial silt. And everywhere in between lay a lush, emerald-green carpet of vegetation on the east- and north-facing slopes, while the more arid south- and west-facing slopes were adorned with desert shrubs and outcroppings of muted orange rock, which, early in the morning and late in the afternoon, looked as if it had been dipped in molten gold. Not far from the mortar pit, there was even a waterfall cascading down through a section of gray stones and surrounded by a grove of ancient, twisted trees.

In a word, the place was gorgeous. Yet even as we remarked that it reminded us of Colorado's Rocky Mountain National Park, we never forgot that we were outsiders and that this place did not welcome our presence.

In more ways than we could count, that hostility was reflected not only in the land itself but also in the things that flourished there. You couldn't place your hand on a single surface without getting a fistful of barbs, because there were thorns everywhere. Each plant or tree seemed armed with spikes or claws—and the same was true of the wild creatures. All along the slopes of the mountains were enormous porcupines, larger than dogs with quills to match, and ill-tempered bands of monkeys that would perch on the cliffs and pelt us with rocks as we shuffled past. What was truly freaky, however, were the insects.

There was a type of black ant that that had legs like those of a spider. They could move so fast that if you sat down near a cluster of them while you were on patrol, they would swarm all over you. We couldn't find them listed in any book, so we called them "crack ants." As for the *actual* spiders, they were enormous, with yellow-gray bodies the size of hot dogs that looked big enough to kill and eat birds. We couldn't find any references to them either, so we dubbed them "vomit spiders," and when we were bored, we would place one of them in a coffee can together with a scorpion and watch them battle each other to the death.

There were plenty of other creatures too. Snakes that had horns coming out their heads. Giant prehistoric-looking lizards with forked tongues and sharp claws. And a mysterious creature that only showed up on our surveillance system at night as it ghosted through the forest, and that Jonesie was convinced was a snow leopard, although none of us believed him.

As unnerving as all of that was, what made these nature walks most disturbing was that when we were out on patrol, we finally got a bird's-eye view of just how vulnerable we were. You'd be shuffling along a stretch of ridgeline somewhere up by the Diving Board or the Switchbacks or the North Face, and suddenly you'd gaze down at the outpost and realize just how many places there were, right there, from which to hide and shoot. To confirm that, you'd carefully raise your weapon and look through your scope down at the base, and then whistle softly to yourself.

Damn, you'd say, *they could do some real damage from here . . .*

Then you'd walk a hundred yards away, or maybe just fifty feet, then stop and stare through your scope again.

Jesus, you'd murmur. *This spot's even better than the last.*

But the creepiest thing of all, by far—the thing that messed with our minds more than the crack ants and the vomit spiders, more than the rock-throwing monkeys or the imaginary sniper posts—was when we'd stumble across a little patch of matted-down grass, an area that was maybe littered with one or two wrappers from Afghan candy bars, and you could tell someone had been there, looking down on us through the scope of their own weapon, drawing the same conclusions that we had, and making note of it all.

IN BETWEEN GUARD DUTY and going out on patrol, we were responsible for an endless range of chores that ran the gamut, from unloading the Chinooks and resupplying the battle positions with ammo to rounding up all the garbage in camp and hauling it to the burn pit, a shallow hole that was on the far western side of the camp.

The burn pit was continuously smoldering; its fires never seemed to go out. Sometimes, it seemed like you would go up there and look in and see the same piece of trash that had been burning for weeks. And there were several Afghan guys hanging out there all the time because that's where they kept their stash of porn magazines. They had a bench to sit on, and they had their own umbrella. We envied those guys greatly, not just because of their quality porn and their leisure time but also because they never seemed to get shot at, which was something that happened to us pretty much every time one of us went up there.

We also got shot at when we went to get water, which we started having to do multiple times a day after Kirk took out the camp's water-delivery system one afternoon when he tossed a hand grenade and accidentally hit the pipe about ten yards beyond the wire. From that point on, we had to send one of the junior guys like Mace or Davidson or Gregory out to the river just beyond the front gate, where he would fill up two plastic five-gallon buckets in which the fuel had been delivered, haul them back, and then return for more. The Taliban had so much fun shooting at the water guy that we had to establish two-man teams so that one guy could carry the water and the other guy could return fire. When it was hot and everybody was thirsty, they would schlep water all day long.

As unpleasant as that was, however, it couldn't hold a candle to the most unpleasant chore of all, which was servicing the latrines.

The "shitter," as we called it, was a small shed fashioned from cinder blocks that sat on an open stretch of ground about 150 feet from our shower trailer. Inside, there were plywood benches running along both walls, each of which featured a row of six holes with its own plastic toilet seat and a green-and-blue privacy curtain that never closed all the way except for one, which was obviously the choice stall. (The worst seat was the second one in on the right side, which had a curtain no bigger than a beach towel, which meant that you gave everyone a lookie-loo.) There was also one open hole, which was used by the Afghan security guards and laborers, who preferred to squat rather than sit.

Underneath each of the holes was an oil drum that had been cut in half with an acetylene torch, which would collect whatever fell into it. The bottom of the building was open so that the drums could be pulled out and the contents upended into a large metal barrel, a duty that fell to whichever of the lower enlisted guys happened to be pissing off me and the other sergeants the most. Once all the drums had been emptied, the boys on the burn detail would then douse the barrel with jet fuel and toss in a match.

It sounds simple enough. But if you just stood there and watched it burn, the flames would incinerate only the top layer inside the barrel. So it was necessary to get a c-wire post—a metal fence post used to support the concertina wire that we strung around the perimeter of camp—and vigorously stir the contents of the barrel while smoke from the aviation fuel and burning particles of poo wafted up into your face.

This process could easily take as long as three hours, although it was accelerated somewhat if you tossed in a couple of "charges," which were packets of explosives that we used to increase the distance of a mortar round by giving it an extra boost. When the mortar guys were willing to part with a few chargers, the guys on the shitter detail would fling them with great satisfaction.

"We're such badasses," Koppes used to brag, talking about Red Platoon, "that we even bring the fight to the poo cans."

Even with the charges, however, latrine duty was still a horrible experience. The smell alone was enough to make you want to throw up. Worse, you could spend the better part of an afternoon incinerating an entire drum of poo, only to discover that at the end of it there were still kernels of corn lurking at the bottom of the burn barrel. (Which is the reason why you never wanted to burn shit if corn had been served for dinner the night before.)

It was amazing to me that the younger guys—especially Koppes and Mace and Jones—somehow found a way to make all of that fun. They told themselves that at least they were mostly burning American feces rather than Afghan feces, and that this made all the difference. And they tried not to think about the fact that while they were standing in hundred-degree heat being coated with poo goo, the rest of the platoon was inside the barracks napping or playing Call of Duty on the Xbox.

MOST OF THE BUILDINGS at Keating were windowless, tin-roofed cubes that had been cobbled together from stacks of rocks and plywood, then reinforced with sandbags—which meant that from June through August, they basically functioned like saunas. Despite the oppressive heat, we had to spend almost all of our downtime indoors, thanks to the fact that virtually

Stephan Mace bringing the fight to the poo cans

every square inch of the outpost was visible from the surrounding hills. There were no football or volleyball games, no relaxation of any kind in the open. If we stepped outside for any reason—to walk to the shed that housed the phones to call home, to use the piss tubes or the latrines—whatever respite we might have felt from the heat indoors was negated by our full "battle rattle," almost thirty pounds of ceramic armor and Kevlar. Wearing armor was mandatory any time we were outside or on the move, so we were continuously drenched in our own sweat—which didn't help our ongoing odor problems.

Thanks to a series of intractable glitches with the power generator and the water pump, we were lucky to get a shower once a week. Before too long, we were holding competitions to see who could build up the most impressive stink. (Ryan Willson, a private who was unmemorable in pretty much every other respect, was the undisputed champion when it came to BO.)

When we weren't sleeping or on patrol, life during our downtime could become almost unbearably dull. To pass the hours, we played endless rounds of Hearts and Spades, and the Xbox was in constant rotation. Some of the guys also flung themselves heavily into fitness by going to the "gym," a ten-foot-by-twelve-foot room located above Headquarters Platoon's barracks that was equipped with a StairMaster, a treadmill, assorted dumbbells, and a broken Bowflex. The regular workout crew included Kirk and Gallegos, plus Daniel Rodriguez and Kevin Thomson, who were part of the gun crew in our mortar pit. (Thomson, a bear of a man who was extremely quiet and deeply fond of smoking weed, had developed a weight problem and was constantly logging time on the treadmill in an effort to shed some pounds.) Mace often showed up too, although he concentrated exclusively on doing curls in order to beef up his biceps in the hopes that his huge guns, together with the effects of the ExtenZe he was taking, would impress the ladies when he went home on leave in September.

By the middle of the summer, Kirk and Gallegos had gotten so fixated on bulking up that they were working out twice a day while pumping themselves full of bodybuilding supplements. The products they were ingesting—N.O.-Xplode, creatine powder, and whey protein—made them so gassy that they farted pretty much continuously, filling the air with noxious fumes.

Excessive flatulence might have presented a problem in the dining hall or the barracks, except for two things. Because at least one RPG had already gone through the roof of the chow hall and taken out the big-screen TV, we almost never ate or hung out there. Instead, we preferred to bring our meals over to our barracks building, which was already so disgusting that some additional cheese cutting had no impact whatsoever.

In addition to a pungent, nostril-clinging stink that featured a layered mix of corn chips, body funk, and ass, Red's barracks was also infested with fleas. The insects had established themselves so firmly that nothing could get rid of them. Despite that we all wore flea collars around our ankles and wrists, and that we'd managed to fly in a pest-control team (they left in disgust), each of us had flea bites all over our bodies.

The hooch in Red Platoon barracks shared by Raz and Larson

Nevertheless, we did our best to make the barracks feel like home. If you entered through the west door, walked down the hall, and peeked into the little sleeping cubicles known as "hooches," most of which featured a single set of bunk beds that accommodated a pair of roommates, you could almost always spot a detail or two which revealed something about the personality of the occupants.

Kirk and Gallegos's zone was relatively clean, reasonably well ordered, and absolutely chock-full of ammunition. While it was true that we all liked to stash what Jones called "a little somethin'-somethin'" in our bunks in case the base was attacked while we were asleep, Kirk and Gallegos took this practice to the extreme. In addition to an impressive assortment of guns, Gallegos had ammo belts hanging from virtually every surface. Kirk, meanwhile, had pulled several raids on our ammo-supply depot and managed to snatch up five AT4s and something like eighteen claymore mines. Together, they were probably hoarding the most impressive stash of munitions and weapons outside of the arms room.

A few feet down the hall was the hooch where Larson and Raz slept. If the curtain wasn't closed, it was best to avert one's eyes because Raz, who detested wearing clothing except when it was absolutely necessary, was almost always naked—a situation that Larson accepted, as he did most things, with his trademark silence.

Just beyond was the cubicle where Jones roomed with Kyle Knight, a specialist from Michigan who was so messy that trash was literally rolling out of his bunk, onto the floor, and into the hall—a state of affairs that earned both Knight (who fully deserved it) and Jones (who was deemed guilty by proximity) the distinction of being "the dirty birds."

Finally, there was the little space that Hardt shared with Mace, who won himself both envy and derision for the impressive collection of tasty snack goodies that his family kept sending him in care packages. When Mace let it be known that his packets of beef jerky and his cans of Chef Boyardee stew were off-limits to anybody who wasn't willing to at least *ask* before scarfing them down, Kirk—who prided himself on never letting anyone tell him what to do or not do—made a point of barging inside whenever Mace wasn't around, selecting something to eat, and ostentatiously leaving the wrapper behind just to let Mace know that he'd stopped by.

Later on when Mace would return and spot whatever Kirk had left behind, he'd pad down the hall, peel back the curtain to Kirk and Gallegos's hooch, and retaliate by farting into their cubicle. Given how much gas the occupants were already putting out, this gesture was both pointless and ineffective. But it seemed to offer Mace some satisfaction because he always returned to his bunk with a canary-eating grin.

Given how close we were living inside those barracks, it didn't take much for us to get on one another's nerves. To relieve some of that tension, me and the other sergeants were constantly offering miniature training seminars in everything from land navigation and radio operation to emergency medicine. We also held what we called "family night," in which the entire platoon would gather around a tiny table in the entryway of the barracks so that we could all watch a movie together.

Those things certainly helped. But to fully relax, it was necessary to step outside the barracks and head over to perhaps the only place in Keating where everyone, regardless of rank or seniority, truly felt at ease—which was odd because it was also the place where we gathered our wounded and dead.

CHAPTER FIVE

Everybody Dies

ALTHOUGH OUR MEDICAL FACILITY was tucked up against the wall of Hescos at the periphery of camp, it nevertheless served as the center of the outpost—the place, more than any other, that was the heart and soul of Keating. It wasn't much bigger than a kitchen in a modest suburban house, and there were no windows, just a plywood door that the medics propped open whenever we got into a firefight so the wounded could be brought directly inside.

The floor was an ugly blue linoleum. The walls were bare and gray. And above the rafters was a storage area that held large quantities of Kerlix for stanching arterial wounds, plus plenty of extra saline and drugs. Toward the back were two sets of bunks for the medics, Chris Cordova and Shane Courville, each of whom slept with a pair of fragmentation grenades next to him in his bed.

Cordova, a captain, was a former X-ray technician from the Washington, DC, area who had become a physician's assistant before joining the army. In addition to being a fitness addict who was deeply into triathlons and CrossFit training, he had the most extensive medical training of anybody at Keating. Courville, a staff sergeant who served as his assistant, was from a town in Vermont so small that he'd had thirteen people in his high school graduating class. In addition to a previous stint in Afghanistan, he'd done two hauls in Iraq, where he'd seen some horrific wounds

Doc Courville, Doc Hobbs, Captain Cordova, and Doc Floyd

inflicted on soldiers who were stationed inside the insurgents' haven between Mahmudiyah, Yusufiyah, and Latifiyah, an area that was known as the "triangle of death." This would be his fourth deployment.

Courville's time in Iraq was important because it had exposed him to so much trauma. By the time he got to Keating, he had dealt with somewhere around fifteen hundred injuries, a mixture of Americans and Iraqis with the balance tipped toward the Iraqis. From the perspective of a medic, however, there was one thing that made Afghanistan fundamentally different from Iraq, which was that you couldn't simply stanch a wounded man's bleeding and expect that a helicopter would appear from out of nowhere to whisk your patient off to a hospital. The battle theaters of Afghanistan were too remote for that. Instead, many medics would have had to wait, on average, at least an hour and a half for a chopper to fly out their casualties. At Keating, it could take far longer, which is why Courville

Chaplin Weathers, Courville, and Cordova in the aid station

and Cordova knew that they needed not simply to offer effective triage treatment, but also to keep their patients alive long enough for the helevac to show up.

The aid station was set up to handle three wounded men at a time. The worst case would be taken directly inside, where there was a wooden frame designed to hold a stretcher at waist height. The other two casualties would typically be carried out to the "café," a wooden deck extending off the west wall of the building. This area was partially covered by a tin roof and camo netting, and it was further protected by a double-stacked wall of sandbags, about four and a half feet high.

The medics had oxygen tanks, a ventilator, and a defibrillator that we never used. To administer saline and intravenous drugs, they would suspend bags from nails on the rafters in the ceiling. The walls also featured two whiteboards. The one by the litter frame kept track of the patients' vital signs. The other board was supposed to display the phone numbers of other buildings, such as the command post and the mortar pit. But instead we used it to run Keating's daily "incoming fire" betting pool.

The betting board kept track of the daily wagers everyone placed on when and where we were going to get hit next. The majority of those bets were logged on Fridays and Saturdays because those were the days the Taliban most liked to nail us. The board also kept track of side bets on more nuanced wagers, like, for example, whether the attack would involve small-arms fire or the B-10, or which gun trucks would get hit, and how many times. There was never money riding on these bets, because most of us didn't have any cash, so the stakes usually involved cigarettes or brass .50-caliber machine-gun cartridges, which could be used as currency to purchase cigarettes.

The aid station was pretty sweet for a number of important reasons, starting with the fact that the medics almost always had electricity because they were connected into the command post's backup generator. This meant that they not only had air-conditioning, but also their own phone as well as Internet with a DSN line, which meant that you could call back home to the States or set up a Skype chat on the computer.

Cordova and Courville were extremely generous with both the phone and the computer, and the guys who were married tended to lean on that generosity pretty heavily even though—in a reflection of how much stress we were all under—their calls home would often lead to absurd and pointless arguments. One night, one of them found himself in a furious dustup with his wife about the placement of a chandelier. Later, another dude got into a screaming match over where his wife had left the remote control to the TV.

"Jesus," muttered Koppes, who had inadvertently overheard part of that call, "please tell me you are not fighting with your old lady about where she left the clicker . . . from *Afghanistan*."

DESPITE THOSE minor unpleasantries, the aid station offered an escape to which anyone who wanted could retreat to bullshit, hang out, drink coffee, smoke cigarettes, and tell stories. Sometimes Courville and Cordova would prop the computer on the litter frame so that everyone could sit around and watch shows like *The Wire* or *The Office*. At other times, Courville would give classes on basic medicine or on how to use PowerPoint, while Cordova, who was deeply into stocks and investing, would offer miniseminars on financial planning. But as nice as all of those things were, what really drew us into the aid station was the tone and vibe of the place.

Because it was neutral ground, and because the medics floated inside a bubble that belonged neither to the world of the enlisted ranks nor to the realm of the officers, the aid station served, in effect, as Keating's de facto therapy shack. This was where NCOs like me would come in order to bitch to Courville about the dumb moves that our officers were trying to pull, and we knew that he'd listen with a willing and sympathetic ear. Those same officers, in turn, would come talk to Cordova about whatever it was that bothered them about the NCOs.

In essence, the medics provided a one-stop shop for both physical and emotional treatment. And, of course, the other draw of the aid station was that it was where we kept perhaps the most important item in the entire outpost, aside from the poster featuring a Hooters waitress from back in Colorado Springs: the pair of lace panties that had belonged to the Russian tennis star.

Her name was Maria Kirilenko, and that summer she would make it to the second round at Wimbledon before later going on to win a bronze medal at the 2012 London Olympics. Even more noteworthy, she had appeared in the *Sports Illustrated* Swimsuit Edition with two other female tennis players in a pictorial titled "Volley of the Dolls."

Our connection to Maria was first formed when a member of Red Platoon who must remain nameless sent her an e-mail whose message more or less said: "You might be able to kick my ass in tennis, but I could whip your ass in Ping-Pong," along with a comment about being stuck in the mountains of Afghanistan, which "you Russians should know all about."

A few days later, a reply showed up that read: "If you guys ever need someone to talk to, you know, I'm always here."

We ignored that, presuming it was either fake or had been sent by one of her handlers. But then a couple of weeks later, a package showed up in the mail whose return address was a house outside of London where female professional tennis players were supposed to live. Inside was a pair of white lace panties, carefully folded into a Ziploc bag. There was also a signed photo.

The arrival of these two objects provoked a massive amount of Googling in an effort to confirm the address and authenticate the signature on the back of the photo. When we concluded that, to the best of our knowledge, the items were legit, we affixed the Ziploc bag to the whiteboard and established a policy that everyone agreed was fair. Anybody who wanted could come by at any time, open up the bag, and take a sniff—as long as he didn't touch the panties with his fingers, and was careful to reseal the plastic.

Those panties had the most *amazing* smell, a perfume that was, to us, as beguiling as it was mysterious and unknowable. As it would turn out, years later and through a strange twist of fate stemming directly from the outcome of the battle that we were about to fight, we would eventually track down and confirm the name of that scent.

But this too is getting ahead of the story.

AS WE APPROACHED the end of the summer, the Taliban attacks slowly increased to the point where Keating was in total lockdown except for the helicopters that were flying in diesel fuel and ammo. When those supplies arrived, the pace could be intense. The Chinooks would land in the middle of the night and dump their loads as fast as possible before dusting off. We'd bring the forklift or the Bobcat across the bridge and onto the landing zone to haul the heaviest items back into camp. But the rest of the stuff would have to be carried by hand, which could take hours. Then the bird would return and we'd load it up with whatever we were sending out.

There were plenty of times when we got done unloading a shipment just as the sun was about to come up and decided that there was no point in even going to sleep because we'd have to head out on patrol within the hour. But what we found even more frustrating than the lost sleep was that we weren't getting our mail.

Sometime in August, after a delay of almost an entire month, we finally did receive one mail pouch—but the helicopter crew was in such a rush to dump the package that they accidentally dropped the thing in the river. After scrambling around in the dark, we managed to retrieve it, but the soaking upset some of the guys enough that a bunch of us decided that it was time to send a message out to the Chinook pilots.

Submitting a formal complaint would have done nothing, so instead we tromped into the aid station, fired up the computer, and found a website called PoopSenders.com. For a modest fee, they would deliver to any address in the world a quart- or gallon-sized package of dung from a variety of animals, including deer, rabbit, moose, cow, gorillas, and elephants, while keeping the identity of the sender anonymous.

After much discussion, we decided to go with elephant dung, which would be delivered to the Chinooks' home base in Jalalabad. We never quite managed to pull the trigger on actually placing that order. But the idea of responding to the shit we'd been taking from these pilots by sending them a consignment of *actual*, honest-to-God shit struck us as brilliant and hilarious.

At the time, we had absolutely no idea how ignorant we were about what was really going on: how brave those men were, the challenges that they were up against, or how important they would be to our survival.

THE HELICOPTER PILOTS of Jalalabad were far more than just airborne delivery boys; they also flew attack helicopters armed with a fearsome array of missiles, machine guns, and cannonry with which they could, quite literally, drench the enemy in hellfire from virtually any position. These men and women were game changers, the undisputed knights of the air. Without them, we would have been sitting ducks.

Those pilots were led by Jimmy Blackmon, a lieutenant colonel from Georgia who had an impressive armada of choppers on the tarmac just beyond his headquarters at Jalalabad Airfield. Task Force Pale Horse,

Courville, Kirk, Gallegos, and Raz

which Blackmon was in charge of, consisted of sixteen Kiowas, six Apaches, six Black Hawks, four Chinooks, and three medevac helicopters, plus a trio of Hunter unarmed aerial vehicles for surveillance. The task force was staffed by almost six hundred soldiers, and on any given week, the demands that were placed on them would be difficult for a civilian to comprehend.

Each night, regardless of weather or moonlight, Blackmon's pilots were moving people, equipment, and munitions around the battlefields along the Kamdesh, Korengal, and Kunar Valleys. This meant that there was a finite limitation on resources, and the decisions about how that limit was managed stemmed entirely from our brigade's priorities.

If the brigade's commanders wanted to stage an air assault at Restrepo, one of the most vulnerable outposts in the Korengal, this meant that half a dozen other outposts might not get resupplied for forty-eight hours. When the resupply was finally carried out, the first priority would be ammunition: mortars, small arms, and .50-cal rounds. After that would come water and fuel. Rations for the men was bumped behind those things, and all the way at the tail end of the line was mail—the item that, as it turns out, has the greatest influence on soldiers' morale.

The reality, which I didn't appreciate until years later, was that this constantly shifting alignment of priorities played havoc with the intricate task of sequencing a small number of aircraft beset by an endlessly exploding array of demands and flown by pilots who accepted appalling dangers.

For a fully loaded Chinook that was carrying ten thousand pounds of cargo, there was one way in and one way out of Keating, and it was right down the Kamdesh Valley, where the Taliban, fully aware of this necessity, made a point of shooting up the helicopters. On almost every mission the pilots launched, they found themselves in the airborne equivalent of a knife fight.

All of this was more than enough for Blackmon and his team to juggle, so receiving a shipment of elephant feces from a bunch of ground-pounders at Keating would not have been appreciated. But late in the summer, a series of events in eastern Afghanistan pushed Pale Horse even further into the red zone in a way that would have made our little prank totally unacceptable.

FROM THE FIRST DAY that we arrived in Afghanistan, our superiors— Colonel Randy George, the brigade commander, and Lieutenant Colonel Robert "Brad" Brown, our squadron commander—had been pushing aggressively to have Keating shut down as quickly as possible. By midsummer, a plan to dismantle not only Keating but also a few other exceptionally vulnerable outposts had been signed off on by General Stanley McChrystal, who was in charge of all US forces in Afghanistan, and there were hopes that we might be pulled out in the early autumn. Unfortunately, those plans were shoved to the back burner in the middle of the summer, when hundreds of insurgents and foreign fighters tried to seize a remote village just to the north of Keating.

The place was called Bargi Matal, and at the request of the Afghan government, which was afraid not only of losing its foothold in the area but also of losing the upcoming elections, the US Army started sending in troops and equipment. That drew off most of the air support we would need in order to dismantle Keating and evacuate, so our departure dates kept getting pushed further and further back.

Meanwhile, Colonel Blackmon juggled his four Chinooks to deliver what they needed to the American soldiers at Bargi Matal while simultaneously continuing to supply all the American outposts in the Kamdesh Valley. When he ran out of aircraft, he somehow managed to keep both missions going by borrowing extra helicopters from Bagram Airfield. By this point, however, yet another wrench had been thrown into the works.

Sometime after midnight on June 30, 2009, a young American soldier from Hailey, Idaho, named Robert "Bowe" Bergdahl slipped off the remote outpost called Mest Malak in Paktika Province on the border with Pakistan. Bergdahl left behind his body armor, weapons, and a note saying he had become disillusioned with the army and was leaving to start a new life. Several hours later, when he was discovered to be missing, soldiers began a frantic search using drones, helicopters, and tracking dogs.

When word arrived that Bergdahl had been seized by the Taliban and that his captors were going to try to move him to Pakistan, orders came down for a full-court press to find and recover the missing American. The mission went to Task Force Attack, an aviation unit stationed at Salerno, a forward operating base in the southeastern part of Afghanistan. Throughout July and August, Attack was banging four and five targets a night, running down intel leads on where Bergdahl might be in the hopes of pulling him out. And that effort sucked up every last Chinook and Apache that Blackmon had borrowed from Bagram.

For me and the rest of Black Knight Troop, this was the straw that broke the camel's back. The army simply didn't have the resources to do more than handle Bargi Matal and Bergdahl, so Colonel George's hope of shutting down our outpost and enabling us to get out of Keating was put on ice.

For the time being, we were stuck.

One could say that this boiled down to a cause-and-effect chain of lousy ideas, poor decisions, and flawed thinking. When it's laid out that way, the logic of this argument seems to hold water. But most soldiers who have experienced combat understand that armchair quarterbacking is shallow and often misguided. It's easy to second-guess decisions based on their ramifications, and then to assign blame. Considerably harder is accepting that in combat, things can and will often go wrong not because of bad decisions, but despite even the best decisions. That is the nature of war.

Of course, none of this changes the fact that, for those of us at Keating, things were about to truly go to hell.

TOWARD THE END of the summer the heat began to abate, which was a welcome change for everyone. As the weather cooled off, a few of the guys in the platoon got on Amazon and started ordering up hoodies. Pretty soon, everybody had one. The logo on the one that Koppes selected was Zoo York, the old-school skateboard-inspired brand that he imagined imbued him with a gritty, urban hip-hop vibe. Most of the other guys opted for their favorite colleges. When we'd get back from a patrol, we'd throw on our hoodies and settle in for another round on the Xbox. As evidenced by the smiles in the selfies we took, morale seemed to be improving.

In some ways, this was an outward manifestation of an inward trend. Despite the difficulties and challenges, we were finally hitting the point in the deployment where we felt marginally comfortable. Partly, this was because we now had a routine firmly in place. But the larger reason was that we were really starting to gel as a platoon in the field. Thanks to the patrols and the gym, we were all in the best shape of our lives. With a few exceptions, most of us liked one another and got along. Finally, we'd honed an impressive skill set, at both the individual and the collective levels, which enabled us to function together like a smooth, well-oiled machine.

If we had a major problem at this point—aside from our lingering security worries—it was keeping ourselves occupied. We were so bored when we were off duty that we were running out of things to say to one another.

One afternoon, mostly to avoid just sitting around in silence, we got into an argument about waterboarding, which had been authorized as a legitimate interrogation technique by the Bush administration during our stints in Iraq, but was now off-limits. Was it torture or not? we wondered. To settle the matter, we decided to try it on four of our own guys. While I poured the water, one of the other sergeants held a shirt over their faces. No one lasted past four seconds except for Koppes, who made it to eight. (After it was over, everyone agreed that it was definitely torture.)

In the end, however, what we did more than anything else—the thing that pushed the Xbox and the gym, the silly tricks and the endless bullshitting to the backseat—was to try to get inside the heads of the guys on the other side of the wire and figure out how they were going to attempt to destroy us. Many an evening, me and the rest of Red Platoon's leadership—a cast of about five guys that included Gallegos, Kirk, Larson, and Hardt—would gather at the café, the protected well just in front of our barracks, light up our cigarettes, and talk about how we'd plan for it to go down if we were staring into Keating from the ridgelines.

We all agreed that you'd want to come in just before dawn and start off by suppressing our mortar pit while simultaneously hitting OP Fritsche, which would silence our biggest guns. Then you'd lay down an impenetrable barrage of fire on all four of the armored Humvees—Truck 1, Truck 2, LRAS1, and LRAS2—with the goal of knocking out our .50-caliber machine guns and our Mark 19s, which would otherwise stop your assault cold. You'd also want to be certain to put an incredibly heavy volume of fire into the ammunition depot to make it impossible for us to resupply the gunners in those Humvees, who would then get picked off one by one as their ammo ran out.

Right after that, you'd start sending successive waves of men down the Switchbacks and directly at the Afghan Army barracks, getting as close as possible to our perimeter so that we'd be forced to hold off calling in our F-15s for fear of getting taken out by our own ordnance.

Your first wave of fighters would absorb the claymores below the Switchbacks and the machine-gun fire from the Afghan soldiers. But your second or your third wave would make it all the way to the wire and breach our perimeter. Once your guys were inside, it would be a turkey shoot. They could sweep through the entire camp, moving from hooch to hooch, eliminating us one pocket at a time down to the last man, whoever that might be.

We ran through variations on this scenario endlessly. When we'd strike. What we'd hit. How we'd coordinate. And no matter how hard we tried to come up with a solid plan to defend Keating, the outcome was always the same.

We'd get overrun and everybody would die.

Little did we realize how accurate those predictions would be when the Taliban decided that it was finally time to pull the trigger.

AFTER DINNER on the evening of the first Friday in October, Courville went up to the gym to work out with Kirk, Gallegos, and Larson. As they moved through their session, everyone noticed that Kirk, who was almost always a total loudmouth, was extremely quiet. Courville was bothered enough by his silence that just before he left, he turned to Gallegos.

"Is he all right?" he asked, nodding in Kirk's direction.

"Yeah," replied Gallegos, "as far as I know."

"Is everything okay with him at home?" continued Courville.

"Yeah, as far as I know."

"Well, okay, then," said Courville.

Stepping through the door, he walked downhill to the aid station. When he got there, he headed straight for his bunk, popped an Ambien because he hadn't been sleeping well, and went to bed.

Meanwhile, Gallegos was on his way back to our barracks, where Bundermann was preparing for bed with the knowledge that his responsibilities over the next few days would be heavier than normal.

Less than a month earlier, the widely disliked Captain Porter had finally been relieved of his command and sent home. His replacement, Stoney Portis, was a hard-charging captain from Texas who displayed promising signs of the aggressiveness and hands-on management that we had found so visibly lacking in his predecessor. As an example of that behavior, the previous morning Portis had hopped aboard a helicopter to catch a lift up to Fritsche, where he was hoping to meet with a group of Afghan elders from the neighboring village of Kamdesh.

He'd planned on returning later in the afternoon, but on the flight to Fritsche an insurgent had fired on the chopper, scoring a direct hit on the bird's fuel line and forcing the pilot to divert to Bostick for repairs. This meant that until Portis could catch another helicopter ride back to Keating, Bundermann was in charge—the de facto commander of Keating.

While Bundermann racked out for the night, Gallegos padded down the hall in search of Raz, who was supposed to sit for a promotion board exam the following morning at nine. The exam would determine if Raz moved up to the rank of sergeant, something he very much wanted, which was why he'd asked for help from Gallegos, who had already passed.

The two men studied together until well past midnight, at which point most of the guys in the barracks were fast asleep. By the time they finally went to bed, it was approaching one a.m.

By two a.m., the only guys inside Keating who weren't asleep were those on guard duty. One of these was Armando Avalos, our forward observer, who was stationed inside LRAS1, the gun truck just outside Blue barracks.

As he stared through his thermal optics from the turret of the Humvee, Avalos saw nothing out of the ordinary. There was no sign of any movement, nor was there any sound whatsoever. The night was as silent and as calm as one could wish.

Unbeknownst to Avalos or to anyone else inside Keating, however, a lot was happening along the slopes and ridgelines that ringed the outpost.

Somewhere out there, concealed by the terrain and cloaked in darkness, roughly three hundred Taliban fighters were moving into position around Keating while another hundred or so fighters climbed the slopes beyond the southern ridgelines to converge on Fritsche. Many of those men were from the surrounding villages, places that had names like Kamdesh and Agassi, Mandaghal and Agro, Gewi and Jalalah. Their numbers were reinforced by a smaller group of seasoned Afghan fighters who had been brought in from outside of Nuristan. It's also likely that there were a handful of foreigners from places like Saudi Arabia and Chechnya.

Around three a.m., a group of these insurgents entered the little village of Urmul, on the opposite side of the river. They ordered the residents to pack their things, vacate their homes, and leave the area. Then they split up and began occupying the buildings, setting up machine guns in windows and doorways that would enable them to shoot directly into Keating.

Two hours later, when their entire force was in position, the insurgents settled behind their weapons and patiently waited for dawn to arrive.

PART II

★ ★ ★

Going Cyclic

CHAPTER SIX

"Let's Go Kill Some People"

AT FIVE IN THE MORNING, the only frontline soldier at Keating who was awake but not on duty was Daniel Rodriguez, who was part of the four-man crew at the mortar pit. D-Rod, as we called him, had been drawn out of the pit by the chance to snatch a few minutes of online time at the aid station computer so that he could check his Facebook page and polish off the application papers for his upcoming leave in November, which he intended to spend surfing off the Gold Coast of Australia.

It was still dark as Rodriguez clomped down the metal set of stairs, fashioned from empty steel ammo cans, that led from the mortar pit and stepped onto the patch of high ground between the mechanics' bay and the trash pit. As he started skirting past LRAS2, the gun truck on the far western end of camp, he caught the glow of a cigarette coming from inside the turret of the armored Humvee, and stopped to exchange a few words with Mace, who was counting down the remaining minutes of his guard shift until Larson showed up.

When Rodriguez left Mace, he headed across the long stretch of open ground leading toward the main cluster of buildings at the center of camp. Upon reaching the aid station, he padded through the dark room as quietly as possible to avoid waking up Courville and Cordova, who were asleep in their bunks, and spent the final minutes before dawn tapping away at the keyboard.

• • •

Brad Larson and Daniel Rodriguez

AT 5:49 A.M., the sun rose.

By this point, a few of the guards on the battle trucks were starting to move. Ed Faulkner, who had been on Truck 1's gunner's turret for more than an hour, wouldn't be going anywhere for almost another two hours. The same was true of Truck 2, where a forward observer from Blue Platoon named Jonathan Adams was sitting quietly watching the first rays of light illuminate the Putting Green and the Switchbacks high above Urmul. But down at LRAS1, Hardt had already radioed for relief so that he could dash off to the latrines, and in response, Koppes was shuffling out with his copy of *SportsPro* stuffed into the go-to zone beneath his armor, anticipating a hot breakfast delivery as soon as Hardt finished taking his morning dump.

Out at the Shura Building, Nicholas Davidson and Justin Gregory were preparing a similar handoff inside the gun turret overlooking the front gate. Meanwhile, out at the western end of camp, Larson had just finished zipping up his fly and was retrieving his helmet and carbine from the hood of his Humvee before climbing into the cab of LRAS2.

The first rays of light were streaming off the tops of the mountains and into the valley when, at 5:50 a.m., Ron Jeremy, one of our Afghan interpreters, approached the front door of the command post to relay some disturbing news.

Shamsullah, the commander of the Afghan National Police station on the far side of the river just in front of Urmul, had sent word that enemy forces had moved into the village. In the middle of the night, according to Ron, the Taliban had begun ordering all the residents to vacate their homes and leave while small groups of fighters had moved in.

At 5:53 a.m., Sergeant Jayson Souter, who was with HQ Platoon, passed this info along to James Stanley, my other section sergeant in Red Platoon, who had just relieved Gallegos as sergeant of the guard and was standing out near the center of camp. Glancing around to see if he could spot anything strange, Stanley immediately caught sight of the commander of the Afghan Security Guards, a man who was normally armed with nothing more than a 9-mm pistol.

The guy was now carrying an AK-47 and several extra mags.

As Stanley made his way over to the command post to report what he'd seen and find out if he could learn more, he radioed the gun trucks to let the guys on guard know what was up. Chatter echoed across the net as, one by one, everyone on the perimeter began acknowledging.

Up inside the gun turret overlooking the front gate, Davidson was about to key his radio when he glanced toward Urmul, which was just emerging in the morning light, and noticed that dozens of armed men were dashing in and out of buildings all around the village.

Then he looked down, spotted the ASG commander with the AK-47 and the rack of extra ammo, and had the same thought as Stanley.

Weird . . .

It was 5:58 a.m. and Davidson was pressing the button on his radio transmitter when a loud bang sounded off to the west and an arrow-shaped missile came hurling toward the outpost with the distinctive trajectory of an RPG.

As the rocket approached, Davidson could see a plume of gray vapor that revealed the location of the shooter on the Putting Green, high on the spine overlooking Urmul. He lined up the M240's gun-sights on the point from which the smoke trail originated, and was about to trigger a burst of return fire when, as if on queue, the mountains surrounding Keating erupted in flames.

Along the ridgelines and across the hillsides, concealed behind rocks and trees as well as the buildings of Urmul, roughly three hundred insurgents opened up with everything they had: RPGs and AK-47s, B-10 recoilless rifles, Russian 82-mm mortars, sniper rifles, and the powerful antiaircraft machine guns known as "*dishkas.*"

Whatever arms the Taliban recruits had managed to scrounge from the surrounding villages, purchase on the black markets of Nuristan, or haul in across the mountain passes from Pakistan were now being brought to bear, with shocking effect, directly on Keating.

TO SAY THAT the initial seconds of the attack were too much for a normal mind to process would be an understatement. From his vantage in the turret of LRAS1, it seemed to Koppes as if someone had seized hold of a fold in the sky, ripped a hole in the thing, and was now dumping all the ordnance and munitions in eastern Afghanistan directly on top of his head.

As Koppes scanned the eastern and southern ridgelines in front of him, he spotted orange-colored muzzle flashes in every direction. There were so many starbursts that he found it impossible to concentrate on firing back at one or two and then moving on to the others. The flickering of gunfire, and the cumulative impact that it was having all over the outpost, overwhelmed his senses and forced him to respond by instinct.

The rounds were now coming in so fast that at first Koppes didn't even have a chance to key his radio and report what was going on. It was all he could do to concentrate on a few discreet flashes of light and try to get some grenades heading toward them.

The same was true sixty yards uphill where, inside the gun turret of Truck 1, Faulkner was hurling burst after burst from his .50-cal over the center of camp and across the river into the North Face.

Like Koppes, Faulkner was confused. Although he could see the smoke signatures of the incoming RPGs from within the tree line, there was no way for him to pinpoint the positions of the machine-gunners and snipers who had him in their crosshairs, and who were concealed by the rocks and vegetation. All he really knew was that it was his job to respond. And so, like Koppes, he furiously raked his gun across his sectors of fire, hoping that some of those rounds would find a target.

WITH THE GUYS on all four gun trucks fully engaged, Keating's outgoing was making a serious bid at keeping up with the Taliban's incoming. Granted, we weren't exactly matching the enemy shot for shot, and unlike the Taliban, we didn't have the luxury of being able to concentrate all of our fire in more or less the same place. Nevertheless, every heavy weapons system inside the outpost was immediately hot and rolling through ammo *hard*.

In addition to Faulkner and Koppes, Davidson had fully opened up from the turret above the front gate, and each of their guns had a distinctive sound. The sharp, piercing percussion of the M240 was underlaid with the bass growl of the slower and heavier .50-cal. Beneath all that, you could also hear the *chug-chug-chug* coming from the open area out near the latrines and the showers where Adams, assisted now by Hardt, was launching a storm of grenades toward the Switchbacks and the North Face from the Mark 19 on Truck 2.

Even amid all of that clatter, however, there was one sound that registered more distinctively than any other. It was the return fire coming from our most exposed battle position, as well as the one that was farthest from the command post: the gun truck on the far western end of camp that housed Keating's second .50-caliber machine gun, the "Ma Deuce" on the turret of LRAS2.

Judging by the sound of that gun, which was a noise that resembled a chain saw tearing through sheet metal, Brad Larson—a man who less than a minute earlier had been standing helmetless in front of the truck with his weasel in his hand—had clawed his way into the turret, thrown back the charging handle, and gone absolutely bat-shit.

MA DEUCE is the nickname for an M2 .50-caliber machine gun, and the working end of the weapon features a pair of grips known as spade handles, each of which has a V-shaped trigger that's called a "butterfly." If a gunner pulls down on the butterflies with his thumbs and keeps the gun on full auto, a well-maintained .50-cal is capable, in theory, of punching out almost six hundred rounds a minute.

This is known as "going cyclic," and it's something you generally want to avoid, except in the most extreme situations. If a gunner maxes out his rate of fire in this manner, it's likely he'll ream out the bore on his weapon within a belt or two. But long before that, the rounds he's sending through the breech can build up enough heat to literally melt the barrel. This is also an excellent way to jam your gun, creating the sort of problem that can be fixed only by climbing out of the turret, standing on the hood of the truck with your rear end exposed to whoever is trying to shoot you, and viciously kicking the loading arm until the thing finally decides to come unstuck, all the while hoping that you don't get drilled in the ass.

For this reason, if you're doing things by the book, you want to keep your cool and let off brief, accurate three-to-five-round bursts. That's the way to maintain good fire discipline and let the weapon do the work. All of which was (more or less) what Faulkner was doing over at Truck 1.

Well, fuck that, thought Larson, who, at this particular moment, couldn't have given a rat's ass what the book said, much less what Faulkner was up to. The only thing Larson wanted was to establish some fire superiority, and the only prayer he had of making that happen was to start dumping as many rounds downrange as he possibly could *right now*.

Going cyclic, in his estimation, was the sanest and most effective response to the tsunami of shit that was being hurled in his face.

Larson's gun truck had three separate sectors of fire that covered a

120-degree arc facing directly west. At the center of that arc lay Urmul, just 150 yards away on the other side of the Darreh-ye Kushtāz, whose tight cluster of flat-roofed, mud-walled buildings were nestled at the bottom of the massive, V-shaped declivity created by the Switchbacks to the left and the Putting Green to the right.

By Larson's best guess—and it was a pretty decent guess because, unlike Koppes and Faulkner, he was meticulously counting muzzle flashes—he was now being targeted by no fewer than twelve separate weapons systems spread across the field of fire in front of him. He could see smoke trails from several RPG teams high in the Switchbacks, the Putting Green, the Waterfall area, and the north side of RPG Rock. He was also facing off against at least three machine-gun crews—one firing from the Waterfall, another working from somewhere up on the ridgeline directly above the Switchbacks, and a third from somewhere deep inside the mosque. Scattered throughout the school and several houses on the near side of Urmul, there were also dozens of guys spraying him with AK-47s. And in addition to all of that, he was sitting directly in the crosshairs of several snipers, each armed with a Russian-made Dragunov that fired a 7.62-mm round capable of blowing through Kevlar body armor as if it were made from the working end of a squeegee mop.

Those snipers were a particular problem for Larson because their rounds were so disturbingly accurate and so menacingly close. They thudded into the bulletproof windshield in front of his knees. They ricocheted around inside the turret that shielded his torso and chest. A bunch of them were even splintering off the plywood shade cover of the .50-cal itself. But what shook Larson more than how close those snipers were to drilling him through the forehead (a job they probably should have taken care of when he was still taking a piss), and more than the proximity of the enemy (he could now see dozens of them moving brazenly inside the village and along the river), more rattling than even the feeling that he simply could not shoot fast enough (the guys he was facing off against were fricking *everywhere*)—the thing that Larson found most sobering was the simple realization of how terribly alone he was in that moment.

To the west, north, and south were a couple hundred Afghans wearing turbans and Chinese sneakers.

Inside the gun truck? One lone dude from Nebraska.

A dude who was now kicking himself for having neglected to bring his chest rack out on guard duty with him that morning—an omission which meant that when Larson finished burning through his machine-gun rounds or when the .50-cal finally decided to lock up (whichever came first), he would have only his M4 assault rifle and seven thirty-round magazines' worth of bullets with which to defend not just himself but the entire western sector of Keating.

Damn, he thought, *I kinda need some help out here.*

This was no time to call for help, though—nor was it the time to ring up the command post and deliver a crisply worded sitrep on precisely how much crap was flying through the air. No, this was the time for only one thing, which was to rock the Ma Deuce to her outer limits, and then see what she'd do when he took her past that point.

And so Larson rammed down the butterflies and sent an entire belt of three hundred rounds running through the gun while working the barrel back and forth in the hope that even if he wasn't being completely accurate— which is to say, even if the spray-and-pray he was putting out didn't find a single viable target—perhaps the demonic manner in which he was riding his gun on full auto would give the enemy a few seconds' pause before they decided to bum-rush the Humvee.

He figured he had about fifteen hundred rounds, and as he neared the end of his first belt and found himself starting to ponder the question— which was an interesting one—of how the hell he was going to survive a reload, he also took note of the odd fact that there didn't seem to be any return fire whatsoever coming from the mortar pit.

As Big John Breeding never tired of pointing out to anyone who would listen, the pair of guns in his pit, the 60-mm and 120-mm mortars, qualified as serious rainmakers. They were, by far, the heaviest casualty-producing assets that Keating had. What's more, those guns were always laid onto specific targets where we knew the enemy liked to set up shop, and the mortar crew had someone awake and on radio watch twenty-four hours a day so that if called upon, they could start hanging rounds immediately.

The response time for Breeding's crew to start getting rounds in the air should, in theory, add up to about two and a half nanoseconds. Which meant that by now, Breeding and his guys should already have started putting a deluge of hurt down on the enemy fighters who were trying to obliterate Keating.

Where the fuck are those mortars? Larson wondered.

Right about then, he caught sight of something moving off to his left.

It was Rodriguez, clad in nothing but a T-shirt and vest, gym shorts, and tennis shoes, running for the mortar pit as if his life depended on it.

Which, at that moment, it most definitely did.

WHEN D-ROD, sitting in front of the computer inside the aid station, had heard the first wave of rockets start to drop, he immediately started clipping on his vest while cursing himself for having failed to bring his carbine.

"What's up?" asked Courville, who had just emerged from his bunk in the rear of the building.

"Gotta run, Doc," replied Rodriguez as he shot out the door. "Wish me luck."

Without his gear to slow him down, Rodriguez moved fast, zigzagging past the showers, the laundry trailer, and the piss tubes toward the western end of the outpost. Taking the open slope beyond at a dead sprint, he started to fire his 9-mm handgun toward the Switchbacks, where half a dozen enemy gunners were doing their best to nail him with their AK-47s.

Bullets were kicking up small stones and bits of dirt around his feet, but the gunners couldn't get a bead on him. Then, as he drew near Larson's gun truck, he heard bullets clanging off the armor and called out a warning.

"Mace! Mace!" he yelled—not realizing that Mace had been replaced by Larson. "Friendly coming!"

Rodriguez was planning to take a pause beside the Humvee before making his final push across the open stretch of ground leading to the ammo-can staircase. But just as he was about to veer over, the truck took a direct hit from an RPG. The rocket plowed into the fender just above one of the tires, exploding with enough force to knock Rodriguez to the ground while sending flames all along the south side of the Humvee.

"*Maaaace!*" he screamed as the figure behind the gun, which was actually Larson, flopped backward and disappeared inside the turret.

Getting no reply, Rodriguez got back on his feet and resumed his race for the pit. When he hit the bottom of the stairs, he emptied the rest of the fifteen-round magazine on his handgun.

Right then, nothing was more important to D-Rod than getting those mortars up.

AS RODRIGUEZ APPROACHED the top of the stairs, Breeding had just extracted himself from his fart sack (which was what he liked to call his sleeping bag) and was punching the keys on the laptop that cranked out the grid coordinates he'd need to lay the guns on a new set of targets.

Meanwhile, Kevin Thomson was already geared up—he'd been monitoring the radios all night while playing a video game on the PlayStation—and racing out the door, weapon in hand, into the pit. His aim was to get to the 60-mm gun tube and put out some suppressive fire with his assault rifle while Breeding determined what charges they would need to place on the rounds.

The mortar pit was protected by a single M240 Bravo machine gun that was mounted on a steel fence post with a pintle on top that cradled the gun while permitting it to swing. The mortar team liked to keep that gun covered with a poncho to protect it from rain and dust, and as Rodriguez came off the top of the stairs and into the pit, he grabbed hold of the poncho and yanked it to the side.

"RPG Rock!" yelled Thomson, shorthand to let Rodriguez know that the pit was taking fire from a massive boulder about two hundred feet above them that looked directly down into camp from the far corner of one of the switchbacks—and that D-Rod needed to lay some fire on it immediately.

Kevin Thomson

Rodriguez seized the gun and was bringing it on target when Thomson, who was standing an arm's length away, let out a soft grunt as a Dragunov sniper round, fired from somewhere up in the Switchbacks, slammed straight into this face.

It's an indication of the extreme angle of the Taliban's plunging fire from the ridgelines surrounding us that the bullet pinholed through Thomson's right cheek, then blew an exit hole beside his left shoulder blade. Along the way, it destroyed his jaw, his tongue, and two of his cervical vertebrae, along with a bunch of the soft tissue at the base of his neck.

Without uttering another sound, the big man with the quiet smile who loved to smoke weed crumpled to the ground, bleeding from the face and head like a steer felled to the floor of a slaughter chute.

Rodriguez, who watched the whole thing unfold in front of him, had already seen death dished out in any number of horrible ways during his time in Iraq. (He'd been on the cleanup team of an armored Humvee that had been blown up by an IED one morning in 2007, scrambling and cooking the contents so badly that the remains of the three American soldiers inside formed what he had described as a "human stew.") Unlike those guys in the Humvee back in Baghdad, however, Thomson was Rodriguez's closest friend. And seeing him cut down, from less than two feet away, cracked open a door in D-Rod's mind that led to a stash of cold rage he didn't even know was there.

Without a word, he put his shoulder into the gun, squeezed the trigger, and didn't let off until he'd put more than three hundred rounds into the Switchbacks, where the shot that killed Thomson had come from. As he fired, the casings from his spent cartridges tumbled from the breech and partially buried the body of Thomson under a blanket of hot brass.

If you don't let off, a 240 Bravo takes about thirty seconds to chew through three hundred rounds. As Rodriguez completed his payback fusillade, the sound of his weapon merged with the baseline sound track of the surrounding battle to form the thunderous, full-throated, symphonic fury that is the audible signature of no-quarters combat.

One hundred and fifty yards downhill to the northeast, inside the tight little cluster of stone-and-plywood barracks buildings at the very center of camp, that sound was now rousing me and the rest of Black Knight Troop from our bunks.

AS I CAME out of my rack in the third hooch from the south end of Red barracks and threw on my battle kit, I could hear that we were taking fire from every sector. What's more, I could tell that the intensity was on a new and different order of magnitude from anything we'd yet encountered. Something about the way those rounds were coming in—I'm not sure exactly what it was, but we all heard it—signaled that this wasn't just serious but *nothing-like-we've-ever-seen-before* serious.

This was no mere hit-and-run, guerrilla-style skirmish, and that awareness—the fact that the Taliban was meeting us in direct, toe-to-toe combat, an all-out assault into which they were funneling everything they could muster to wipe our presence off the map of Nuristan—brought every man to his feet knowing that we needed to throw every gun we had into this fight.

From every hooch, guys were strapping on gear and moving down the hall toward the weapons rack to grab their guns.

At the first cubicle from the north end, Kirk was snatching up his vest as he turned to Avalos at the far end of the hallway.

"They're startin' up early today," said Kirk, stepping into the hall. "Let's go kill some people."

By this point in our deployment, we'd been attacked enough that most of us, especially the staff sergeants and the team leaders, knew exactly where they needed to be. Some of the younger guys, however, paused before heading out the door to take a quick look at the whiteboard to confirm which position they were supposed to man.

"Dannelley, you're with me!" yelled Jones as he pulled one of his Mark 48 machine guns off the weapons rack, shoved it into Dannelley's hands, and started draping hundred-round belts of ammo over his shoulders.

According to the battle roster, Jones and Dannelley were responsible for getting that machine gun out to support Koppes at his Humvee. As both men headed toward the north door of the barracks, Jones almost collided with Kirk.

"Hey, what time is it?" demanded Kirk.

"It's 6:01," replied Jones.

The Battle for COP Keating was exactly three minutes old.

Thomson was already dead. Larson had just gotten smoked. And those nine words that Kirk and Jones had just exchanged?

That would be the last thing those two dudes ever said to each other.

CHAPTER SEVEN

Heavy Contact

WHEN I SWITCHED on my handheld radio, reports were rolling in from every point along our perimeter defenses, and from those sitreps it was clear that each one of our battle positions was overwhelmed with fire from every possible direction.

Because Red Platoon was already on guard duty, it would be our job to man the heavy weapons systems and try to stop the assault. White Platoon would play no part in this effort because they were all up at Fritsche—but it was Blue Platoon's job to support us by delivering ammo, a task that a few of them had already stepped up to by snatching up extra bags of ammo that had been stashed in their barracks and running them out to the gun trucks. The bulk of Blue, however, was now gathering in their barracks with the two sergeants who were their section leaders, Eric Harder and John Francis, and preparing to make a coordinated push out of the ammo supply point, the two rooms built into the Hesco wall on the east side of the Shura Building that contained our primary stash of munitions.

Because Sergeant First Class Frank Guerrero was back in the States on leave, I was the acting platoon sergeant for Red. This meant that instead of jumping into the fight, my first job was to figure out where every man in the platoon was and find out what he needed, starting with my four team leaders: Hardt and Larson for Alpha section, Kirk and Gallegos for Bravo.

One way of getting a head count is simply to monitor your radio and try to piece together an assessment based on what you're hearing from the various sectors of the battlefield. But a more comprehensive picture of how a fight is shaping up can be gleaned by stepping into the command post. So that was where I headed first.

While bullets snapped at the walls and plowed along the ground, I dashed across the fifteen-foot gap that separated Red barracks from our tactical operations center, yanked on the plywood door on the west side of the building, and flung myself inside.

The interior of our command post was unapologetically functional and spartan. The lights were six-foot-long fluorescent tubes, and the place was devoid of any of the frills that you'd see in other buildings. There were no posters like the ones at the gym. No outdated Christmas and Fourth of July decorations like the stuff hanging from the walls of the chow hall. And certainly no Ziploc baggies with tennis-star panties.

The windowless room was dominated by a pair of eight-foot-long tables fashioned from two-by-sixes and plywood, which ran almost the entire length of the room. The first table held several laptop computers, including one reserved for the commander. The second, which also supported several computers, sat directly in front of a bank of half a dozen flat-screen TV monitors mounted on the east wall. Several of those monitors displayed maps of Keating and the surrounding mountains. On the west wall, just a few feet from the door, hung another map that pinpointed the location of every major weapons system inside the outpost, along with its sectors of fire.

The first thing to catch my eye were a bunch of guys attached to Headquarters Platoon, most of whom were sitting on metal folding chairs and hunched over their laptops at one of the two tables. Glaring into the biggest of the flat-screen computers were Private Jordan Wong, our radio operator, and Sergeant Ryan Schulz, our intelligence analyst. Standing behind them were Lieutenant Cason Shrode and Sergeant Jayson Souter, who were in charge of coordinating artillery and air support, along with First Sergeant Burton.

In all, at least ten guys were jammed into the command post, and each of them was doing several things at once. Standing at the center of this mess was Bundermann, who was clad in a brown T-shirt, black shorts, and a pair of plastic Adidas flip-flops, an ensemble that made him look like he was getting ready for a game of beach volleyball. He had no helmet, no weapon, and no chest rack. (Far more problematic, in his view: he also did not have his can of chewing tobacco.)

The second that Bundermann had been awakened by the torrent of incoming fire, he'd leaped from his rack and sprinted over to the command post without bothering to grab a single piece of his battle kit. But the fact that he was now so wildly out of uniform reflected something larger than an understandable lapse of attentiveness regarding his gear—which was that he wasn't really supposed to be inside the command post at all.

As the lieutenant in charge of Red Platoon, Bundermann's normal battle position—the place to which he was accustomed to going and, in fact, the place where he felt that he truly belonged—was the LRAS2 gun truck. This was his go-to spot, the destination to which he'd raced at the start of virtually every engagement since the first day we'd arrived at Keating.

LRAS2 was also where Bundermann *preferred* to be because, among other reasons, he was convinced that this was where we would win or lose a major battle like the one that was now unfolding. But like it or not, with Captain Portis still stranded at Bostick, the command post was where he belonged.

From this moment forward, every tactical decision—where we funneled our remaining resources; which areas we defended and which sectors we ceded to the enemy; how we coordinated the assets we still had with those that were, hopefully, on their way—all of that responsibility, all of that burden, rested directly on Bundermann's shoulders.

He had neither asked for nor aspired to this role. But nevertheless, it was now his show. And the way that show played out would be determined, in large part, by how Bundermann handled the most potent and far-reaching weapons system at his fingertips.

KEATING'S PRIMARY MEANS of communication with the world outside the wire involved a military Internet-relay chat system that was known by its acronym, mIRC. In essence, mIRC functioned like an instant-messaging app on a cell phone, except that multiple users could hop onto and off of the net at the same time. During the heat of battle, this form of tactical chatting (or "tac-chat") was more efficient than phone lines or even radios.

Inside the command post, the way the tac-chat worked was that Bundermann would instruct Wong, his radio man, what to type under the call sign of Keating's commander, which was "2BlackKnight." As Wong pecked away at his keyboard, other members of HQ Platoon—Schulz, Shrode, Souter, and Bundermann himself—would also be weighing into the system under their own call signs. While that was happening, the system was also logging a stream of responses, orders, and questions from command posts at other bases that would be scrambling to get us help. This included not just Bostick, but also Jalalabad, Kandahar, and Bagram. The network even extended as far away as Ramstein, Germany, where a satellite relay station enabled air force specialists in Nevada and New Mexico to communicate—using the same tac-chat network—with armed Predator and Reaper drones that were patrolling the skies directly above Keating.

If this instant-messaging system went down for any reason, we had SATCOM as a backup, which was essentially a phone with a satellite uplink. This was reliable, but unlike the tac-chat, there was a limit to how many people could be on the SATCOM line at the same time. So we tended to lean most heavily on tac-chat—a fact that was now evident on the forty-two-inch flat-screen on the east wall of the command post.

Looking up at that monitor as I walked in, I could see the messages scrolling onto the screen as they were being logged. This provided a running record of the battle, starting with our initial call for help and including the first response we were just now receiving from Task Force Destroyer, the call sign of our immediate superiors in Bostick:

6:02 a.m.
<2BlackKnight_TOC>
>>> Keating in heavy contact . . .

121

>>> *We have mortars pinned down and fire coming from*
everywhere . . .
>>> *We need something*

6:02 a.m.
<TF_DESTROYER_BTL_CPT>
>>> *We are working to get rotary wing and close air support.*

While Bundermann juggled these external communications with Bostick, Jalalabad, and beyond, he was also receiving a steady stream of reports from—and issuing orders to—the American soldiers inside the wire at Keating. To do that, he had five radio channels, or "nets," each keyed to a separate frequency that was reserved for a particular group of soldiers. The Force Pro net, for example, connected Bundermann to his section leaders within each of the platoons inside Keating's perimeter, while the Platoon net was restricted to platoon leaders such as myself and Jonathan Hill, who ran Blue. If Bundermann wanted to speak to anyone up at Fritsche, he had to switch over to the Troop net, while the Fires net was reserved for Keating's mortar pit. Finally, there was a separate channel, the CAG net, which stood for "combat applications group." This would patch him through to aircraft flying overhead, enabling him to speak directly to the pilots of any fixed-wing aircraft or helicopters that were within communication range of Keating.

What made this especially challenging was that while Bundermann managed all of this internal and external talk, he was also making decisions—in many cases, split-second decisions—that would help to determine who among us survived, and who did not.

WHEN I BURST into the command post and slammed the door, Bundermann was standing in front of the target-overlay map, which depicted the sectors of fire that corresponded to Keating's defensive battle positions. He was holding a radio to one ear, his gaze was locked onto the map, and he was speaking into the SATCOM mike, which he held in his other hand.

His remaining ear was cocked to a green speaker mounted on the east wall, which was broadcasting all the radio traffic coming across the Force Pro net.

It wasn't easy to make sense of the Force Pro net because everyone was trying to talk at once. Reports were tumbling in from all four gun trucks and the front gate, as well as from various other men who were on the move.

Red Five: Truck One is almost black on ammo!

Red Five-Delta: The ECP is taking heavy, accurate fire from the North Face, the Putting Green, the ANP Station, and north up the LOC!

Red Six: Calling for immediate suppression on targets 4525 and 4526!

Those voices on the radio were laid on top of the sounds of battle reverberating through the walls of the command post. The volume of fire and the varying pitches of the different weapons—the incoming PKM machine guns and RPGs; the outgoing M4s and Mark 48s—all of it rose to a level of intensity that to a civilian would have sounded like total chaos. But to Bundermann's ear and mine, that multilayered cacophony made sense on several levels.

The concussions that were rattling the walls and the roof of the command post told us that we were taking fire from every cardinal point of the compass, and that although the RPGs were coming in at a rate of roughly one every fifteen seconds, the machine-gun and small-arms fire was pretty much continuous.

At the same time, the radio traffic was letting us know that Koppes's truck was being hit by a torrent of fire, that Faulkner needed an immediate resupply of .50-cal ammo in order to keep his gun in action, and that Davidson's turret above the front gate was now engulfed in smoke, and thus in danger of being overrun.

When those two streams of information merged—the rockets and bullets slamming into the outside of the building, the increasingly agitated voices coming across the Force Pro net—it was evident that our return fire wasn't having much effect, because the enemy was able to continue pouring it on without pause.

The upshot was clear. If we didn't get some help soon, we weren't going to last much longer—which was why Bundermann was now ordering Wong to send out a series of requests for help, starting with an immediate call for with air support.

He wanted both fixed-wing jets and attack helicopters—in short, anything that army aviation in Jalalabad and the air force in Kandahar and Bagram were willing to send us. The urgency of those requests was reflected in the messages that were being logged into the system:

> *6:03 a.m.*
> *<2BlackKnight_TOC>*
> *>>> We need air ASAP . . .*
> *>>> We need air assets . . .*
> *>>> HEAVY CONTACT*

While awaiting a response from Bostick, Bundermann turned to the next order of business.

Big John Breeding was calling in on the Fires net with a report from the mortar pit.

"I GOT ONE KIA," declared Breeding from his position inside the mortar team's bunker, which was directly adjacent to the pit. "Thomson's dead."

"Roger," Bundermann replied. "Can you get out to the pit and get your guns up?"

"Negative, we're taking too much fire," said Breeding. "The pit *cannot* come up."

"Okay, B," said Bundermann, invoking his nickname for Breeding. "Stand by."

Another call was coming in on the Force Pro net—this time from Gallegos, who was standing out by the latrines on a piece of higher ground that gave him a good overview of what was happening at LRAS2, where Larson had popped back up in the turret after the RPG hit that Rodriguez had witnessed. (As it turned out, Larson had been struck in the neck, shoulder, and bicep by bullet fragments that had spalled off the top of the truck, but the turret shield had protected him from the worst of the blast.)

While Gallegos watched, Larson was now attempting to reload the .50-cal—an awkward process that involved leaning forward to pry open the cover of the machine gun, feed in a new belt of ammo, and then close the cover—moves that left him dangerously exposed.

Gallegos could see that if Larson didn't get some help and get the gun working quickly, his gun truck was in danger of being overwhelmed. He also understood that in the absence of air support, the best way to assist Larson was by bringing the mortar pit's guns up and targeting them on the Switchbacks—which was exactly what he was now demanding on the radio from Bundermann.

Unfortunately, there was a bit of a catch-22 in meeting this request, because if the mortar pit was pinned down, the only gun truck that was positioned to provide suppressive fire to free up the mortars was, as luck would have it, LRAS2. In a nutshell, the mortar pit and Larson's gun truck worked in tandem, sort of like the wings of an airplane: if one was taken out of action, the whole deal pretty much fell apart. Right now, each of the two battle positions required the very thing that the other could not provide.

In response to Gallegos's requests, which were getting more insistent with every second, Bundermann jumped back on the Fires net to find out if, by some miracle, anything had changed on Breeding's end.

"Hey, B, can you get to your guns?" he asked.

Breeding glanced out the doorway into the pit.

The incoming fire was so intense that Rodriguez, who was now inside the bunker with Breeding, couldn't even pull Thomson's body out of the field of fire and drag it into the mortar team's hooch. Each attempt he

John Breeding

made triggered a massive barrage of fire from RPG Rock. The entire pit was now a kill zone.

"Sir, we are straight-up pinned down," replied Breeding. "Everything is exploding inside the pit. The only way I can get out there and get those guns up is if you ask me to kill everybody else up here. It can't be done without us dying."

As Breeding spoke, Rodriguez was scrambling outside for one more attempt to retrieve Thomson. As he seized his friend's legs, an RPG smashed into the top of the 120-mm mortar shack.

The concussion caught D-Rod and hurled him through the air and straight through the open doorway of the hooch, where he crashed to the floor.

"I want to help, sir," Breeding said to Bundermann, "but I can't do it without killing the rest of my men."

"Roger that," said Bundermann. "Hold tight."

• • •

BY THIS POINT, I'd learned as much as I could from inside the command post about where my guys were and how the battle was shaping up. It was now time for me to get outside. As I slipped out the door, Wong was still sending out pleas for help through the tac-chat:

6:04 a.m.
<2BlackKnight_TOC>
>>> Still taking heavy contact. Need something. Our mortars
can't get up . . .
>>> We are taking casualties . . .
>>> GET SOMETHING UP!

There was no mistaking those requests. But given how rapidly things seemed to be spinning out of control, Bundermann wanted to convey the seriousness of our situation directly to our superiors—and the best way to do that, it seemed to him, was by speaking one-on-one to Captain Portis at Bostick.

Keying the mike on the SATCOM, he put a call through to the radio-telephone operator in Bostick's command post. Upon hearing the request, the operator asked him to hold the line, explaining that Portis had just been woken up and would be there in a few seconds.

As Bundermann waited, the line suddenly went dead.

Outside the walls of the command post, the Taliban commanders had been directing a portion of their RPGs and their B-10 shells at our electrical generators, knowing that without those units, we had no power—and that without power, we had no communications. It was a smart plan—conforming, almost to the letter, to the way we'd imagined the first phase of an all-out attack like this would play out. And now that strategy was paying some rich dividends. An RPG had just landed a direct hit on our 100kW generator, which sat next to the mosque and powered pretty much everything at Keating that ran on electricity, including almost every piece of equipment in the command post.

First the big screens on the walls—the maps of the outpost and the tac-chat dialogue—winked out and went dark.

Next, the video screens from the motion-sending cameras on the southern perimeter started blanking out, one by one.

Finally, we lost the lights, the radios, and the coffeepot.

Although we still had our battery-powered communications inside the outpost, we were now cut off from the outside.

UP AT THE MORTAR PIT, Breeding and his remaining men had taken up defensive positions just inside their hooch with their M4s pointed out the two doors, their eyes peeled for any sign of movement that would signal a Taliban assault.

"*Hey*," Rodriguez whispered to Breeding and Sergeant Janpatrick Barroga, the third member of their crew, "I think I hear something."

From above the concrete roof of their hooch, there were definite signs of movement. It sounded as if a group of enemy fighters was approaching the outer wire from the south, most likely from a large boulder directly behind the mortar pit.

Then the men in the pit started hearing voices.

As the enemy passed by, no more than fifteen or twenty feet from the pit, pushing east toward the mechanics' bay and the shower trailers, they were laughing and cheering one another on.

Judging by those voices, Breeding figured that there were probably two dozen men, far too many for the mortar crew to fight in close quarters. Breeding did, however, have one thing up his sleeve: the mines that were seeded at the edge of the wire about fifty yards away.

Those claymores could pack enough of a wallop to blow some holes in the line of attackers before they reached the concertina wire that formed the southern perimeter of the outpost. The only catch was that the mines had not been tested or replaced in more than a year, despite our repeated appeals to Captain Porter to let us do exactly that.

Moving quietly, Breeding reached for the clacker, an electronic triggering device that would detonate both mines, squeezed it together like the handles on a set of pliers, and . . .

Nothing.

Neither of the claymores blew.

As Breeding seethed at the incompetency of our former commander, Barroga—who had arrived at Keating only two days earlier, and had never before been in combat—turned to him with a question.

"Hey, Sergeant," Barroga asked, "are these attacks always this bad?"

"No, dude, not at all," Breeding declared emphatically. "They have *never* been this bad."

"Well . . . is everything gonna be okay?" asked Barroga, unable to connect the dots.

In his eighteen years in the army, John Breeding had never been a dispenser of bullshit. He saw no need to change now.

"I don't know if we're going to get outta this one," he replied, looking Barroga in the eye. "All I can tell you is that if we go, we're taking some of these motherfuckers with us."

Combat Kirk

TO SAY THAT JOSH KIRK found the prospect of a let's-take-the-motherfuckers-with-us gunfight less than intimidating would not, perhaps, be entirely accurate, because this was precisely the sort of standoff—desperate, outmatched, furious—that Kirk lived for. It was the thing that lit his fuse like nothing else.

As far as Kirk was concerned, we were finally getting a taste of the real deal. And as such, this moment marked the arrival of the kind of test that no true soldier could fail to embrace. Which is why Kirk's primary aim—aside from venting the impulse to get the hell out of Red barracks as quickly as possible so that he could start returning some fire—was to race directly to one of the most vulnerable points in camp.

It's hard to imagine anywhere more important to Keating's defense than the Shura Building. While the east wall of that structure formed the ammo supply point where all of our munitions and explosives were stored, the Shura's roof housed the machine-gun turret from which Davidson was desperately trying to protect the front gate. The building had already taken the brunt of the very first wave of RPGs. It was here, Kirk knew, that his particular brand of aggression was most needed now.

As it happened, the battle roster indicated that Gregory and Knight were also supposed to be heading to the Shura Building. But as all three men clustered at the front door of the barracks and Gregory, who was first in line, started to push the thing open, he was greeted with a storm of gunfire that raked the stairs, the roof, and the ground directly in front of him.

Leaping back, Gregory collided against Kirk.

"We gotta find another way out," barked Kirk, heading for the back door on the east side of the building.

He peeked through the door to make sure it was clear, then turned to his team.

"Gregory, grab that AT4," he ordered as they headed out.

The three of them clattered down the alley in front of the command post, hooked a sharp left at the corner of the barracks, and squeezed past a Bobcat, a small front-loader that had been abandoned on the corner of our ammunition supply shed, partially blocking the path to the aid station. Then they moved along the wall of Hescos that formed the northern perimeter of the outpost and turned toward the Shura Building, roughly ten yards away.

Instead of a flat-out sprint, they bounded—each man moving forward, in turns, while the others covered him. With every pause, Kirk shoved another round into the breech of his .203 and pumped a grenade across the river toward the North Face while simultaneously letting loose with his M4. It look less than two minutes for them to complete their maneuver.

When they came through the back door on the east side of the Shura Building, they couldn't see more than a few feet ahead because the air inside was filled with dust created by the RPG rounds that were pounding into the outer walls. As Kirk approached the ladder on the west wall leading to the entrance to the turret where Davidson was manning the M240 machine gun, he peered through the haze and spotted an Afghan Security Guard who had abandoned his fighting position just beyond the front gate, and was now taking shelter in the turret entrance.

"Get out of there, you fucking *coward*," yelled Kirk as he grabbed the Afghan and shoved him out of the way. Then Kirk stepped to the side of the doorway and ordered Gregory to cover him while he punched a round from the AT4 up into the Putting Green.

Both men stepped into the open doorway, and Kirk raised the barrel of the single-shot rocket launcher to his shoulder.

As he took aim and prepared to fire, an RPG plowed into the side of the building and exploded, spraying shrapnel everywhere. The concussion, which was immense, hurled Gregory into the wall while slapping Kirk to the ground. As Kirk went down, a Taliban sniper somehow managed to put a round straight through his face.

Horrified, Gregory and Davidson—who had climbed down the ladder to help—seized Kirk's vest and dragged him inside. As Kirk's head slid along the ground, the dust was smeared with a streak of crimson. Meanwhile, Knight clawed his way up into the turret with the intention of getting the machine gun back in action.

When he reached the top of the ladder, Knight seized the pistol grip on the M240 and raised himself up to take a look down the barrel. As his head cleared the top of the turret, hundreds of rounds began slamming the turret shield from several directions at once, fragmenting off the steel flanges and generating a shower of sparks and tiny shards of metal that struck him in the face like a shovelful of gravel.

Stunned by the intensity of the fire, Knight withdrew from the turret and scrambled back down the ladder. When he reached the opening at the bottom, he was pulled up short by the sight of Kirk's feet, which were stretched out on the floor, and the alarmed voice of Davidson, who had snatched Kirk's radio from his combat vest and was now putting out the call for help.

OVER AT THE AID STATION, Courville was listening to the combat radio, which was tuned to the Force Pro net, while he peeked out the door and observed continuous muzzle flashes flickering up and down the Switchbacks and across the entire North Face.

"Bro, it's fucking *bad* out there," Courville reported to Cordova, who was standing with the phone in his hand, having just had his connection to the aid station at Bostick—where he was trying to warn the medical team to prepare for mass casualties—severed by the destroyed generator.

The second they realized that someone had been hit in the Shura Building, and needed help, Cordova seized the trauma bag, which was reserved for grab-and-go emergencies, and flung the thing straight at Courville.

Courville, who was already halfway to the door, caught the bag on the run and was gone in a flash. He was moving so fast that he didn't even think to grab his gun.

Instead of proceeding cautiously as Knight, Gregory, and Kirk had done just a few minutes earlier, Courville flung himself into a headlong dash toward the Shura Building. As he ran, bullets pounded into the dirt around his feet.

When he reached his destination, he spotted Kirk lying on his stomach directly inside the front door. Courville rolled him onto his back and gently shook his shoulders.

"Kirk! Kirk!" he yelled. "Dude, can you *hear* me?"

Kirk's eyes were closed, and he made no response. The sniper's bullet had smashed through the cheekbone directly under his left eye, drilled through his head, and exited through the base of his skull. On the floor next to his head were small chunks of brain matter lying inside a shallow pool of dark, frothy-looking blood. He was bleeding profusely from his nose as well as from the wound at the back of his neck. And yet, remarkably, his lungs were still working. Every few seconds his chest would heave, forcing out a short, choppy breath that sounded labored and wet.

Kirk was still alive.

The trauma bag that Courville had hauled with him was jammed with enough medical supplies—combat gauze, pressure dressings, needles, and airway openers—to set up what we called a "mass-casualty" center inside the Shura Building. The idea was that we would best be able to protect our wounded and our medical team by spreading them between two locations rather than concentrating everyone in the aid station.

That was the theory. But when Courville took a look around the room he was in, it was clear that the notion of collecting and treating patients in this space was ludicrous. The ceiling was made of plywood and it already had several bullet holes through it. Given that the enemy could fire almost directly down on the roof, no patient would be safe lying in the center of the room.

Even worse, now that the machine-gun turret that was supposed to be protecting the front gate had been abandoned, Courville knew that there was no way we could hold and defend this position. So he decided right there, on the spot, that there would be no secondary trauma center. Instead, he would have to get Kirk back to the aid station—which meant a reversal of the gauntlet he had just run. But this time he and three other men would have to haul, at full speed, the unconscious body of the second-biggest soldier at Keating.

Courville didn't hesitate.

"Hey, Davidson, can you run back to the aid station?" he called out as he unfurled a thick roll of gauze, tucked a few pieces of Kirk's brain back into the exit wound, and began wrapping his patient's head.

"We're gonna need a stretcher."

WHILE DAVIDSON SET OFF, I was trying to prevent some additional casualties from happening about two hundred yards to the east.

After leaving the command post, my first goal was to get to Koppes's gun truck, LRAS1, which was still being targeted by some incredibly intense fire from the Diving Board. It was distance of only sixty feet, and I arrived to find that Jones and Dannelley were already there, crouched in front of the gun truck and firing their M240 toward the Diving Board.

That was a bit strange.

The front of Koppes's gun truck was pointed south so that he could shoot directly up at the Diving Board and the Waterfall, which meant that his back was exposed to the North Face. So Jones and Dannelley's job was to set up their machine gun *behind* the truck and start laying down fire on any snipers or RPG teams to the north that tried to shoot Koppes from the rear.

As it turned out, that's exactly where they'd posted up when they'd first reached Koppes's truck. But the Taliban, who had done their homework, had been waiting for this exact moment, because about thirty seconds after Jones and Dannelley got in position, a massive barrage of rocket and small-arms fire started hitting the ground around them.

"Dude, this is not good," exclaimed Dannelley, who was manning the gun while Jones fed him ammo. "We need to move *now*."

As they muscled the gun to the front of the Humvee and prepared to resume laying down fire on the North Face, an RPG from the Diving Board plowed into the patch of dirt that they had just vacated, and exploded. If they'd stayed there, it would have pureed them both.

A half second later, Jones looked to his northeast and caught sight of a second RPG. It was heading directly toward a guard tower on the near corner of the Afghan National Army side of camp, less than fifteen yards away.

That tower, which was made of two-by-sixes and plywood, sat six feet above the ground and looked like a rickety gazebo. Perched on a chair inside the tower was one of the many ANA soldiers whose apathy and indifference had so infuriated Jones during the previous four months. Oddly enough, that man's demeanor didn't seem to have changed, despite that we were now facing an all-out assault. Kicking back in a casual pose and staring placidly away from the direction in which the RPG was arrowing, he displayed the kind of vapid stare that made Jones wonder if the man wasn't stoned out of his mind.

If so, it was probably a blessing. When the rocket slammed into the guard tower with a ferocious *pa-WOOOSH*, the entire structure, along with the soldier inside, was blown to pieces.

Jones had no chance to even register the horror of that moment, because a second later another rocket exploded directly in front of him, sending a jagged piece of shrapnel into Dannelley's helmet and a second one into Jones's leg.

Both men were knocked to the ground, and Jones, who was now writhing in pain, screamed, "my knee, my *knee!*"

"Keep your heads *down*," yelled Koppes from the turret, where he was launching one grenade after another toward the Diving Board while sniper rounds from the North Face struck the back of the turret and bounced around inside the gun shield, sending frags of hot lead into his hands.

That was when I showed up.

• • •

AS I POSTED up along the west side of the gun truck by the hood, I could see that neither Jones nor Dannelley had any cover whatsoever. And although Koppes was working his Mark 19 for all it was worth, he wasn't stopping the incoming fire that was targeting those two guys. There was so much RPG and B-10 fire coming down on them from the Diving Board that a cloud of flying dirt and moondust completely surrounded the front of the Humvee.

In another minute or two, they'd both be dead.

"You and Dannelley—displace back to the barracks *right now*," I ordered Jones, whose knee was tormenting him but still intact.

"Wait there until we can develop this situation a little better and figure out where we're gonna flex you guys to next."

As they grabbed their machine gun and took off, yet another RPG drilled into the top of Blue Platoon's barracks and dropped a piece of the roof directly onto Jones, crumpling him to the ground.

"Jones!" screamed Koppes, who had caught the whole thing out of the corner of his eye and was sure that Jones was down for good this time. But a second later, Jonesie was back on his feet and staggering behind Dannelley through a shallow trench that ran along the north side of Blue's barracks.

Pushing Jones and Dannelley back to the barracks seemed like the right move. I assumed that if we were going to suffer a massive breach in our perimeter, it would probably take place on the western side of camp at either the front gate or out at the furthermost gun truck, where I could still hear Larson's lone .50-cal hammering away. If that happened, we'd need to send most of our extra men, including Jones and Dannelley, into that sector. What this meant, however, was that I was about to leave Koppes all by himself, which I hated to do in the middle of such an intense firefight.

Sometimes there are no good choices in combat.

Just before I followed Jones and Dannelley, I reminded Koppes that he was only thirty feet from the command post, and that the guys inside Blue barracks were even closer. I confirmed that his truck was fully stocked with ammo, and that there was a Kevlar blanket on the rear of the turret, which was designed to protect him from getting shot in the back. Finally, I told him that the Afghan National Army troops were holding up the eastern side of the camp, so he had friendlies in the area.

"Sorry I pulled your machine-gun team off of you," I said, looking up at him in the turret one last time before I made my run for Red barracks.

As I took off, I could hear Jim Stanley over the radio letting Courville know that a stretcher was on the way to the Shura Building to assist with moving Kirk.

THE MOMENT WORD got out that Kirk needed help, several of our guys, including Stanley, Raz, and Francis, had all converged on the aid station to help form a litter team and make the run.

As Davidson laid the stretcher next to him, Courville and Raz started cutting off Kirk's gear, leaving nothing but his T-shirt and his underpants. They stripped his boots, his vest, and his chest rack, setting those items next to his weapons and his helmet, which had been blown off his head when he was shot.

While they did this, the enemy continued pounding the Shura Building relentlessly, hammering at the walls with RPGs and bullets and blowing more holes in the roof. The reverberations made the air so thick with dust that they could taste it.

One of the unwritten rules of combat is that you don't get to reflect on loss until it's over. So as Courville and his team completed preparations for what they would do next, none of them paused to consider just how outrageous this was or how unthinkable they found it that Josh Kirk, one of the toughest and most fearless soldiers any of them had ever known—a man who was universally regarded by everyone with whom he had served as all but indestructible—lay gasping in a pool of his own blood.

And yet Raz, being Raz—which is to say, being a man who combined brutality and empathy in a way that we all found odd and endearing in equal measure—what Raz did, in that moment, was to permit himself a few seconds of reflection that boiled down, in essence, to a wish.

A wish that the fucker who had just drilled Kirk in the face with a single shot, and who was probably still wedged between some rocks somewhere up there on the North Face, had killed Kirk instantly so that those who cared most deeply about him, those who loved him best, did not have to watch him struggle to breathe as they hefted his body from the floor of the Shura Building and loaded it onto a stretcher while chunks of his brain lay marinating in the dirt.

WHEN THEY FINISHED prepping their patient and got him loaded on the litter, Raz and Francis stepped outside with their guns and hurled out a curtain of suppressive fire from an overwatch along the Hescos that the Afghan Security Guards had abandoned. Then the rest of the guys grabbed on to the handles and headed through the door with Kirk.

When you're running with a stretcher, it's generally a lousy idea to weave or zigzag or to try anything fancy. Moves like that are an excellent way to dump your patient onto the ground. What you want to do is to chart the simplest, most direct line to where you need to get him, and then haul ass at a dead-out sprint. Which was pretty much exactly what they did.

There were four men on the stretcher, and as they ran, the bullets of the enemy gunners who were trying to take them out thudded into nearby walls and kicked up small clods of dirt around their feet.

Courville, who was berating himself for having failed to bring his weapon, held on to one of the front straps, and the entire way he recited a little one-word prayer that he made up, right there on the spot, in the hopes of keeping them all safe. It went like this:

Fuck-fuck-fuck-fuck-fuck-fuck-fuck-fuck-fuck-fuck-fuck-fuck-fuck-
fuck-fuck-fuck-fuck-fuck-fuck-fuck-fuck-fuck-fuck-fuck-fuck-
fuck-fuck-fuck-fuck-fuck-fuck-fuck-fuck-fuck.

Kirk's body was facing forward as they ran, with his shattered head lying at the front of the litter. He was completely limp, and the jostling of the litter team caused his arms and legs to flop over the sides of the stretcher and bounce crazily as they made a sharp left-hand turn and passed in front of the ammo supply point, then broke to the right to cross in front of John Deere's room, then ran down the alley with the wall of Hescos off their left shoulders—and, abruptly, came up on the abandoned Bobcat.

With the Bobcat in the way, the passage was too narrow to allow two men to run through it abreast. So Knight, who was on the front right handle, was forced to let go, almost dumping Kirk onto the ground.

Somehow, Stanley seized the empty handle and took that corner of the stretcher the rest of the way in: past the west door of Red barracks, past the café, and straight through the front door of the aid station.

IT OFFERED a telling reflection of how the first few minutes of this battle were shaping up that when Kirk's little team arrived, there was already a cluster of half a dozen wounded men on the porch in front of the aid station, with another half dozen or so inside.

Doc Cordova was juggling several injured Afghan soldiers plus a handful of Americans, all of whom had some combination of gunshot or shrapnel wounds to the head, chest, abdomen, or extremities. The sheer number of casualties was pretty startling. But what shocked Courville even more was that everyone who wasn't laid out on the floor seemed to be crouched on their knees.

"What the fuck is *wrong* with you guys?!" he exclaimed as Kirk's stretcher cleared the doorway.

"We just got hit," explained Cody Floyd, the medic for Blue Platoon. "I got one in the armpit. Stone's leg is pretty cut up. Hobbs has got shrapnel in his neck and his chest, and somehow he got himself nailed in the *ear* too." (Specialist Andrew Stone was one of the mechanics, and Sergeant Jeffery Hobbs was the medic for Headquarters Platoon.)

As it turned out, shortly after Courville had departed for the Shura Building, an RPG had slammed into the aid station's doorjamb, sending shrapnel spraying throughout the interior. Although the entire medical team except for Cordova had been hit, none of them was injured seriously—which was sort of hard to believe given that a piece of the RPG had whacked Stone's combat vest with enough force to snap two of his magazines in half.

As Courville helped move Kirk to the middle of the room so that they could start working on him, he realized that most of the blast had been concentrated on the metal box on which Courville typically sat whenever they were waiting out an engagement. That was enough to make Courville pause for a moment. If he had been sitting there, his face would have been taken off by that blast.

In a very real sense, Kirk had probably saved his life.

Now it was time to try and return the favor.

When Doc Cordova performed his initial assessment, he could see that the sniper's bullet had caused multiple fractures along the right side of the base of Kirk's skull. Thanks to the RPG that had slammed into the wall of the Shura Building, Kirk also had multiple ballistic impact points on his right arm and the right side of his chest. Because his brain wasn't getting enough oxygen, he was experiencing a form of respiratory distress known as agonal breathing, which would require one of the medics to respirate for him using a bag-valve mask to perform the work that his lungs no longer could. Finally, noted Cordova, Kirk was bleeding like a stuck pig.

While Courville worked to control the bleeding, Cordova was trying to get an IV into one of his veins. After several failed attempts, he turned to a device called a FAST1, which is designed to access a patient's vascular system by driving a line directly into his sternum.

The FAST1, which looks like a flashlight, has ten needles protruding from the business end. When it is slammed home, the central needle punches all the way into the marrow of the chest bone. It's a fairly brutal procedure, but once Cordova rammed the line through, the medics were able to start getting saline solution, blood expanders, and other fluids into Kirk's body. Then they jammed a tube down his throat so they could get him on oxygen, and started chest compressions in an effort to keep blood moving through his body.

While all of this unfolded, Kirk's eyes, which were now open, remained glazed and fixed on the ceiling while lungs continued to emit labored, gasping breaths.

Courville had no time to take any of this in, because more wounded men were already pouring through the door.

Almost all of these were Afghans, and one or two of them involved some horrific casualties, the worst being a soldier who no longer had his eyes. He appeared to have taken a blast directly to the face from either a hand grenade or an RPG. His right eyeball was dangling from its socket, still attached to a whitish-looking nerve. The other orb had been punctured, and its contents—a clear, gel-like fluid—were smeared down the side of the man's face.

Even with all of the butchery he'd witnessed in Iraq, Courville had never seen anything quite like this. He didn't even try to put the eyeball back in its socket, deciding instead to cup it gently in a bandage and then wrap the man's head in gauze.

While he completed the job, a few more Afghans rolled in—men who, unlike the blind soldier, appeared to be suffering from only minor cuts and scratches or faking more serious injuries. Their aim, it seemed, was to take shelter in the aid station and hide from the enemy.

Courville and the rest of the medical team had no way of knowing that this onrush of frightened Afghans had been set in motion by a defensive collapse among our allies on opposite sides of Keating. Nor did the medics realize that in addition to sending some of those soldiers running for the aid station, this collapse had resulted in two groups of panicked men who were now racing across the camp in different directions.

Those human wave trains were about to come together within direct view of Zach Koppes, who, thanks to the fact that I'd pulled away his machine-gun team, was now all by himself.

ON THE MORNING of the attack, there were thirty-six Afghan National Army soldiers at Keating, including a platoon sergeant who was serving as the unit's commander. When the ANA guard tower was blown to smithereens in front of Jones, that marked the moment that every one of these men ceased fighting and abandoned their posts on the east end of the camp.

We would not discover until much later that a number of these soldiers—somewhere between ten and fifteen—had thrown down their weapons and actually run through the breach in the concertina wire *toward* their attackers, presumably in the hopes of surrendering. Most of them were gunned down on the spot, although a few were captured or managed to disappear into the trees. Meanwhile, a larger group turned tail and started running as fast as they could toward the center of camp with the aim of seeking cover in whichever building looked most inviting: the barracks, the aid station, the command post.

At the same time that this rout was unfolding, the Afghan Security Guards who were responsible for holding the front gate on the opposite side of Keating also abandoned their post en masse and were now engaged in a similar stampede. While a handful of these men sought shelter in the buildings on the west side of the outpost—the mosque, the latrines, the showers—the bulk of them decided to run in the direction of the ANA encampment, having no clue that the defense of this entire sector had just collapsed.

Neither of these events came as a huge surprise to me or the rest of my guys. Not one of us believed the ANA or the ASG possessed either the will or the ability to hold and defend their ground. But no one had ever imagined that they might all bail out at the same time, then set off running *toward* one another—which was the spectacle that was now about to unfold before Koppes.

A couple of yards in front of his gun truck, these two groups of Afghans—the soldiers running from the east, and the security guards sprinting from the west—approached one another, converged . . .

. . . and kept right on going.

It was one of the strangest things Koppes had ever witnessed. Neither group of soldiers seemed to have the slightest effect on their counterparts. The two bands of men simply ran through each other like herds of cattle stampeding in opposite directions, each convinced that it was headed away from danger and toward a safer place.

As Koppes watched this cross-tracking, he realized two things: that the eastern side of camp was now wide-open, and that therefore the defense of that entire sector now consisted pretty much of himself and the Mark 19.

There was nobody else.

As bad as that was, Koppes was no less disturbed by what seemed to be taking place within the abandoned ANA compound to his left.

The half-dozen barracks buildings inside that compound had already absorbed some tremendous blows from the RPGs and B-10 rounds that had been raining down from the Diving Board. Most of those buildings, which were spaced close together and separated only by narrow footpaths, were composed of little more than sheets of plywood and scrap lumber. Inside this warren, the incoming ordnance now appeared to have ignited several fires, and flames were licking greedily at the wood and canvas. (According to a report published after the assault, the attackers employed gas-filled RPGs with the specific aim of setting Keating on fire.)

It wasn't a conflagration, at least not yet. But it was gaining strength— and it seemed to be headed in Koppes's direction.

AS FOR ME, the moment I'd left Koppes I headed directly for Red barracks because I'd heard that Kirk's prognosis wasn't looking good, and I knew that I'd need to provide his blood type in order to call for a medevac and get him headed toward the military hospital at Bagram, which was the only place that could handle his wounds.

As I darted through the alley between the gun truck and the barracks, I juked left and right in the hopes of throwing off the gunners who were trying to nail me.

The entire way, I could hear Bundermann going back and forth on the radio with Gallegos, who was now preparing to make a run from the latrines in the hope of assisting Larson.

"We need mortars, air support—anything—" Gallegos was yelling, "or we're gonna die here!"

Gallegos was the kind of man who almost never lost his cool on the radio. So this could mean only one thing.

My best friend, Brad Larson, who was still stuck by himself out at the most vulnerable position in the entire battlespace, was in big trouble.

CHAPTER NINE

Luck

BY NOW, LARSON should have been dead several times over. Against some appalling odds, he'd managed to survive a fusillade of machine-gun fire, several snipers, at least one direct RPG hit, and perhaps most amazing of all, two reloads of the .50-cal. But as he started running through his third and final belt of linked machine-gun ammo, things seemed to be getting worse.

While there was still no sign that our mortars were up, the enemy fire was growing more intense and more accurate. The combined effect of it all was enough to make him think that his luck had finally turned and was now heading downhill in earnest, when two things happened that made him reconsider.

First, Mace showed up. About twenty seconds after that, Gallegos did too.

The front of Larson's Humvee was shielded by a four-foot-high wall of gray-and-blue plastic sandbags. Tucked directly between this bulwark and the hood of the gun truck was an M240 machine gun, mounted atop a piece of steel pipe just like the one up at the mortar pit. When Mace arrived, a bit breathless from his run from the area near the latrines, he grabbed the machine gun and was racking back the charging handle when Gallegos, who had seniority, pulled him off and took his place.

Peering over the sandbags, Gallegos now had a direct view into Urmul, where he could see dozens and dozens of muzzle flashes exploding from the top of the mosque and the school, as well as from numerous windows and doorways in the houses along the near side of the village. Although Larson had already been firing into the village for more than ten minutes, Gallegos was a bit hesitant to start machine-gunning what he presumed to be the residents—Afghan civilians—without getting a green light from Bundermann.

"We're getting attacked from the village," he shouted into his ICOM radio. "Do I have permission to fire back?"

"Absolutely," replied Bundermann. "Light it up."

With that, Gallegos started pouring the 240's entire three-hundred-round belt directly into Urmul while Mace took aim with his M4 at the fighters who were concentrated inside the Afghan National Police station, which was just outside the village and opposite our helicopter landing zone.

Adding two more guns to the fight certainly helped. With the extra firepower, Larson was able to focus more carefully on the individual RPG and machine-gun teams. But with no more than two thousand rounds for the 240, Gallegos knew that he could sustain fire for only another four minutes or so, and that Mace's seven thirty-round magazines wouldn't last any longer. After that, their guns would be useless.

"We need ammo *right now*," he yelled into his radio. "This is *no bullshit!*"

As he spoke, you could hear explosion after explosion after explosion in the background. It sounded horrific and unrelenting.

ALTHOUGH THERE WERE a handful of ammo bags scattered in various different buildings around Keating, almost all of our munitions were stored in the ammo supply point, or ASP. This was actually two separate structures, both located on the east side of the Shura Building. Each was made out of Hescos arranged in the shape of a rectangle about twelve feet deep and twenty feet wide. Both rooms were protected by a roof made of heavy beams and plywood topped by three or four feet of sandbags, all covered by blue tarps for waterproofing.

The building on the north housed hard-case munitions that were fairly stable and therefore unlikely to blow up. This included all the ammo for our machine guns, as well as the bullets for our carbines and sidearms. The more volatile stuff—grenades, AT4s, and claymores, along with our entire stash of TNT and C4 explosives—was warehoused in the building next door. Inside both structures, crates were stacked to shoulder height and sat atop wooden pallets running along each wall, which left a pathway running down the middle of each room.

In many ways, these two buildings were the linchpin to Keating's defense because they contained everything we needed to stay in the fight. If they were to fall into the enemy's hands, our guns would soon go silent, at which point the battle would devolve into a hand-to-hand affair as the Taliban moved from building to building shooting us down point-blank until there was no one left.

When the radio calls for ammo started coming in from the perimeter, the section leaders of Blue Platoon gathered their men to form a team whose mission was to get out to the ammo supply point, grab whatever was required, then fan out to the battle positions that needed resupply.

Sergeant Eric Harder and Sergeant John Francis were poised to lead this group, which numbered seven guys, including themselves. And from the second they burst through the west door of Blue barracks and started their run, they started taking contact from every direction, both small-arms fire and RPGs.

Harder was in the lead, followed by Francis and then the rest of the team. They covered the distance quickly, and thanks to the fact that a good portion of the route was partially concealed by leafy tree branches or camouflage netting strung between the buildings, they didn't absorb a real hit until they took their first pause, between the command post and Red Platoon's barracks.

As Harder peeked around a corner formed by the Hescos to confirm that the rest of the route was clear, an RPG exploded directly in front of him.

Although the concussion was powerful enough to knock Harder to the ground, the shrapnel missed him. Francis picked him up, and together they completed the final twenty-five yards of their rush and stacked up in a line along the wall of Hescos bisecting the camp. It was here that they ran into Ty Carter, a specialist from Blue Platoon who had arrived just a few seconds earlier and was preparing to enter the southern building.

Both structures had a plywood door framed with two-by-fours anchored into the Hescos. Each door was fronted with a crude wooden handle and a small metal clasp onto which one could place a lock. For the bulk of our stay at Keating, those doors had been unlocked. But just a few days earlier, First Sergeant Burton had ordered the locks fastened as part of the general effort to corral all of the weapons in camp prior to Keating's impending shutdown. This wasn't a popular move—and when Harder and Francis reached the ammo supply point, the reasons became obvious.

No one had thought to bring the keys, which were kept back at the command post.

Fortunately, the handles and metal clasps on the doors were flimsy enough that when Harder grabbed hold, he had no problem ripping the doors open with his bare hands.

As he pulled the lock off the door to the north building, yet another RPG hit the Hesco wall directly across from him and exploded, blowing Francis into the wall while flinging Harder through the open doorway, in the process peppering one of his legs with shrapnel.

A bit stunned, both men picked themselves up and got to work tearing into the crates and handing their contents off to the men behind them. Along with instructions to return to Blue's barracks after he'd completed his run, each soldier was told what he was being given and where it needed to go:

Here's two thousand rounds of 7.62 for the Mark 48. Get this to the Shura Building. Go!

Here's a case of Mark 19 for Koppes. Get this to LRAS2 now!

Carter, here's a crate of linked 7.62 for the 240. Get this out to Gallegos. GO-GO-GO!

When Francis and Harder finished passing out what was needed, they retraced their run back to the barracks. Once again, they found themselves under fire the entire way.

Although neither man was hit, the fact that bullets and rocks were kicking up so close to their feet left them convinced that the enemy had taken note of their initial run and anticipated their move. Next time they were ordered out to the ammo shed and the gun trucks, they might not be so lucky.

As bad as it was in the center of camp, however, things were even worse out at LRAS2.

ONE ODDITY OF LARSON'S .50-cal machine gun was that it wasn't anchored securely to the turret of his gun truck. The weapon rested inside a steel yoke, which had a two-inch pin protruding from the bottom that fit loosely into a hole in the turret. As Larson got down to the last five linked rounds in his third belt of ammo, the drawbacks of this system were revealed when another well-aimed RPG came torpedoing in from Urmul, slammed into the sandbags in front of the truck, and exploded with enough force to lift the eighty-four-pound gun into the air and fling it off its mount while destroying its receiver housing and feed tray.

As an added bonus, the same RPG sent shards of metal into Larson's right armpit.

By this point, the Taliban snipers were so fixated on Larson that it was impossible for him to lean out of the turret and retrieve the gun. As he took a final glance at it before ducking down into the Humvee, he saw a sniper's bullet strike one of the last five rounds hanging from the breech, and cleanly take the head off the bullet's casing.

Dropping from the turret and settling into the driver's seat, Larson couldn't help but feel like someone had just punched him in the gut. The loss of the .50-cal was a heavy blow, possibly even a game changer. But his run of bad luck was just getting started.

At this point Gallegos, who was still standing outside behind the M240 and firing for all he was worth, now became the focal point for much of the enemy's attention as Taliban snipers, machine-gunners, and RPG teams from inside Urmul, up in the Waterfall area, and behind RPG Rock all began homing in on him. As the density of their fire increased, rounds from several snipers and AK-47 shooters punched past the sandbags shielding his gun. At least one of these scored a direct hit on the M240's feed tray and foregrip, instantly rendering the weapon inoperable, which meant that Gallegos and Mace had no choice but to abandon their position in front of the Humvee and join Larson inside the truck.

LRAS2 had now lost both of its primary weapons systems, and the men inside had only their carbines to fight with.

This they tried to do, lowering their windows just enough to accommodate the barrels of their M4s and taking careful aim at their attackers. But when the snipers realized what was happening, they started placing rounds through the two-inch gaps at the tops of the windows, forcing the three men to pull their weapons back inside and close the windows up tight. The Taliban snipers then continued shooting directly into the bulletproof glass. The heavy 7.62 rounds from their Dragunovs couldn't penetrate the three-inch-thick glass, but they left indentations the size of baseballs and created dozens of starburst patterns that made the windows almost impossible to see through.

"Holy shit, there's a lot of them out there," remarked Gallegos.

As they tried to take stock of where things stood and decide what to do next, the passenger door on the right side of the truck swung open to reveal Ty Carter, who had just made the seventy-five-yard sprint from the ammo supply point, and was now standing there holding two bags of ammo for the inoperable M240.

"I got your ammo!" Carter announced. He was surprised that no one was outside manning the machine guns.

"Either get in and shut the door, or get the hell out of here!" yelled Gallegos.

As Carter climbed in and shut the door, Larson asked if he had any M4 rounds. Carter was handing over his extra mags when the door swung open again.

It was Vernon Martin, a sergeant attached to HQ Platoon who was Keating's chief mechanic, responsible for every motor-driven machine on the outpost.

"I heard you guys need ammo?" said Martin.

"Get in or get the hell out of here!" Gallegos yelled again.

Martin handed in the bags of ammo he'd been lugging, then climbed in straight over Carter and squeezed himself into the gunner's platform underneath the turret, whose hatch was jammed open by the damaged .50-cal.

Mace was in the process of divvying up the magazines from Martin's M4 when an RPG slammed directly into the turret, sending flames and shrapnel through the open hatch. Martin absorbed most of it: hot, jagged pieces of metal penetrated his legs and hips in numerous places.

While Martin screamed in pain, Gallegos keyed the pork chop, the handheld mike that controlled communications through the truck's radio, to let Bundermann know that the mainspring defense on the entire western side of Keating was useless, and that the men inside his gun truck were now sitting ducks.

ALTHOUGH THE HEAVY WEAPONS systems on LRAS2 were out of action, the remaining battle trucks were still in the fight. But all three of those gunners—Faulkner, Koppes, and Hardt—were about to go "black on ammo" (which meant they were out) and were issuing urgent radio calls for a resupply. To the section leaders of Blue Platoon, whose men had only just returned to the barracks, it was clear that they needed to make another push to the ammo station. With that in mind, Harder and Francis started forming up a second team.

First on deck to go through the door were two young specialists: Michael Scusa, followed by Jeremy Frunk.

As with many of the younger soldiers in Blue Platoon who had spent the first month and a half of our deployment up at Fritsche, I knew little about Scusa other than the occasional remark one of my own guys dropped. If there was anything about him that stood out, it was that he seemed the opposite of what one imagines a warrior should look like.

Michael Scusa

With his glasses and the awkward, boyish smile that he wore, a lot of the guys said that Scusa looked like someone from the cast of *Revenge of the Nerds*—although Koppes (who had strong opinions about things like this) argued that he was instead a dead ringer for Ralphie Parker, the goofy nine-year-old kid in the movie *A Christmas Story*.

Regardless, the two points on which everyone agreed were that Scusa cared deeply about his wife, and that nothing could make him stop talking about their young son. It didn't matter whether he was on guard duty, standing in line for chow, or burning poop out at the latrines, if you were there with Scusa, it was pretty much a guarantee that you'd be treated to a lengthy and excruciatingly detailed update on every aspect of his little boy's world. How many naps he was taking each day. How far he'd been able to crawl. What he'd eaten for breakfast every morning since last Tuesday. These lectures could get so tedious that many of the guys had started making jokes behind Scusa's back, and sometimes even to his face. But it said something about both them and about what they really thought of Scusa that although the teasing was often vulgar it was never mean or cruel. Unlike the rest of us, he seemed too decent for that.

Despite his gentle vibe, however, Scusa was a competent soldier, which was why he didn't hesitate when Hill ordered him to make a push through the west door and get to the ammo station for another resupply.

He was running the second he got outside, and he was moving fast enough that he got five steps down the alley before the Taliban sniper who was hidden somewhere along the North Face, and who had that doorway lined up in his crosshairs, managed to shoot him down. It happened right in front of LRAS1, where Koppes, who caught the whole thing, heard only a single sound—a sharp little expression of surprise that came out like "*heh!*"—as Scusa went to ground, hard.

The bullet, which had pierced the right side of his neck, severed his jugular vein and his brachiocephalic artery, then cut his spinal chord in two before blowing an exit hole in his back.

Frunk, who was only a step or two behind, was preparing to grab Scusa when a series of three separate shots were fired from the same location along the North Face.

The first round clipped the nylon sling on Frunk's assault rifle. As he sensed the weapon starting to fall and lunged to catch it, the second shot passed directly over his neck and plowed into the wall behind his head. That sent him diving to the ground, where fragments of the third bullet drove into his arm and leg after clanging off the side of Koppes's gun truck.

Frunk crawled back to the door, arriving just as Harder and Francis were about to head out.

"Scusa's shot in the face," reported Frunk as they dragged him inside.

With that, Harder and Francis each seized a smoke grenade, pulled the pin, and popped it into the alley—one in front of Scusa and the other behind.

When the grayish-white smoke was dense enough to cloak their movements, the two sergeants dashed outside, scooped Scusa's body off the ground, and ran him to the aid station.

For the moment, there would be no more resupply runs going out to Hardt, Koppes, Faulkner, or the five men out at LRAS2. They would all have to make do with whatever they had left.

ALTHOUGH GALLEGOS was the sort of man who was driven by the darker forces at center of his soul, he also had a sense of humor. A lot of the younger guys initially found this surprising, but it was true. More than any of us, I think, he had a flair for staring misery and fear straight in the face, and laughing.

This was more than just an expression of Gallegos's defiance (although that was surely another signature aspect of his character). Instead, the laughter arose directly from Gallegos's appreciation for the way that the world can sometimes smash horror and levity together with such force that you can't even tell them apart. And a good example of how that worked was right now, because as Gallegos took stock of how thoroughly and utterly *fucked* he and his four companions were, he found that he couldn't stop giggling.

"*Ho-ho-ho*," he chuckled as another sniper round tried to punch through the glass right next to his head. "*WHOA . . . damn*, was that close!"

In some ways, this was helpful. It lowered the tension inside the truck by a notch or two—especially, perhaps, for Martin, who was grimacing with pain as he pulled a piece of dressing from his aid pouch and tried to bind the shrapnel wounds on his leg. But it didn't do a thing to change the fact that they were trapped inside an undrivable Humvee whose armor had been scalded by dozens of rockets, whose turret was wedged open by a useless machine gun, and whose windows were so smashed up that one could barely see out. But perhaps the most intolerable aspect of their plight was that there was absolutely nothing they could do other than sit there and listen to the Force Pro net, which was blaring over the speaker mounted up in the turret.

Although they had piled into the truck in no particular order, they were positioned in a manner that roughly reflected their relative authority. Gallegos, the senior soldier, was in the front passenger seat that's typically reserved for the tactical commander, and was holding the pork chop. Larson was in the driver's seat, and in the backseats were the two junior specialists—Mace behind Gallegos, and Carter behind Larson—with Martin, the mechanic, wedged between them.

In a testament to the importance of luck in combat, the places where each man was sitting would soon seal his fate—although they had no way of knowing this. All they really understood was that together they were confronting one of a soldier's hardest and most frustrating predicaments, which was being forced to sit back passively while hoping that somebody was putting together a plan to pull their chestnuts out of the fire.

As it turned out, I was working on something along those lines. The only problem was that, given the way the odds had been stacked, I wasn't sure that it had a prayer of working.

CHAPTER TEN

Tunnel Vision

IF YOU THINK of combat in terms of football—which is not a bad analogy—then the role played by a platoon sergeant is closest to an offensive coordinator, a guy who is in the game but not on the field. Instead, his job is to stand back, watch closely, and make sure his team has everything it needs to keep moving the ball toward the end zone.

Up to this point in the battle, that's pretty much exactly what I was doing. My task was to figure out where my guys were, what they needed, and how to deliver those resources to them. This meant that despite all the running around I was doing, I wasn't engaged in any actual fighting, much less figuring out how to stage a counterattack. Instead, I was simply monitoring the radio in an effort to get accountability: a head count and location for every member of the platoon. Which is why, during the twenty minutes that followed the initial attack, I never even fired my weapon.

One of the many ways in which combat is *not* like football, however, is that if things start heading downhill fast, a platoon leader needs to come off the sidelines, jump onto the field behind the center, and make a throw. This doesn't happen often—and if it does, there's no manual for when and how it occurs. More than anything else, it boils down to a gut instinct, an innate understanding that it's time to transition out of one role and into another. And perhaps that's why, looking back on that morning now, I have no memory of making a conscious decision to set aside my responsibilities as a platoon sergeant and take direct action. There wasn't really any thought involved at all—nor, for that matter, was there any hesitation or second-guessing. All I can say for certain is that after leaving Koppes at his gun truck and dashing through the alley toward the back door of our barracks, something about what I was hearing on the radio—in particular, the increasingly strident requests for help coming from Gallegos—convinced me that I had to try to make something happen.

When I stepped inside the barracks, the first person I spotted was Gregory, who was standing in the center of the room holding a Mark 48.

Although the Mark 48 is classified as a light machine gun, it's heavy enough that its nickname among the guys who have to carry the thing is "the pig." It's a devastating weapon capable of putting out eight hundred rounds per minute with extreme accuracy.

"Hey, gimme that," I said, reaching over and grabbing the gun. "How much ammo have you got?"

"About two hundred rounds," Gregory mumbled. His face displayed the kind of blank, dull-eyed expression, which suggested that events were happening too swiftly for him to process.

Two hundred rounds wasn't even close to what I needed. And although Gregory was a perfectly nice young guy, he was about as far from A-Team material as you could get and still be in Red Platoon. But the Mark 48 was the right tool for what I had in mind, which was to throw out a lifeline to the guys who were trapped with Gallegos—and that was the only thing that mattered right then. The rest would just have to sort itself out.

"All right," I said to Gregory. "Follow me."

We went out the same door I had just come in, which looks directly onto the rear door of the command post. We were both running, so I had only a split second to absorb what was going on, but as Gregory and I hooked a sharp right and raced south toward the gym and the mosque, I could hear enraged shouts:

"Get back to your positions and defend your country!"

As I turned to look, the door of the command post opened and the body of an ANA soldier was hurled into the alley.

Inside, I could see Janis Lakis, the enormous Latvian first sergeant who was in charge of training the Afghan Army soldiers, seizing hold of a second Afghan and flinging him outside, where he sprawled in the dirt next to his companion.

"Where are your weapons?!" Lakis yelled in an accent that made him sound like Arnold Schwarzenegger. "Get out and fight for your country!"

Jesus, I wondered, *what the hell's going on in there?*

The answer to that question was something I was able to piece together only later, and understanding it requires knowing a bit about what had been taking place inside the command post since I'd left.

DURING THE FIFTEEN MINUTES that had elapsed since Keating's main generator had been taken out, Andrew Bundermann had found himself dealing with a cascade of crises, each bigger and more unsolvable than its predecessor.

As soon as the command post had lost power, First Sergeant Burton scrambled to get the SATCOM back up and running by switching the system over to battery power. Then he brought the tac-chat system back online by shunting it through the feed to our satellite antenna.

These moves had restored our external communications. But right around this time, the Fires net had gone down as another antennae—one that was positioned on top of the mortar pit—was obliterated by an RPG. Without any way of speaking to the men at our mortar pit, Bundermann had no idea whether Big John Breeding and his team were simply cut off or if their position had been overrun and they were now dead.

Fortunately, the radio connection between the command post and Fritsche still worked, so Bundermann contacted Lieutenant Jordan Bellamy, his counterpart at White Platoon. Bellamy was now the acting commander at Fritsche, which was equipped with a pair of mortars exactly like those at Keating.

What Bundermann didn't yet know, however, was that the men at

OP Fritsche

Fritsche had been subjected to an assault no less vicious than the one that had been unfolding at Keating. Just like us, they'd been awoken by a massive bombardment of rockets and machine-gun fire coming from all directions. And like us, they immediately understood that this was no mere hit-and-run, but a sustained effort to overwhelm them.

As Bellamy now explained to Bundermann, his post was being hit from all directions with massive fire, much of which was concentrated on the mortar pit in order to prevent Fritsche's biggest guns from coming up to support Keating. The attackers, who were now within seventy-five yards of Fritsche's perimeter— almost at the edge of their wire—had the pit under such intense fire that Bellamy's men couldn't even get within thirty feet of their mortar tubes.

Once again, the Taliban were coordinating their attack in a manner that neatly conformed to what we all had anticipated, and the strategy was proving every bit as effective as we'd feared it would:

6:17 a.m.

<Keating2OPS>

>>> Fritsche and Keating taking heavy contact.

>>> It is coming from everywhere: the Switchbacks, from
Urmul, the Diving Board and North Face at Keating . . .

>>> Fritsche is surrounded as well.

With Fritsche's mortars neutralized, at least for the moment, the enemy had not only robbed us of our most effective weapons system, but also cut off our plan B.

ALL OF THAT was bad enough—but just as disturbing, from Bundermann's perspective, was that his initial requests for air support had yet to yield any results.

When the attack broke out, the nearest Apache helicopters were on the tarmac in Jalalabad. Their crews were responding as fast as possible—indeed, the first sortie would be in the air within the next three minutes. But those aircraft, which were the army's most effective tools for dealing with a crisis like this, would take almost an hour to reach us.

While the choppers were scrambling to get airborne, Bundermann's request for air support was relayed to Bagram Airfield just outside Kabul. A pair of the air force's F-15E Strike Eagles were sitting at the end of the runway and preparing to launch when they were notified by satellite radio that their current mission had been scrapped.

"Proceed directly to COP Keating," said the call. "It's being overrun."

As this pair of Bagram-based planes got airborne, two more F-15s that were just coming off of a night sortie, and thus already in the air, were also ordered to assist. All four of those fighters were armed with two five-hundred-pound laser-guided bombs, three five-hundred-pound GPS-guided bombs, and one two-thousand-pound GPS-guided bomb, plus 20-mm machine guns. Those planes wouldn't be enough to stop the Taliban's attack in its tracks. But they could slow the enemy down and buy Bundermann some time to regroup.

That was all good news.

The bad news was that it would be at least another ten minutes—maybe even fifteen—before the first of those aircraft was on the scene. And thanks to some additional communications complications that occur whenever the army and the air force are attempting to coordinate, it would take another five minutes to clear the airspace and provide positive ID on the targets before those fighters could drop their bombs or conduct a strafing run.

That sounds like a short amount of time. And it is—unless you're about to be overrun, in which case it feels like forever.

WITH BOTH KEATING'S and Fritsche's mortar pits pinned down, with the first fighter jets still twenty minutes away, and with only two of our four battle trucks now returning fire, Bundermann knew that it was only a matter of minutes before the enemy breached the perimeter at Keating. And apparently the Afghan National Army soldiers who by now had abandoned their positions on the eastern side of camp understood that danger too—because it was right about then that nearly a dozen of these men burst through the door of the command post.

"Where are the helicopters?" demanded the Afghan commander. "We need to leave!"

At first, Bundermann was so shocked by the absurdity of this request that he didn't know how to respond.

"Uh, that's not gonna happen," he finally stammered. "You and your men need to get back out there and defend your side of the perimeter—*immediately.*"

At this point, the Afghan commander started acting in a manner that would later be described in the official after-action documentation as "somewhat detrimental to the command and control of the troop." What this translated into was that the dude totally lost his shit while Bundermann and the rest of the team inside the command post stared in amazement.

In the midst of this rant, Lakis, the Latvian military advisor, burst through the door and urged the Afghan commander to get his men back into the positions that they had deserted.

"Hey, we need to get out of here and do our job," declared Lakis. "Let's get outside and shoot some people!"

This had no effect whatsoever on the ANA commander, who continued to call for helicopters to evacuate him and his men.

Finally, with a nod from Bundermann, Lakis seized the Afghan soldier standing next to him, opened the door with his shoulder, and hurled the man outside into the alley—just as Gregory and I were exiting the barracks with the machine gun.

When I saw that man land in the dirt, I knew nothing of what had just taken place inside the command post. But it didn't take much for me to connect the dots and draw the obvious conclusion:

If there was a way to turn this situation around in the next few minutes, no one—not even our supposed allies—was going to help. Instead, we were going to have to figure things out for ourselves.

WITH GREGORY AT my heels I raced south, moving along the alley between our barracks and the command post before heading uphill toward the chow hall. As we ran, we kept close to the walls and did our best not to draw attention to ourselves, because I was hoping to sneak into a place and set up our machine gun without being spotted by the enemy.

As we approached the chow hall, we made a sharp right turn and hooked around the side of the mosque, at the far corner of which lay a drainage ditch that was about four feet deep and two feet wide. On the opposite side of the ditch was a concrete slab on which sat a rectangular metal structure that was four feet high and painted lime green. This was the diesel-operated 100kW generator that had already been disabled by rocket fire.

Because it was wedged right next to the mosque and our toolshed, the generator was somewhat concealed from the north, the south, and the east. From the top of the generator, however, you had an unobstructed view of the entire western side of camp, all the way out to the gun truck where Larson, Gallegos, and their teammates were trapped. There was also a direct line of sight to the Switchbacks and the Waterfall on the left, the Putting Green on the right, and wedged between them, the village of Urmul.

It wasn't the perfect spot for a machine gun, but it was the best place I could think of—and hopefully it would fit the bill for what I had in mind.

Gregory and I slithered on top of the generator and got busy setting up the Mark 48. As we worked to get the gun in place, I could hear Gallegos and Bundermann going back and forth on the radio: Gallegos still forcefully calling in his requests for mortar fire and close air support; Bundermann continuing to reply that the mortars at both Keating and Fritsche were suppressed, and that the fighter jets would not be on station for another ten minutes.

When Gregory fed the first hundred-round belt of ammo into the left side of the gun's feed tray, I stared down the barrel and got my first good look at what we were facing.

There were several RPG teams along the Switchbacks and the Putting Green, along with at least one sniper team inside the Urmul mosque. The enemy also had one machine gun concealed behind a clump of rocks at the Waterfall area, another team tucked behind the foliage in the Switchbacks above the mortar pit, a third one laying down fire from a house on the north side of Urmul, and a fourth team that was nestled behind a large boulder on the slope just above the subgovernor's house, the highest structure in the village, directly beneath the Putting Green.

Every one of those positions was hurling as much fire as they possibly could at the LRAS2 gun truck, which was being hit from so many directions that the Humvee was all but obscured by a haze of dust and smoke. As appalling as all of that was, however, what really took my breath away was just how many fighters there were moving around the hillsides. They were descending from the ridgelines in every direction, and as they moved through the rocks and the trees, clad in their loose-fitting robes and turbans and carrying their weapons, they looked like an army of ants coming down the mountain.

There was so much noise coming from both the attackers and from our remaining two gun trucks—one explosion after another—that there was no need for me to keep my voice down as I keyed the mike on my radio to interrupt Bundermann and Gallegos.

"Hey, G, I sneaked into a place where I've got a machine gun on pretty much every sector you're taking fire from," I said. "I'm gonna open up and start suppressing, and if I can lay on enough fire to keep their heads down, you and your guys can make a run for it. Can you do that?"

It was clear to Gallegos and his team in LRAS2 that they needed to find a way to break contact and make their way back to the Shura Building. Their best chances of survival—as well as of keeping everybody else inside the wire alive—was to make a push to the Shura Building, secure the ammunition stored next door, and then fight from there.

The plan that Gallegos had come up with—and which he'd already thrown out to the rest of the group for their reaction—was based on where they were sitting. Since Gallegos and Mace were positioned on the north side of the truck, they would open their doors and, together with Martin, who would join them, they'd make a direct run for the latrines while Larson and Carter, shielded on the south side of the truck, would provide cover fire.

Once Gallegos, Mace, and Martin were in position behind the latrines, they would then lay down cover fire to enable Larson and Carter to make the run. Then they would repeat the same set of moves to reach the safety of the Shura Building.

"Right now, we're just taking too much fire to move," replied Gallegos.

"Okay, I'm gonna open up with the Mark 48," I declared. "Move when you can—I'm engaging now."

With that, I took a deep breath, racked the bolt on the rear of the weapon and opened up.

Back in Carson during our battle-drill training, one of the most important things I always tried to impress on my guys was that when you're facing an attack from several directions, it's important not to allow yourself to become locked on a single individual or group. Don't get tunnel vision, I'd tell them. Even though you'll be fighting against your instincts to finish the job, never allow yourselves to fixate on annihilating any one target. Send out an accurate burst toward each one, then move on to the next; otherwise you'll get hit by someone coming at you from a direction you're not even aware of.

Doing my best to adhere to the advice that I'd dished out others, I started on my left and began punching rounds into pockets of men throughout the Switchbacks, then started worked my way toward the village in the center and eventually swept to the Putting Green on the right. Then I moved back to Urmul, then returned to the Putting Green, then jumped over to the Switchbacks.

Urmul—Putting Green—Waterfall—mosque—Switchbacks—Urmul again—Putting Green—Urmul again.

Some of this was effective. I was able to eliminate two machine-gun teams—one high on the Switchbacks, the other lower down on the slopes just above our mortar pit. But as fast as I suppressed fire from one pocket of insurgents, two or three others would resume, and with each new burst from the Mark 48, I was drawing more and more attention to myself. Also, there were so many targets—and so many additional fighters now taking aim at me—that there was no way for me to keep up. If I'd been able to put another gun in place and coordinate some crossfire, it might have been possible to shut them down hard. But one gun simply wasn't enough.

As I burned through our first belt of ammo and Gregory was loading up the second, I could hear Gallegos calling me on the radio.

"You can't lay down enough fire for us—you're not being effective!" he shouted. "There's just too many."

That wasn't at all the message I wanted to hear, so I bore down tighter, focusing more intently with each additional burst in the hopes that I could tear some permanent holes in the Taliban line. And in the process of doing that, I totally forgot the advice that I'd pounded so relentlessly into my own guys, allowing myself to get zoned in too narrowly on a single target—a one-story mud house on the north side of Urmul whose windows were bright with continuous muzzle flashes—while losing sight of the bigger picture, until—

Buh-WHAM!!!

To my far right, about forty yards downhill, a Taliban RPG team had made it to Keating's front gate—which was no longer protected by the machine-gun turret atop the Shura Building—unlimbered their weapon, and sent a rocket directly into middle of the generator. The rocket hit the main motor housing just a few feet to my right, and the blast—which was ferocious—picked me up, hurled me into Gregory, and dumped both of us together with the machine gun off the far side.

I picked Gregory off the ground and confirmed that he hadn't been hit.

"Get back to the barracks, try to find some additional machine-gun ammo, and bring it back here," I ordered. Then I scrambled on top of the generator with the Mark 48, got the gun back in place, and started cranking through my final hundred rounds on the last belt of ammo.

"You're not bringing enough firepower to allow us to move," reported Gallegos. "They have too many guys—we can't move. We just can't move!"

By now, the enemy gunners had a bead on me, and as I reached the end of my third burst, rockets and gunfire were striking the metal surface of the generator all around me.

"Hey, G, I can't hold this position any longer," I radioed as my final rounds were expended. "I'm outta ammo, they know where I'm at, and I just can't cover you. I'm sorry!"

"Roger that—thanks for trying," he replied. "I guess we'll just hang out here for a bit longer."

As I climbed down from the generator, I had a horrible feeling that I'd just failed on two fronts. I'd been unable to deliver Gallegos, Larson, and the rest of their guys what I'd promised, while simultaneously doing absolutely nothing to relieve Bundermann and his team of the mess that they were trying to solve. A mess that, from what Bundermann could now see and hear back at the command post, only seemed to get worse with each passing second.

EVEN BEFORE the Afghan National Army soldiers had been booted into the alley outside the command post, Bundermann was already searching for another way to get Keating some artillery support. The person he turned to was Cason Shrode, his square-built, 220-pound fire-support officer.

In addition to having been West Point's lead tackler during his senior year, Shrode was exceptionally good at the intricate and technical challenges of coordinating air support, artillery, and mortars—in essence, anything that might be moving through the air around or above Keating.

Bundermann and Shrode both knew that the fastest way to get some relief for Keating was to find a way of freeing up Fritsche's mortar pit—and perhaps the best way of solving that problem was by turning to the massive gun emplacements at Bostick.

Inside the center of Bostick were several howitzers, each of which was capable of hurling a 155-mm explosive shell well over ten miles. That was close enough to put a shell just outside the wire at Keating. But at that range, the margin of error for Bostick's artillery was eight hundred meters—which meant that any shell they fired was just as likely to obliterate us as to destroy whatever target we were asking them to hit.

On the other hand, Fritsche was slightly closer to Bostick than Keating, and therefore within accurate range of those big guns—albeit just barely. So Shrode immediately started pulling up all the information we had on how to target Bostick's howitzers onto Fritsche's attackers. If the gun crew at Bostick could get some of their 155 shells close to those attackers, Fritsche's mortar team might be able to lay *their* guns onto targets like the Putting Green, the North Face, the Diving Board, even Urmul itself—places from which we were getting hit the hardest—and thereby take some of the heat off Keating.

While Shrode punched up the data and crunched the numbers, Bundermann turned to answer a series of calls that he'd been getting from the command post at Bostick, where Colonel George was monitoring the battle.

Several minutes earlier, the colonel had awoken to the news that Keating was in danger of being overrun. When he stepped into the command post, his team already had a map of the outpost up on the board. Based on the information that was pouring in, they were filling in the sectors that the Taliban controlled with red markers. When George looked at the board, everything but the aid station, the command post, and Red Platoon's barracks was colored in.

For the first several minutes, while George's battle captain and his second in command ran the fight, the colonel concentrated on ensuring that the requests for fixed-wing and rotary air support were given full priority as they went up the chain of command. Now, with a range of aircraft bearing down on Keating from several different directions, George took over the SATCOM to assure Bundermann that help was on the way, and then turned to the next item on his list of concerns.

"Do you have accountability?" he asked.

Accountability isn't necessarily the first priority during an attack, but the moment that things are under control, it's one of the first things that high command wants to know:

Even if they are wounded or dead, have you figured out where all your people are at?

Unfortunately, when that request came in from Colonel George, things at Keating were very much *not* under control. And so Bundermann's first impulse—the thing that he most wanted to do, not only because it would have been the truth but also because it might have helped convey some of the balls-to-the-wall urgency that the situation demanded—was to repeat the question back to Colonel George—*Do I have accountability?*—and then explain that in light of the fact that our Afghan allies had just left two entire sectors of the outpost wide-open to anyone who might want to waltz through the wire, and given that two of his key battle positions were now completely cut off—one of which, the mortar pit, he had no communication with whatsoever, while the other involved five guys who were wedged into a toasted piece of armor on the far side of camp; and furthermore, given that his command post had just been bum-rushed by a dozen Afghan dudes whose only interest lay in finding out when they were getting chauffeured out of the place by private helicopter; and also given that the enemy's fire was continuing to pour down from the ridgelines from every direction and that he'd just had three soldiers shot in the face—what Bundermann really wanted to tell George was that, *Hell no, he did not have accountability.* Absolutely not. No accountability whatsoever—and furthermore, if accountability was something that George wanted him to provide, then the colonel needed to find a way of getting some fucking air support on station right now.

That's what Bundermann wanted to say.

His actual response was a simple no, delivered in a manner that was controlled and professional. But despite his best efforts, Bundermann couldn't quite suppress the tone of his voice, which sounded increasingly desperate.

Even if George had been the sort of commander who didn't tune in to that sort of thing, Bundermann's rising anxiety would have been obvious to him from the messages that were scrolling on the tac-chat system in front of his screen, which were reaching a level of stridency that is not often seen except when men are facing extremis:

> *6:39 a.m.*
> *< BlackKnight_TOC >*
> *>>> We need something.*
> *>>> Trucks are pinned. RPGs are being taken every time we try something. Mortars can't do shit. We are taking indirect fire.*
> *>>> We took another casualty!!!*

When the classified transcripts of these communications were eventually dumped onto the Internet by WikiLeaks, the *New York Times* would describe them as a "frightening record" that depicted a group of young American soldiers "isolated and overwhelmed on enemy turf."

I suppose that's more or less true. What mattered at the time, however, was that the sense of desperation that is so clearly evident in those text messages was about to set off a chain of dominoes, the first of which was already toppling in my direction.

I WASN'T PRIVY to any of Bundermann's communications with Colonel George, nor did I much care as I pulled the machine gun off the generator and told Gregory—who had returned with more ammunition—to take cover in the adjacent drainage trench. At that moment, I was primarily concerned with ensuring that Gregory could hold this position if the enemy started coming through the front gate and tried to cut us off from

Gallegos and his crew out at LRAS2. And to do that, he'd need some additional help.

"I'm gonna get some more guys," I said, handing off the gun.

Then I took off, tracing the same route alongside the mosque, then past the command post back to the barracks.

Just as I got to the east door of the barracks, I was spotted by Raz, who had finished helping to deliver Kirk to the aid station and was now headed back to the barracks for more orders.

"Ro, dude—you're hit!" he exclaimed.

One of the weirder aspects of combat is that it's quite possible to get shot and not have the faintest idea. You get so amped up on adrenaline that you tend to focus on everything but yourself. As if to underscore how true this was, I didn't have a clue what Raz was talking about until he pointed to my right arm, which had a hole on the outside of the forearm about the size of a silver dollar, courtesy of a piece of shrapnel from the rocket that had blown me off the generator.

There didn't seem to be much blood, perhaps because the wound had already been cauterized by the heat of the metal. The edges were raised and at the center was a small crater. It almost looked as if someone had taken a welding torch and shoved it into the skin.

My main concern was assuaged when I wiggled my fingers to ensure that I still had the use of my hand. My second worry was relieved when I flipped my hand over, rotating the forearm, and saw that there wasn't any blood coming out the bottom, which meant that it wasn't a through-and-through.

I was set to brush the whole thing off and keep moving, but Raz was insistent about wrapping it and had already reached into my aid pouch, on the nonshooting side of my left hip, grabbed a dressing, and was now winding it around my arm as if he were cinching down the girth strap on a pony. It felt far too tight, but I had bigger things on my mind as I rolled through the door, stepped into the barracks, and spotted Jones standing by the west door awaiting orders.

"Jonesie, I need you to get up to the trench by the mosque and help out Gregory," I told him, knowing that Jones was a much better machine-gunner than Gregory and would be far more effective at laying down suppressive fire.

"Get on the Mark 48, hold that position, and don't let them get any closer."

Then my attention was pulled over to the west door by the sound of a heated argument. Stanley, our platoon's senior squad leader, was standing in a nose-to-nose face-off with Hardt.

From the tone and volume of their voices, they'd been going at it pretty hard. Hardt looked angry, while Stanley appeared exasperated. When Stanley caught sight of me, he took a step back and pointed in my direction.

"You need to go talk to Ro," he barked.

Hoo boy, I muttered to myself as Hardt headed in my direction.

What he laid on me in the next minute or two was an idea whose flawed assumptions and tactical misguidedness were exceeded only by the fact that it was so incredibly brave.

PART III

★ ★ ★

Overrun

CHAPTER ELEVEN

The Only Gun Left in the Fight

WHAT HARDT HAD IN MIND arose from his awareness that we had lost all momentum and initiative. Our force was now fragmenting—breaking into small, isolated pockets of resistance like the mortar pit, Gallegos's gun truck, and Fritsche—which could no longer support one another. But instead of reversing that downhill slide, it looked like we were now about to pull back further and give up even more ground. Before that happened, Hardt was determined to go and get our guys at LRAS2.

The key to his plan was Truck 1, where Faulkner was still manning the .50-cal from the gunner's turret. What Hardt wanted was to start up the Humvee and drive the thing from its current location all the way over to the western end of camp, a distance of about sixty yards, in order to relieve Gallegos and his team.

"That's a bad idea—Truck 1 is almost out of ammo," I declared after he laid it out. "We need to come up with a better plan than driving a Humvee that's almost black on ammo right into the middle of heavy contact."

"We just found some more .50-cal ammo, and I've got two guys coming with me," replied Hardt, pushing back. "We'll run the Humvee over there, and we'll either throw Gallegos and his guys in the truck, or they'll run alongside and we'll give them cover that way as we bring them back."

Part of the problem with arguing against this was that the idea actually had merit. If Hardt could get Truck 1 all the way over to Gallegos, he'd place another heavy weapon system back into the fight at the far end of camp. At that point, he and Gallegos could decide if they wanted to stay there and use the .50-cal to lay fire on the Switchbacks in the hopes of enabling Breeding and his crew—assuming they were still alive—to bring their guns back up at the mortar pit. Or Gallegos and his team would have the option of falling back to the Shura Building under the protection of Truck 1. Either way, we'd be in a stronger position than where we were now.

My concern wasn't the idea itself, but the way it would be executed.

As Hardt and his team made their way toward Gallegos, they would be partially protected on their left flank, where the Humvee would be screened by the trees and other vegetation along the southern perimeter of the outpost. His right flank, however, would be completely exposed to the enemy gunners on the North Face, plus any RPG teams that might be massing around the front gate. Hardt's crew would have absolutely no protection from that sector, and even if his gunner on Truck 1's .50-cal was lightning fast, it would still be impossible for that shooter to focus on all the targets directly in front of him—the Waterfall area and the Putting Green—while simultaneously swinging over to fend off an attack coming from his right. Finally, there was simply no way that I could put a machine gun in place to support Hardt, because I'd just been driven off the one spot from which we could do that.

"Look, I can't do anything to secure your right flank," I explained. "The generator's the only place where we can do that—and me and Gregory just got blown off of the thing. It's a *bad* idea."

As I laid this out, I caught something coming off of Hardt—partly a look but also a vibe—that told me it was pointless to keep pressing my case because he had no intention of allowing himself to be talked out of his plan. He was determined to try something—anything—that might help Gallegos and his guys, and he wasn't going to let anything stand in his way, not even chain of command or a direct order. The only way for me to stop him from going would have been to coldcock him to the ground.

I also knew something else—something that, for lack of a better

176

expression, boils down to what you might call the calculus of combat. I knew that despite the obvious risks, despite the very high likelihood that this would not end well, there was a slim chance that Hardt might be able to pull it off. Under normal conditions, I would never have sanctioned something so sketchy. But right now, given how much we were up against and how close we were to being overrun, it was a chance we might have to take.

Hardt's best bet, I knew, would be to drive the truck along the back side of the mechanics' bay, which faced south. The building would shield him from the shooters along the North Face, as well as anyone trying to come at him through the front gate. So that's the message I tried to drive home.

"Look, if you're gonna do this, then you have to use the mechanics' bay as your shield," I declared. "Whatever else you do, do *not* take the truck between the mechanics' bay and the shower trailers and put yourself in a position where your dick is out there flappin' in the wind. Got it?"

"Roger."

"Okay," I said. "Do it."

While Hardt took off to get his team together, I took a second to weigh my options. I assumed that the Shura Building and the front gate were still under our control—an assumption that I would soon discover was dead wrong. Not knowing that yet, however, I decided to use the next few minutes to dash over to the aid station to see how the medics were doing with Kirk.

BY THIS POINT, most of the Afghan soldiers who had sought admission to the aid station with fake injuries had been booted out of the building. The only exception that I could see as I came through the door was the ANA platoon sergeant, who was curled on the floor in the fetal position and refusing to move. Even without the malingerers, however, the place was still overflowing. Inside, there were seven Afghan patients who were suffering from a variety of gunshot wounds and lacerations, plus one man whose abdomen had been eviscerated. There were also several Americans with shrapnel or gunshot wounds. In fact, so many guys had been hit that the medics had started moving those with less severe injuries to other areas. The Americans who could still walk were being sent to the command post, while the Afghan soldiers were being placed outside on the café, the small deck on the west side of the aid station that was partially surrounded by sandbags.

The patients left inside the building were taking up every square inch of the blue linoleum floor, which was covered with blood. Most of those men were sitting or lying quietly. But one soldier in particular—the Afghan who had been blinded by the blast to the face—was making things difficult by continuously getting up from his chair, despite repeated requests by the medics to stay put. Eventually, Courville had grown so frustrated that he'd seized the guy by the shoulders and shoved him into his seat while telling him to "sit the fuck down." In response, the man had hauled off and kicked Courville in the leg. It's a measure of how frustrated Courville was that he barely managed to restrain himself from punching the blind soldier in the face.

Part of the reason Courville was so on edge was that the challenge of treating these patients was exacerbated by the fact that the medics didn't have their supplies on hand. Just a few days earlier, as part of the preparation for shutting down Keating, Doc Cordova and his team had been ordered to start dismantling their operation. They'd bundled whatever wasn't worth saving into trash bags, while packing anything of value inside more than a dozen plastic footlockers that could be loaded onto the Chinooks when the time came to evacuate. This meant that the shelves in the aid station were now all but empty, except for a cursory stash of the most essential supplies.

Fortunately, the contents of each storage box had been carefully labeled. Those boxes, however, had all been stacked outside on the far side of the café. This meant that whenever the medics needed something—bandages, tourniquets, pressure dressings—Courville and Cordova would have to consult their list to figure out which box needed to be opened up, and then Courville would dash out the front door, race into the most exposed part of the café area, and frantically rummage through the correct box until he found what he was looking for while praying that he didn't get picked off by a sniper or blown to pieces by an RPG.

After Courville's third or fourth retrieval trip, he started calling these missions "retard runs" because they were so terrifying and so stupid. At one point when Courville was rooting through a box looking for more bandages, he heard an ominous *thunk-thunk*. Looking up, he spotted a grenade rolling toward him along the ground and flung himself through the door of the aid station. He landed directly on top of the Afghan soldier with the abdominal evisceration.

In the midst of these challenges, about ten minutes earlier Harder and Francis had burst through the door carrying Scusa. Cordova dropped what he was doing, examined the gunshot wound to Scusa's throat, and felt for a pulse or a heartbeat. Finding neither, he pronounced Scusa dead—the first time that he'd ever done such a thing—and, with one of the other medic's help, took Scusa into the sleeping area, where they zipped him into a body bag and placed him next to Courville's bed.

Meanwhile, as rockets continued striking the exterior of the aid station, the plastic smoke alarm on the wall blared incessantly, competing with the gunfire and all but drowning out the groans of the wounded. Eventually, things got bad enough that somebody had turned to Cordova and asked the inevitable:

"Hey, Doc? Can we smoke in here?"

"Only if you give me one," replied Cordova, in total violation of his strict no-smoking-in-here-ever policy.

"Hell yeah," Courville sighed in relief as he lit up a Marlboro Red and inhaled deeply.

It was right about then that I came through the door and spotted Cordova, standing at the head of the litter frame on which Kirk was stretched out, lying on his back.

When Cordova looked up and spotted me, I raised my right fist and made a thumbs-up/thumbs-down motion to ask how Kirk was.

Shaking his head, Cordova gave me a thumbs-down. Then he and Courville hefted Kirk's body and staggered toward the sleeping quarters to get him into a body bag and place him next to Scusa.

Under different circumstances, I might have been able to go up to Kirk's body and offer some sort of gesture—a hand on his shoulder, a word or two to bid him farewell. At that moment, however, such a thing didn't even cross my mind. Instead, I was fully attuned to the radio calls coming through on the Force Pro, where Hardt was trying to report his movements to me.

"You don't need to be talking to me—you need to coordinate with the guy you're heading *toward*," I barked. "Talk to Gallegos!"

Then I turned to the other radio call that was coming in for me, which demanded my immediate focus.

Zach Koppes was in trouble.

DURING THE FEW MINUTES that had elapsed since I had taken away the machine-gun team that was supposed to protect his gun truck, Koppes had been hit with a lot. He had watched the exodus of fleeing Afghan soldiers running in opposite directions. He'd seen Scusa executed directly in front of him. He'd been subjected to unrelenting fire from the Diving Board throughout these events. And during this entire time, he'd been completely alone.

He held up well to those challenges, in part because the Mark 19 was perhaps the ideal tool for dealing with his attackers, most of whom were hidden high above him behind rocks and trees, and moving like cats from one piece of cover to another. Thanks to that, it was especially challenging to shoot straight at them, which is what he would have been forced to do if the truck had been armed with a machine gun. With the grenade launcher, however, he'd been able to catapult his rounds over and behind the enemy. He was also helped by the killing-burst radius of his grenades, which could do serious damage to anyone within fifteen yards of their blast.

The other thing that Koppes had going for him was plenty of ammo: the back of his Humvee was packed with boxes of Mark 19 grenades. He'd started out the morning with more than six hundred rounds, and although he was working through them at a steady clip, he was still in better shape than any other gun truck. Unfortunately, though, a problem had cropped up that he had no way of solving.

For the better part of the past fifteen minutes, the sniper who had taken down Scusa had been doing his best to eliminate Koppes. The shooter was tucked somewhere up inside the steep and densely vegetated slopes along the North Face, directly behind Koppes, and his aim was to fire through the foliage of a clump of ash trees, located directly behind the truck, in the hopes of drilling Koppes in the back of the head.

Although the rear of the turret was protected by a heavy piece of Kevlar tarp that was capable of absorbing shrapnel fragments and most small-arms rounds, Koppes had no way of turning around and returning fire. In addition to the fact that the turret of the Humvee could not rotate all the way to the rear, the lone tree directly behind him not only provided concealment but also prevented him from seeing where the sniper was shooting from. What troubled Koppes even more, however, was that the Kevlar tarp was coming to pieces.

Each bullet that skipped off the top of the tarp would take off another piece of the fabric while sending a tiny puff of air against the back of Koppes's neck. That was disconcerting enough, but the rounds that struck the tarp directly were now leaving tiny holes, through which the sunlight was boring. With each additional shot, another beam of light shot through the Kevlar. Koppes knew that it was only a matter of time before the sniper got lucky and put a bullet straight into his brainpan—and that the only way to turn the situation around was to get another sniper out to the gun truck.

Catching Koppes's message as I turned to exit the aid station, I glanced to my left and spotted the blind Afghan soldier who had been giving Courville such problems. He was now slumped in a chair that had been placed right next to the door, and his entire head was covered in thick strips of gauze that Courville had wrapped around his face to support his ruined eyeballs. The blood running down his cheeks from his eye sockets had soaked through the gauze and formed crimson-colored lines that made it appear as if he was shedding tears of blood. The scene was horrifying enough to make one want to look away. But something about him made me pause on my way to the door.

Resting in his lap was a leather bandolier lined with copper-tipped bullets, and leaning against the wall directly to his left was a Dragunov sniper rifle.

Looking back on that moment now, I'd like to say that my heart went out to the wounded soldier. But in truth, the only thing I registered was that his weapon, for which he no longer had any use, was exactly the thing I needed. And then there was another thought too:

Cool—I've always wanted to shoot a Dragunov.

I plucked the ammo belt out of the man's lap, snatched hold of the sniper rifle, and headed out the door to make a run for Koppes's truck.

As I took off, I could hear Gallegos's voice on my radio. He sounded agitated, and he was now barking at Hardt:

"We *do not* need you. Get the hell out of here—it's a death trap!"

I had no idea what was taking place. But if Gallegos's words were anything to judge by, things were not going well out on the far side of camp.

TO GRASP the full measure of what was about to befall Hardt and his team, it's necessary to pause and take a step back to the moment just before Hardt and I got into our argument in the barracks—the moment when I ordered Chris Jones to head up to the trench by the mosque and lend a hand to Justin Gregory.

As soon as Jones was given that command, he flung himself into a fifteen-yard uphill sprint toward the back side of the mosque, drawing fire the entire way. His run was interrupted by several rockets, one of which landed close enough to knock him on his butt.

"Greg, what's goin' on, man?" he gasped as he'd finally arrived and slid into the shallow trench where Gregory was huddled. "Where are they at?"

Although Gregory was a veteran with more than five years of experience, he'd spent most of his army stint in Fort Knox, Kentucky, where much of his nonduty time had been devoted to sharpening knives, which were something of an obsession with him. Unlike Jones, he was timid and often withdrawn. Prior to this deployment, he'd never even been shot at. And thanks to all of that, he wasn't responding well at all to his current predicament. In short, he was flat-out terrified.

"They're fucking *everywhere*," replied Gregory.

"Well, yeah," conceded Jones, who felt as if he'd stepped into the center of a circular firing squad. "You know, they *are* pretty much everywhere."

At that moment, an RPG slammed into the mosque, blowing out all the windows on the south side of the building and sending the pieces down on both men. The shower of shattered glass seemed to underscore just how cut off they were, and because neither of them had a radio, they didn't have the faintest clue what was happening elsewhere. (To avoid the chaos that would be created by everyone attempting to communicate at once, we normally restricted radios to team leaders, who would communicate verbally with soldiers like Jones and Gregory.)

Unlike Gregory, Jones understood that it wasn't acceptable to simply keep their heads down and cower at the bottom of the trench in the hope that things would somehow improve. Whatever else might be happening, they needed to put up a fight and return some fire.

"All right, Greg, let's do this," said Jones, taking hold of the much heavier Mark 48 while Gregory switched to a squad automatic weapon, which we referred to as a SAW. "On the count of *three*, we're gonna jump up, and we're gonna *suppress*."

The plan was for Jones to concentrate on the Switchbacks while Gregory focused on the front gate and the North Face.

Jones jumped up, laid the Mark 48 along the top of the trench, and began spraying disciplined three- to five-round trigger bursts, taking aim at the myriad muzzle flashes he could see across the Switchbacks and the Waterfall area. As he fired, he also spotted something much closer at hand.

Hardt and Chris Griffin, a young specialist from Blue Platoon, seemed to be in the midst of an ammo run. Both men were carrying boxes of .50-cal bullets, and they were racing as fast as they could for Truck 1.

Jones tried his best to lay down cover fire for the two runners, who made it safely into the truck. Within seconds, however, Jones could see that he had drawn the attention of several enemy gunners, who were now zeroed in on him. It was at this moment that he also realized, to his frustration, that he was all by himself.

Gregory had never even bothered to stand up.

Disgusted, Jones flung himself back into the trench. He lay there for a moment, staring up at the sky, and was wondering what his next move should be when suddenly, Josh Dannelley's head appeared over the lip of the trench.

Dannelley and two other guys from Blue and HQ Platoons had been taking cover behind the toolshed, twenty yards away. Now they too were about to attempt to make a push up the hill to Truck 1.

"We're gonna run some ammo up to Faulkner," Dannelley yelled as rounds snapped the air on both sides of his face. "We need you to guys to cover us."

To Jones, this seemed weird. Hadn't Hardt and Griffin just pulled off that very job? Did Dannelley have a clue what the hell he was doing?

Without a radio, there was no way to make sense of anything, so Jones figured it was best to do as he was told. When Dannelley and his guys started running for Truck 1, Jones popped back up with the machine gun—and this time, Gregory joined him.

Because Gregory was facing in the direction of the front gate and the North Face, he missed what happened next. But Jones caught the whole thing.

As Dannelley and his guys took off, they drew a ferocious amount of fire. By some miracle, none of them were hit. But within a few steps, they realized that Truck 1 was no longer there.

Baffled by the empty space, they turned in confusion, raced downhill, and piled back into the trench with Jones and Gregory.

Jones had no idea why the guys in Truck 1 had pulled the vehicle out of its established battle position. He knew nothing about where they might have headed, or why. But he did know one thing, which is that Hardt, Griffin, and Faulkner were now driving into the teeth of a ferocious shit storm that had enveloped the entire western half of the outpost.

Where did they go, he wondered as he slammed himself back into the trench with Gregory, *and what the hell are they trying to pull off?*

WHEN HARDT AND GRIFFIN tumbled into the cab of Truck 1, Hardt took the front passenger seat while Faulkner dropped into the driver's seat.

As Griffin climbed into the turret and got behind the machine gun, Faulkner turned the ignition key and threw the truck into gear.

Hardt ordered Faulkner to pull away from the side of the massive, potato-shaped boulder that protected the west flank of the gun truck, and drive toward the showers by cutting along the north side of the mechanics' bay. Significantly, this was exactly the route I'd urged him *not* to take. Instead of snaking along the back side of the mechanics' bay, which would have shielded his movements, he would be out in the open and visible. The right side of his vehicle would be completely exposed to rockets and gunfire coming off of the North Face, as well as from the direction of the front gate.

I can't say anything about why Hardt elected to take that route, except to speculate that he may have been lured by the desire to get to Gallegos and his team by the quickest and most direct line available. Regardless, the moment the gun truck left the protection of the rock and emerged into the open ground just beyond, which was now a kind of no-man's-land, it became a fat target. All across the North Face, the Switchbacks, and the Putting Green, Taliban gunners started training their weapons on the truck and showering it with everything they had.

As sniper rounds and sustained bursts of machine-gun fire struck the windshield and the turret, Griffin did his best to return fire. But he was hampered by the need to swing the weapon in three directions. Within a minute, he found himself forced repeatedly to duck down inside the turret.

When Gallegos, who was communicating with Hardt on the radio, realized that the Humvee was moving along the most exposed and dangerous route, a new tone of stridency entered Gallegos's voice as he ordered Hardt to turn back before it was too late. And it was now that Hardt's strengths as a soldier—his stubbornness, his resiliency, his refusal to back down without having finished what he had set out to do—started working against him.

Ignoring Gallegos, he told Faulkner to keep rolling.

They crept along at five miles an hour as Faulkner methodically threaded between obstacles that arose in his path. Despite the heavy incoming fire, the truck made steady progress. In less than ten minutes, the front of Truck 1 had pulled to a stop about five yards behind the rear of LRAS2.

There are so many blind spots from the cab of a fully up-armored Humvee that you can't really see anything that isn't directly in front or squarely off to the sides, so Gallegos had no way of observing Truck 1, even through his rearview mirror. Nevertheless, he knew exactly how much danger Hardt and his team were in—which is why he started flat-out screaming into the radio:

"Get the *fuck* outta here," he yelled. "Go now! *Go-go-go-GO!*"

As if to drive home Gallegos's order, an RPG scored a direct hit on the front windshield of Truck 1, engulfing the hood of the vehicle in a wall of flames while sending a torrent of shrapnel over the turret and into Griffin's face and chest.

Now, finally, Hardt fully understood that the firepower that was being brought to bear on this battle position was simply too intense to permit the men trapped inside LRAS2 to withdraw safely.

"Sorry we couldn't help," Hardt radioed to Gallegos as he ordered Faulkner to back up and get them out of there. "We're leaving."

Unfortunately, that wasn't going to be possible.

MONTHS EARLIER, the unit that was deployed at Keating prior to our arrival had begun erecting a new building directly to the west of the mechanics' bay. The purpose of this structure had never been explained to any of us, and it didn't really matter, because the walls were only partially finished when orders came to halt construction.

One of those walls, which was less than ten feet behind Hardt's gun truck, had started coming apart under the impact of the dozens of rockets that had landed in the area, crumpling to form a mound of rocks and rubble. In his haste to get out of the kill zone, Faulkner now proceeded to reverse Truck 1 directly into this berm, hitting the pile of debris with enough force that his vehicle shot all the way to the top of the mound before coming to an abrupt stop.

Faulkner made repeated attempts to ram the truck backward and forward, but it wasn't going anywhere. The chassis of the Humvee was high-centered and its wheels were no longer touching the ground. Firmly stuck, they were now little more than sitting ducks.

"Hey, we can't maneuver," Hardt radioed to Gallegos. "Hold on."

Gallegos had been right. It was a death trap.

CHAPTER TWELVE

"Charlie in the Wire"

THE ROUTE THAT I TOOK to get from the aid station to Koppes's gun truck led directly across the dirt alleyway where Scusa had already been killed. I'm not sure why that same sniper didn't nail me too—perhaps some residual haze from the smoke grenades was still hanging over the roofs of the buildings. But regardless of the reason, I was able to dash across the fifteen-foot gap without incident and reach the side of Koppes's Humvee.

When I looked up, I could see that rounds were striking the turret and the doors from every direction. Hunched inside and trying to keep as low as possible, Koppes looked absolutely miserable.

"Hey, dude," I called out, trying to sound as casual as possible. "You doing okay?"

"Not really," he replied. "I've got this sniper at my back."

From the sound of his voice, it was clear that Koppes was deeply scared.

"Oh, man, you don't need to worry about that," I joked. "We're *all* gonna die today."

The expression on Koppes's face suggested that he was weighing the possibility that I might have lost my mind in the heat of combat. (His impression of my sanity probably wasn't helped by the fact that while getting blown off the generator by the RPG blast, I had apparently taken a knock to the front of my face, and my teeth were now covered in blood.)

There was no point in trying to explain things, so I told him to just keep his head down and maintain his sector of fire while I got to work trying to weed out the sniper.

I had only a crude knowledge of the weapon I'd pulled off the Afghan soldier, but my main concern was that its owner might not have zeroed in the scope, which meant that I couldn't be sure of its accuracy. However, the Dragunov's 7.62 round was significantly heavier than what my M4 fired, so I could reach out a lot farther and, even if I only clipped my target, do considerably more damage to him.

I started off on the back side of the truck. Standing next to the bumper, I scanned the North Face through the scope, looking for spots that might conceal the sniper, mainly by trying to pick out positions that I knew I would use, while keeping an eye peeled for any sign of a muzzle flash. I picked a few areas where he might be hiding and placed a few rounds into those spots. Then I pulled back, moved to the front side of the truck, and repeated the process, darting back-and-forth between the bumper and the area where the windshield met the hood. It was strange game to play, and it was made doubly surreal because as I was conducting these moves, I could hear Gallegos still yelling at Hardt through the radio in my ear:

"Get out of there. Do *not* come. Turn around. Go back!"

It wasn't long before I caught the shooter's attention and we found ourselves involved in a deadly, high-stakes game of peekaboo. I'd dash to the back of the Humvee and fire off a few rounds. Then I'd sprint to the front and throw a couple of head fakes without actually firing before returning to the back and trying to pinpoint his location as he continued shooting at the place where I'd just been. My aim was to stay on the move, vary my pattern, keep him guessing.

After several minutes of this hide-and-seek routine, I'd gotten a reasonable bead on where I thought he was—a stack of rocks that was heavily concealed by foliage—and I put a series of seven shots directly into that spot. At no point did I see the sniper's profile in the scope of the Dragunov—nor, after nailing those shots home, did I spot anything to indicate that I'd taken him out. All I can say for certain is that after unloading the better part of a magazine into the place where I thought he'd wedged himself, the gunfire subsided and Koppes's tarp stopped absorbing rounds.

With the job taken care of, at least for the moment, I looked up at Koppes, who appeared grateful for the help, even if he was still wondering about my sanity.

"You good?" I asked him. "You got ammo?"

"I'm good for now," he called down.

"Okay, dude, now listen to me," I said. "The Afghan Army guys have abandoned their positions, so there's just one thing blocking the Taliban from rolling in off the east side. Right now, you are the only gun in this fight, and the only guy who is watching our back door. Do you get that?"

As he confirmed that he understood, our exchange was interrupted by a series of sharp concussions, one after the other, coming from beyond the aid station toward the western side of camp, where Hardt and his team were.

My God, Hardt, what have you done? I wondered as I peeled away from Koppes's gun truck and started running west with the Dragunov.

WHEN THE ENEMY realized that Truck 1 was immobilized, they directed every ounce of fire they had at Hardt's Humvee. As the body of the vehicle was struck from all sides, Hardt realized that he and his team had very little time and almost zero options. Their best move, he decided, was that Faulkner and Griffin would make a run for it while he climbed into the turret and tried to lay down some cover fire for their escape.

Hardt was poised to get into the turret when Griffin opened the rear passenger door on the right side of the vehicle and jumped out. This exposed him to the enemy gunners who were preparing to storm the front gate, and they were on him so fast that several of the rounds they were firing at him went into the Humvee before Hardt could even shut the door.

As with Michael Scusa and many of the other junior enlisted guys in Blue Platoon, I barely knew the first thing about Chris Griffin. We had probably spoken directly on less than a dozen occasions. What little I'd

Chris Griffin

seen had impressed me—unlike many of his peers, he didn't complain, he never seemed to get rattled, and he was *always* where he was supposed to be. But other than that, he was a bit of an enigma.

Thanks to the predicament in which Griffin now found himself, neither I nor anyone else would ever be able to discover much about what happened during the final seconds of his life. But here's what I can say.

Griffin's body wound up roughly a hundred yards away from where he stepped down from the truck, lying in an open spot of ground right outside the Shura Building, which is the area where his killers were coming from—and therefore the last place toward which he should have been running. There's no way of knowing whether he was killed right next to the truck and then was dragged down toward the Shura Building, or if he simply became so disoriented that he ended up running directly into the enemy. Those are details that we would never be able to assemble into anything that made sense—but we did piece together a picture of how he was killed. And, by God, it was brutal.

Griffin was shot twice in the face. The first bullet went through the left side of his temple and the other punched through the left side of his jaw. Both caused extensive skull fractures while tearing the inside of his brain into pieces. He took a third shot to his back, which shattered several of his ribs and blew out his liver. The fourth shot fractured his left forearm, while the fifth shattered his right femur. The sixth and seventh went through his left buttock, and the final round hit him in the left thigh.

In all, he was shot eight separate times. It was a horrible and violent death, and perhaps its only note of grace is that it may have purchased a few additional seconds of breathing space for his two companions—although this is questionable, given that the main threat that Faulkner and Hardt were now confronting was coming from the opposite side of the truck, where Faulkner had just spotted three Taliban by the laundry trailer.

They were clad in Afghan Security Guard uniforms, and one of them was taking aim with a rocket launcher.

"They're shooting at us!" yelled Hardt as the rocket smacked directly into the driver's-side windshield, penetrating the bulletproof glass and driving shards of shrapnel all along the left side of Faulkner's body, from his arm and shoulder blade down to his thigh.

As Faulkner screamed in pain, Hardt did his best to reassure him. "You're good, you're good!" he yelled.

With the enemy now poised to swarm the truck, it was imperative that they evacuate. But there was no plan, other than the vague notion that Faulkner would exit on the driver's side, crouch down, then open the rear door on that side, which would shield him from fire while enabling Hardt to get out.

Instead, Faulkner, who was now so disoriented that he couldn't even figure out where his gun was, opened the door and simply started running.

He had no idea where he was going; all he knew was that he needed to move as rapidly as he could, and that he wanted to get as far away from the Humvee as possible. Without even turning around to confirm whether Hardt had made it out of the truck, he sprinted east as fast as his legs would carry him.

It's hard now to imagine how Faulkner actually survived that mad dash, unarmed and blinded by pain, across the most exposed part of camp, around the mosque, down the alley between Red barracks and the command post, and through the front door of the aid station. When he stumbled inside, he looked as if he'd just been dragged through hell on a chain. His face was lacerated and absolutely covered in blood. Even worse was his left arm—an arm that had already been flayed open two years earlier in Iraq, and was now torn in the exact same places as before.

"They got me in the arm," he kept saying. "They got me in my *arm*!"

While the medics set about patching him up, they tried to get Faulkner to share some information on what had happened, but he was so traumatized and confused that he wasn't able to share any details that made sense. He had no idea what had become of Griffin. He seemed to be under the vague impression that Hardt might still be out there by himself and perhaps still in the fight, but he couldn't offer a single coherent thought about where Hardt might actually be. Nor could he provide any info on how the guys from Gallegos's team were faring.

Suddenly, a voice could be heard coming over the radio—

"Holy *fuck*!" cried Hardt.

Everyone in camp who was still alive and tuned to the Force Pro net heard what followed:

"They've got an RPG pointed right at me!"

Then the radio went dead.

IT'S IMPOSSIBLE to say whether the Taliban rocket team that Hardt was staring at was part of the same group of men who had slaughtered Griffin just a few minutes earlier. It's also impossible to say whether Hardt managed to get any shots of his own off before they unleashed their RPG. All we really know is that the rocket that they fired at him was an armor-defeating round, and that it punched through the rear door on the right side of the truck, spewing shrapnel everywhere.

Somehow, Hardt survived that blast and made out of the truck, probably by scrambling through one of the two doors on the opposite side. Then he started running south in the direction of the maintenance shed, which was about five yards away from the truck.

At some point during that desperate race, he was shot twice in the left side of his chest. One bullet passed through his left lung, diaphragm, and spleen before exiting his back, while the second shot shattered his first three ribs. He was also shot once in the left arm, and once in the left leg.

While all of those wounds caused extensive damage and blood loss, they probably didn't kill him. Instead, as we would later discover, he was finished off by three gunshots that were administered to the left side of his head.

WHEN I HEARD Hardt's radio transmission, I knew nothing about what had happened to Griffin or Faulkner. My only goal, as I raced away from Koppes's gun truck, was to get to someplace where I could see Hardt and support him—and the best place to do that was the café, which afforded a view of the western end of camp and might enable me to get a sense of what was going on.

When I posted up with the Dragunov at the café's wall of sandbags, I could just barely see the back hatch of LRAS2, which looked like a scorched hunk of metal. There was no sign of any movement around it. As for Hardt's gun truck, my line of sight to it was entirely blocked by a "hippo," a huge water-holding tank that was located on the south side of the shower trailers.

As I took in the scene, a movement in the foreground caught my eye. A trio of heavily armed Taliban fighters was emerging from around the back of Truck 2, the Humvee from which Jonathan Adams had been laying down fire with an M-19 grenade launcher during the first several minutes of the battle before being forced to abandon his position.

It was a three-man rocket team, and it was clear that they had come through the front gate and around the corner of the Shura Building. The man in the front and the man in the rear both had chest rigs and were carrying AK-47s. The middle guy was toting an RPG on his shoulder, and he had a pack with his extra rounds strapped to his back. The RPG shooter was wearing a black headband with Arabic writing on it.

As I took in these details, Janis Lakis, the Latvian military advisor, moved into the café area and took a position by my left elbow. By this point, Lakis had abandoned his efforts to get the Afghan Army soldiers under his supervision to help defend the camp. Instead, he'd concluded that the most effective thing he could do was link up with us and lend a hand. It was a decision that I welcomed because, in addition to his skills and experience, he'd brought along his H&K G-36 rifle, which was fitted with a .203 grenade launcher.

"Hey, Lakis," I asked softly, "there's no way that these three guys could be your Afghan Army dudes, is there?"

As Lakis shook his head, the man with the RPG rested his weapon on the back of the Humvee, leaned against the gun truck, and started making an adjustment to his headband.

What shocked me even more than the presence of an enemy fighter standing directly in the center of camp was the casual manner in which he was behaving. He and his companions were stopping for a little tactical pause to catch their breath and regroup before continuing their advance. It was clear that they weren't expecting any resistance, and that they had no idea they were being observed.

Then it hit me:

This was probably the team that had just taken out Hardt.

From where I was standing, the insurgents were roughly fifty yards away. Through the scope of the Dragunov, however, the distance seemed to shrink to no more than about ten feet. The setup reminded me of what it used to be like at night back home on my dad's ranch when you shined a spotlight on some jackrabbits and they just froze and let you line up your shot.

Damn, this is an absolute gimme, I thought as I exhaled to steady the gun and curled my finger around the trigger.

The man with the RPG had the biggest weapon, so my plan was to deal with him first, swing to the right to catch the second guy before he realized what was happening, then finish the job by picking off the third dude as he started his run.

At such close range, the sniper rifle would probably fire a notch or two high. So as the RPG shooter finished messing with his headband and straightened up to present a full-on silhouette, I put the crosshairs of the scope at the bottom of his sternum, directly on the bony nub known as the xiphoid process, and touched off the shot.

It turned out I was right—instead of nailing the center of his thorax, the bullet tore through the man's left clavicle, just above his heart.

As his two companions registered what was happening and exchanged an *oh, shit!* look, I was already swinging right and dropping the front guy by punching him with two shots, one in the left lung and the second in the hip.

As he went down, I swung left and tried to pop the third member of the team just as he bolted around to the back of the truck, where I could see him trying to hide between the wheels.

Under normal circumstances, it would have been a simple matter to take him out by putting some rounds underneath the truck, which sat at least eighteen inches off the ground. However, most of this clearance was obscured by a short terrace of stacked rocks that ran around the front of the truck.

Knowing that I couldn't peg the insurgent with a straight shot, I started skipping rounds, aiming at the ground just a few feet in front of the truck in the hope that one of the bullets would bounce up into him. As I fired repeatedly, I could see the Taliban shooter making frantic motions along the ground with his hand, beckoning back toward the front gate, where it seemed likely that his companions were massing.

"Lakis," I called out, "hit him with your frickin' *grenade!*"

"How far do you think?" Lakis asked as he opened the breech and threw in a .203 round.

"Dunno. Can't be more than fifty meters."

The grenade launcher gave off its distinctive *doonk!* and the snub-nosed projectile sailed across camp in a graceful little arc to land perfectly on the far side of the gun truck and detonate with a satisfying *thump* and *crack*.

The Taliban soldier vanished.

"Fifty meters!" exclaimed Lakis in his Schwarzenegger accent, nodding with approval. *"Ja!"*

LOOKING BACK ON that moment now, I suppose I should have been pleased at having taken out the guys who had probably nailed Hardt. But at the time I had more pressing things on my mind, chief among them the shocking realization that a team of enemy soldiers had just waltzed through our front gate.

Up until that moment, I don't think I truly understood how compromised we were. The idea that we might be overrun was no longer just a dreadful possibility. It was actually happening.

And what's more, the process had already started in earnest just uphill to my left, where an isolated little pocket of men that included Jones, Gregory, and Dannelley was struggling to hold the trench next to the mosque.

This group included some of the youngest and least experienced soldiers in the outpost. Thanks to the fact that they didn't have a radio, they'd received no word of what was taking place elsewhere, including Hardt's final transmission. And unbeknownst to me, they were about to confront an even bigger pack of Taliban.

PART OF THE IRONY of Hardt's failed rescue attempt is that his mission may have inadvertently triggered the very thing that he was trying to prevent, which was a concerted bid on the part of the enemy to breach the western part of our camp. Hardt's high-centered Humvee had presented such a compelling target that it had encouraged several groups of fighters to pour through the wire from both the north and the south. With Truck 1's team now taken out of the picture, those enemy fighters saw no reason not to keep pushing directly toward the center of camp—which put a group of them on a collision course with Jones's team in the trench.

During the past ten minutes, the situation confronting Jones and his guys had gone from bad to worse. There were now almost half a dozen men inside the ditch—Jones and Gregory, plus Dannelley and his companions—and all of them were pinned down. The moment that one of them would raise his head or the barrel of his weapon above the lip of the trench, the enemy gunners along the ridgelines would direct a furious burst of fire in their direction.

That was fearsome enough, but the grenades that had blown out the windows of the mosque next to them had also ignited a fire that was now consuming the building, and someone was evidently trapped inside. Jones and his companions had no idea who this might be. But judging from the wild, high-pitched screams that the man was emitting in either Pashto or Nuristani as he burned to death, he was an Afghan construction worker, an Afghan soldier, or perhaps even the imam himself.

Despite the risks, Jones and his companions had been popping out of the trench every couple of minutes to return fire—usually selecting a different spot in order to confuse the enemy gunners.

"Okay, guys," Jones would say, "let's pop up real quick and see what's going on. No big deal."

Up went their heads and their weapons. Sometimes they'd be able to put out some return fire; other times they'd be driven back down by sniper fire before they could get off a shot.

During one of these moments, Gregory spotted something.

"I see two dudes over by the showers!" he exclaimed as he ducked down again.

Jones had caught sight of them too. They were no more than fifteen feet away. Both men were clad in the brown "man-jam" robes that were standard-issue garb among civilians.

Jones's first assumption was that they were Afghan workers who had somehow gotten trapped within the outpost. But they were so close that not only could he hear their voices—he could also detect the distinctive click/ pop as they pulled the pins on the grenades they were preparing to throw.

"Holy shit, those are *Taliban*," he thought. *"Inside our wire."*

With that, Jones, Gregory, and Dannelley popped up in unison, weapons raised, and took them down. (Gregory fired almost fifty rounds from his SAW, emptying an entire belt of ammo). A beat of relief quickly gave way to the realization that there surely must be more—a fact that was confirmed by the arrival of Kenny Daise, a soldier with HQ Platoon, who breathlessly slid into the trench with Kyle Knight.

"We've got guys on the COP!" Daise reported breathlessly.

Daise just come from the Shura Building after failing to hold his position there and being forced to fall back. On the way up to the trench leading to the mosque, he had met and locked eyes with a bearded Taliban fighter clad in a dirty overshirt and a white turban who was carrying an AK-47. The man was no more than seventy-five feet away. Both he and Daise had raised their weapons to fire, but the Taliban's gun had jammed, while Daise was too slow and didn't get off a shot until his target ducked back around the corner.

Dude, of course we've got guys on the COP, thought Jones. *Tell me something I don't know.*

That wasn't the only news Daise had, however.

"Kirk didn't make it—he's dead," he reported.

Then Daise reached for his radio, keyed the mike, and said something that none of us had ever expected to hear, except maybe in a movie:

"Charlie in the wire!" he yelled. "Charlie in the wire!"

ALL OVER THE OUTPOST, guys on the Force Pro net found themselves doing a double take and, despite the fact that the current state of battle represented a kind of nadir of direness, cracked a smile and shook their heads.

Staff Sergeant Daise had the less-than-stellar reputation of being a little slow—the kind of older guy who was, both literally and symbolically, perpetually a step or two behind everybody else.

Daise had been in the army for more than fifteen years, which was plenty long enough to earn him the label of a relic among most of the younger guys. And now, for reasons so unfathomable that it seemed pointless to even try to parse them, Daise had pounded that reputation home by invoking a phrase lifted from the jungles of Vietnam and applying the thing to a firefight in the mountains of Afghanistan.

This was one of the few comic-relief moments in the day.

Down inside the trench, however, one man didn't find this funny at all. Jones, who hadn't known that Kirk was dead, was filled with an implacable rage over the news that the man he had most looked up to, the person who had taught him the most about being a soldier, had just gotten smoked.

It was the kind of rage that Kirk probably would have admired because, in addition to being all consuming, it refused to be corralled by prudence, instead demanding immediate release. And so, despite the fact that they were still pinned down, Jones rose up, laid down his machine gun, and started firing nonstop.

This probably wasn't the smartest move in terms of conserving his shots for the inevitable moment when the Taliban decided to overwhelm the trench. But right then, Jones really didn't give a flying fuck about fire discipline.

What's more, the need to conserve ammo vanished a few seconds later when a Taliban RPG drilled into the generator alongside the trench and set the damn thing on fire, producing a dense, black column of smoke that provided a perfect screen for the entire group to break contact by low-crawling to the north end of the trench and making a run for the barracks buildings.

This fallback move, which they performed one at a time while covering one another, reflected a larger reality, which was that instead of pushing our lines *out* to retake the portions of the outpost that we'd lost during Hardt's failed rescue attempt, we were doing the opposite and pulling farther *in*.

Needless to say, this isn't the way you fight if you want to win. It's what you do if you're preparing to make a last stand.

CHAPTER THIRTEEN

The Alamo Position

ONE OF THE strangest hallmarks of combat is that it is so chaotic that sometimes the turmoil it engenders in the mind never fully resolves. Soldiers can spend the rest of their lives trying to parse out a sense of exactly how a battle in which they participated unfolded: what came before, what happened after, and which events collided into one another simultaneously to create a tangled mishmash of confusion.

Another salient feature of war is that it is often impossible to go back and fit the pieces of what happened neatly together. The absence of a comprehensive record, the fallibility of human memory, and the fact that the most important eyewitnesses to key events may have been killed—all of these elements can make it extraordinarily difficult to call any subsequent rendition of events definitive.

It is my belief that this is the case with what unfolded at Keating, particularly during the initial attack. It's quite possible that at the heart of this battle there's a level of truth that is fundamentally unknowable.

In light of that, perhaps the best thing that I can do now, with the benefit of hindsight and the impressions that many of my fellow soldiers have shared with me, is to acknowledge that while I was dealing with my own challenges, a complex set of parallel events were unfolding—events that I had no knowledge of at the time, even though a number of them were about to smash up against me. In order to get to those events, I want to lay out a sense of what was happening beyond my immediate awareness. And perhaps the most effective way to do that is to take you into the mind of Andrew Bundermann, who, by virtue of his role in the command post, probably had the best overall picture of what was unfolding.

While my comrades and I were engaged in half a dozen separate duels all across the outpost, the members of HQ Platoon who were stationed inside the command post were caught up in their own whirlpool of challenges, many of which were swirling around a single urgent and overriding fact: if Bundermann didn't figure out how to mobilize some assistance and swiftly hurl those assets against the enemy, our chances of surviving this ordeal were slim.

At the moment, this goal was being thwarted by two problems, the most glaring of which was that Fritsche's mortars still weren't functioning.

For the better part of the past forty minutes, the soldiers up at our OP had been withstanding withering machine-gun and RPG fire while contending with at least one sniper. The fact that none of those men had been killed offered a testament to the advantage of holding the high ground. But that advantage was unexpectedly undermined when Staff Sergeant James Clark, who was probably the sharpest soldier in White Platoon, was hit in the chest with a round that went straight through one of his magazines.

The bullet was stopped by Clark's ceramic chest plate, but not before striking a tracer round inside the magazine and igniting his vest. Suddenly, Clark found himself dealing with an emergency he'd never even known was possible: he was on fire, and if he didn't extinguish the flames immediately, they would ignite the remaining ammo on his chest and turn him into a Roman candle right there on the gun line.

As Clark furiously patted down his vest while continuing to return fire on the Mark 19 that he was manning, he realized that the round that was still lodged in his chest plate had come from the only place on top of the mountain that sat above Fritsche: a tiny auxiliary post that housed six members of the Afghan Border Patrol. Like the ANA soldiers down at Keating, these allies were supposed to provide additional support for Fritsche. And like their ANA counterparts, the Border Patrol soldiers had apparently abandoned their positions. In so doing, they had permitted their post to be commandeered by a group of enemy fighters who, as Clark could now see, were using the superior vantage to direct the bulk of their fire onto Fritsche's mortar pit.

It also meant that Fritsche's attackers were now less than fifty yards from the perimeter.

Clark, who was as competent and as cool-headed a man as you could wish for in a staff sergeant, called for the claymores on one side of Fritsche to be detonated while simultaneously pulling one of his 240B machine-gun teams off of his wall and sending them over to the mortar pit in the hopes of establishing some fire superiority in that sector.

When combined with the assistance that Fritsche was finally receiving from the 155 howitzers at Bostick, whose shells were now exploding thunderously across the open ground on the southeast side of Fritsche, Clark had hopes of being able to get his mortar pit up shortly and start sending some rounds downrange in support of Keating. But for the moment, his team was still too preoccupied with defense to provide anything in the way of offense—a state of affairs that Jordan Bellamy, Clark's lieutenant who was in command of Fritsche, was now communicating to Keating.

"I still can't get to my mortar pit," Bellamy radioed to Bundermann.

"Okay, but the moment you guys can get there, I gotta have it," replied Bundermann. "I *gotta* have it!"

With that, Bundermann turned to his second big problem, which was that although air support had finally arrived, the planes weren't yet able to engage.

The first pair of F-15Es, the two Strike Eagles that had been ordered to Keating just as they were coming off of a night sortie, were now directly above the outpost. What's more, a priority target package—the set of coordinates that would help direct the laser-guided and GPS-guided bombs on board those fighter jets onto the Putting Green and the Switchbacks—had already been selected by Bundermann and sent out to Bostick by Cason Shrode, who was in charge of artillery and air support. Unfortunately, however, moving this information from the army to the air force involved a delay that struck everyone inside the command post as understandable but nevertheless maddening. Thanks to the mountainous terrain, it was impossible for the fighter pilots to radio Bostick and receive clearance for their bomb drops while they were flying directly over Keating. So the F-15s were forced to make a detour to Bostick to confirm their targets via line-of-sight radio, and then return to Keating before they could release their ordnance.

In the midst of a battle when a few seconds can make a difference between men living and men dying, a lag of even a minute or two can seem interminable. For Bundermann, who was listening to one sector of Keating's defense after another either collapse and fall back or go silent on the radio, the nine minutes that passed between the arrival of the first two F-15s and the release of their first bombs seemed like an eternity.

When the bombs finally did land, the explosions were swallowed up by the roar on the enemy's incoming fire and never even registered among myself and the other defenders who were outside. Within the walls of the command post, however, the knowledge that the jets were unloading ordnance offered some satisfaction to Bundermann and his team. But their relief disappeared a few seconds later as the Strike Eagles radioed that they would have to disengage and return to base (they were extremely low on fuel).

The handful of bombs that they'd managed to drop were in no way game changers. They'd done little to deter our attackers and virtually nothing to slow them down. And as if to underscore this fact, Kenny Daise was now sending out his radio alert to let everyone know that we had "Charlie in the wire," confirming just how thoroughly we'd been compromised.

From the reports that Bundermann was receiving, he concluded that Keating had been breached in not one spot, but three. Somewhere between ten and fifteen Taliban had penetrated the eastern gate and were taking up positions inside the abandoned Afghan National Army barracks. On the opposite side of camp, a group of fighters had driven past the mortar pit, across the minefield of defunct claymores, and through the wall of concertina wire in the vicinity of the maintenance shed. And at more or less the same time, a third group had rushed the main gate and run past the Shura Building. Having destroyed Hardt's team and then forced Jones's team to fall back, elements from these latter two groups were now scurrying around the sector that we had just abandoned and, presumably, were preparing to attack the very center of camp.

It was at this point that Bundermann decided it might not be a bad idea for him to change clothes.

By now, he'd already taken the precaution of borrowing an extra set of armor from Shrode, whose bunk was at the back of the command post, and was wearing it over his shorts and T-shirt. But in addition to the fact that Shrode's gear was three sizes too big for him, Bundermann was clomping around in this oversized outfit while still wearing his flip-flops. The entire getup struck him as ridiculous, so he asked one of the guys in the command post to go back to the barracks to grab his boots, helmet, and rifle.

When his kit arrived, Bundermann was still wildly out of uniform, but at least he was geared for what came next. While continuing to man his radios and the SATCOM, he ordered guards posted on both the west and south doors. It was time to prepare for the very real possibility that the insurgents were about to assault the command post.

In a situation like this, it turns out that the army has a special code you're supposed to transmit that summons all available aircraft to drop whatever they're doing and rush to wherever the code originates. This is known as a "broken arrow" call, and it's reserved for a ground unit that finds itself surrounded and facing imminent destruction. When I later checked, I was surprised to learn that the call has been invoked only once—in November of 1965 when the US 7th Cavalry (ironically, the very same unit that had fought under Custer at the Battle of the Little Bighorn eighty-nine years earlier) was encircled by a regiment of North Vietnamese regulars in the Ia Drang Valley. Despite overwhelming odds, the commander of that unit, Colonel Hal Moore, and his men held out against repeated North Vietnamese assaults and managed to persevere.

The reason I had to look all that up is that I'd never heard of such a thing before. Nor had anybody else at Keating, including Bundermann. If there'd been a memo on what sort of announcement you're supposed to send out just prior to having your teeth kicked through the back of your skull, nobody in Red Platoon had ever bothered to read the thing.

In real life, whenever a situation skids out of control and you're a step or two away from getting totally shellacked—which was pretty much where we were headed in that moment—the kind of statement that goes out over the radio tends to be as blunt and as devoid of symphonic resonance as what Bundermann ordered sent up through the tac-chat:

> 6:50 a.m.
> <2BlackKnight_TOC>
> >>> ENEMY IN THE WIRE ENEMY IN THE WIRE!!!

As that call went out, virtually every soldier in the center of camp was preparing to do the prudent and sane thing, which was to batten the hatches and hunker down. The single exception to this strategy was LRAS2, the battered gun truck at the westernmost end of the outpost where Gallegos and his team were cut off from the rest of us and almost out of ammo. Instead of pulling further into their shell, they were about to do the opposite in the hopes of exploiting an odd opportunity that had arisen from Hardt's failed rescue mission.

Because Hardt's stricken gun truck had served as such a powerful a magnet for the fighters who were slithering through the concertina wire and the front gate, Gallegos's battle position underwent a brief and fleeting lull. The Humvee was still taking fire from the surrounding ridgelines— but for the first time in nearly an hour, it seemed that it might be possible to open a door on either side of the vehicle and step outside without instantly being shot to pieces from six different directions.

Granted, this wasn't much of a letup, and it clearly wasn't going to last. But it was enough to make Gallegos think that this might be their moment to make a move. And then something happened that drove any remaining doubt from his mind.

Through the cracks and the bullet craters in the Humvee's front wind-shield, Gallegos and Larson both spotted a quartet of Taliban slithering over the top of the Hescos roughly fifty yards to the west of them. These men had probably come up through the trash pit, and one of them was carrying an American M249 SAW, a weapon whose distinctive profile is unmistakable.

By the looks of them, all four of these men—who were sporting brown robes, chest racks loaded with bullets and hand grenades, and tennis shoes—were intent on pushing toward the center of camp, and there were undoubtedly more insurgents behind them.

Gallegos had already framed up their exit plan, the key to which was that Larson and Carter would dismount on the left side of the truck and use their M4s to provide cover fire while Gallegos, Mace, and Martin poured out of the right side of the truck and made a dash for the latrines. When they arrived, they'd immediately lay down enough fire to enable Larson and Carter to make the same run. From there, the team would split again and bound down to the Shura Building.

The other guys in the truck had all been polled to see if they were on board, and while everyone agreed that there was no way they could stay, nobody had been able to come up with a better idea for how to get out of the mess they were in. Hence, the only question was whether this was the time to launch.

"Hey, G," Larson asked Gallegos, "do we need to go now?"

"Yeah," replied Gallegos. "We *gotta* go."

In addition to being the highest-ranking enlisted man in the truck, Gallegos had the most combat experience.

"Your call, dude," said Larson.

"All right, guys, it's now or never," announced Gallegos, turning to the men in the backseat and giving everyone a hard look.

He received three crisp nods.

"Okay, let's go."

DURING THOSE FINAL moments inside the Humvee, everybody was reasonably convinced that the plan was actually going to work. Gallegos and Larson seemed especially confident, and the three guys in the backseat picked up that vibe and fed off it. Their attitude toward the situation they faced could best be described as: *Right on, bro—let's get this done and we'll see each other on the other side.*

The second the doors opened and they stepped out of the truck, that brittle sense of optimism shattered like glass.

Because Larson was in the driver's seat, he posted up along the hood of the truck with the intention of engaging the snipers he'd spotted inside Urmul and along the Putting Green. At the same time, Carter was positioning himself between the front of the truck and the wall of sandbags.

Alerted by their movements, the Taliban gunners who had been concentrating on Hardt and his team abruptly switched their focus away from Truck 1 and swung back onto the crew of LRAS2. The effect was immediate and devastating.

In the same moment that Larson and Carter started laying down cover fire, an RPG struck a steel shipping container next to the gun truck and exploded. The blast completely enveloped Mace and Martin, coating both men with smoke and dust. Mace, who also took a full load of shrapnel to his legs and abdomen, was slammed to the ground while Martin started running, scrambled over a drop-off, and disappeared around the far corner of the latrines.

"I don't know what to do!" cried Mace as he lay on the ground.

"Follow Gallegos!" yelled Larson, who at this point had no idea that the impact from the rocket had all but demolished Mace's legs.

As Mace struggled to obey Larson's command, Gallegos stepped over, lifted his injured comrade to his feet, and stumbled with him around the far side of the latrines.

On the opposite end of the truck, Carter was poised and waiting for a signal from Larson to start his own run toward the latrines when he heard a series of shots coming from the same spot where Gallegos and Mace had just disappeared. The next thing Carter knew, Gallegos was rounding the corner by himself—Mace wasn't anywhere in sight—and racing back to the truck as a Taliban gunner opened up on him from just above the mortar pit.

As Carter watched, Gallegos took multiple bursts of fire to his chest, stomach, left arm, and right foot. When the first shots hit, he tried to return fire. He kept shooting as he was drilled by the second volley. The third burst put him on the ground.

Meanwhile, one of the Taliban snipers inside Urmul drew a bead on Larson and shot him directly in the head.

I have no idea what thoughts might have been going through Carter's mind in that moment as he scrambled back into the truck. But if it had been me, I know of at least one thing that I'd have been asking myself:

How much time is left before they roll through me?

THAT WAS ONE of the main questions that Bundermann was pondering as he stepped outside the command post for the first time that morning to get a firsthand view of what things looked like. The impression he got offered little more than a confirmation of the reports that he'd been receiving over the radio since the battle had kicked off: the entire camp was getting jackhammered from all sides, and that our perimeter was steadily compressing inward.

Without massive air support, it was pointless for Bundermann to pretend that we could continue to defend our lines. As commander, he could therefore see that his only recourse was clear: allow the outer wire to collapse, pull back to the inner Hesco barrier, and concentrate on defending Keating's core for as long as possible in the hopes that some robust air support would check on station before the Taliban ran us over.

As it turns out, the army has a name for the final defensive posture that's adopted by a unit which is facing the possibility of being overrun—and unlike the broken arrow call, most of us knew what this was. Fittingly, it's called the Alamo Position.

Bundermann was coldly aware that falling back to the Alamo Position would leave nearly ten men—a fifth of his command—to fend for themselves.

He also knew that most of those men were probably already dead.

WITHIN EACH OF the three buildings where we would make our final stand, guys were now gathering up their remaining ammo, getting down on the floor, and aiming their guns at the doors as they prepared for a hand-to-hand fight for the final square feet of the outpost.

Inside Red Platoon barracks, Raz turned to Kyle Knight—who had his machine gun aimed at the south door—and told him to kill anybody who tried to come through.

Next door, the remaining members of Blue Platoon were gearing up to do the same in their barracks. But perhaps the most graphic indication of how far our backs were pressed against the wall was unfolding inside the aid station, where Shane Courville was ruefully casting his mind back to an exchange he'd recently had with First Sergeant Burton.

Three or four days earlier, Courville had been part of a group of guys who were ordered to inventory all of the weapons in the arms room in preparation for Keating's decommission. As they sorted through the mix of rockets and guns, Courville had stumbled across something unexpected: a footlocker stuffed full of shotguns.

He had no idea how they'd gotten there, but there were more than ten of them, and they were pretty sweet—twelve-gauge pump-action Mossbergs with pistol grips and fourteen-inch barrels. And for no particular reason other than that they seemed cooler than hell, Courville decided right there, on the spot, that he really wanted to have one—despite the fact that in a place like Keating, a shotgun was about the most useless weapon you could possibly think of.

"Hey, First Sergeant," Courville had called out to Burton. "How about you let me grab one of these things?"

"Negative," Burton had replied, shaking his head. "If we ever get to where you actually *need* one of these motherfuckers, Doc, we're all gonna be in a world of hurt."

As the medics grabbed their carbines and leveled them on both doors, the memory of that conversation came back to Courville.

Damn, he thought to himself, *wish I had me one of them Mossbergs right about now.*

CHAPTER FOURTEEN

Light 'Em Up

AS MY COMRADES were busy forting themselves up inside the trio of buildings within the Alamo perimeter, I was making a run from the café to the command post, the structure that would be the most heavily defended and thus the last to fall. When I burst through the door, I saw Bundermann standing there in the darkness—the generator was still down—with a battery-powered radio in each hand. Hovering next to him was Jonathan Hill, the sergeant who ran Blue Platoon. Both men were trying to make sense of the information that was pouring in from the radios, the SATCOM, and the tac-chat network.

"We have no indirect fire," Bundermann barked as soon as he saw me—which meant that neither our mortars nor Fritsche's were up, "and we're still waiting on full air support."

Given that we were still on our own, the three of us needed to make some quick decisions about what to do next. But first we had to resolve a fundamental disagreement over whether we were going to accept the mess we'd been shoved into, or start shoving back.

"We need to hold our ground, dig in our heels, and wait for support," declared Hill.

I didn't agree. In my estimation, hunkering down and waiting for whatever was coming at us might be seem like a smart move on the surface, but it felt like a lousy approach—especially if the goal was not simply to survive but to win. Plus, I didn't like where that road led, because we'd be ceding all maneuverability to the enemy while consigning ourselves to a passive role. If help didn't arrive in time, we'd be looking at hand-to-hand combat as the enemy systematically worked its way from one structure to the next, killing us off pocket by pocket. The last group of guys would wind up transmitting the grid lines for the center of camp and calling in a bomb drop on top of themselves with the hope that one of them might survive inside the rubble long enough to be able to tell the story of what happened.

"Fuck that," I told Hill. "We need to retake this camp."

"Okay," said Bundermann, "what do we need to do?"

That question wasn't entirely necessary, because Bundermann already had a pretty good idea of what I was thinking. He was asking partly because doing so was in keeping with his inclusive style of leadership, and partly because he suspected—correctly—that he and I harbored slightly different notions of how to get to the goal that we shared.

What we both had in mind was a counterattack spearheaded by a single squad that would halt the Taliban's assault and set the stage for turning the tables on them. But while Bundermann wanted to go about this in a mea-sured and methodical way, I was keen to get the first set of moves done in one go. Nevertheless, each of us harbored the same basic vision, at the heart of which lay a fairly simple idea that would require quite a bit of skill and a full shot of luck to pull off. Plus, each man who volunteered for this job would need a set of brass-plated balls.

When Hill declared that he was game to give whatever I had in mind a try, the three of us then turned to the map of Keating on the west wall and started walking through how it would go down.

First, Hill would need to send a team from Blue Platoon to lock down the east side of camp by either clearing all of the Afghan National Army bar-racks or, failing that, blocking the pathways leading into the center of camp with anything they could find in order to slow down the enemy. Meanwhile, a team from Red Platoon would launch west with the aim of taking back the ground we'd lost.

We were almost out of ammo, and we needed that to stay in the fight. So

212

the first thing the guys from Red would do was make a push to the Hesco wall, about thirty yards from the command post, and then use that wall for cover as we forced our way to the ammo supply depot and retook the thing.

Once we did that, we'd start kicking ammo back to the center of camp. Then we'd set up a pair of machine guns—one pointing across the river toward the Afghan National Police station, the North Face, and the Putting Green; the other looking uphill toward the maintenance shed, the Waterfall and Switchbacks, and most important, the area just inside of the front gate. When those guns were in place, we'd start laying down some serious fire.

Our next move would be to make a second push, this time from the ammo supply point to the Shura Building. We'd enter and kill whoever was inside. Then we'd retake the front gate, close it down, and seal the thing off with claymores.

"And after that?" asked Bundermann.

"Well . . ." I replied, "we'll figure out what comes next after we get all that done."

AS PLANS GO, this wasn't super sophisticated, nor was it wildly innovative. In fact, what it really boiled down to was one of the first maneuvers that every soldier is taught within his first few weeks of joining the army: reacting to contact by setting up a support-by-fire maneuver. That's all it really was—although the "support" element was the key feature, which was the reason I then turned to Hill.

"When we get near the ammo supply point, we'll be rolling blind," I said. "We won't be able to tell if there are any fighters around the Shura Building or up by Gallegos's gun truck, so I need you to set a machine gun on our left flank to watch out for us."

The machine-gun team I was asking Hill to provide would need to set up somewhere around the chow hall so that they could look into—and shoot up—the piece of ground that me and my team wouldn't be able to see but would be charging toward during our two-part push to retake the ammo supply depot and the Shura Building. Once we wrested back control of those structures, one of my machine guns would then be able to fire uphill toward a section of camp—the area between the mechanics' bay and the mortar pit—that would be invisible to Hill's guys.

Those two intersecting triangles of fire would transform the ground extending from our mortar pit to the front gate into a kill zone for any insurgent who tried to enter it. The crossfire would also enable the rest of my team to complete the final part of our move: hurling ourselves through the east door of the Shura Building, and seizing back control of the front gate.

Hill and Bundermann nodded in agreement.

"Split your team," Bundermann ordered Hill, "and put a machine gun up by the chow hall to cover Ro and his guys."

As we confirmed that the plan was solid, Burton, who had been watching this exchange unfold, stepped over to our huddle.

"Hey, are you all right?" he asked me.

Burton had picked up on the fact that as we drew up our plan, I'd been shaking my wounded hand, the one that Raz had wrapped in a bandage a few minutes earlier, which now seemed to have gone numb.

"Can't feel my hand anymore," I replied.

"Let me see," said Burton, who started unwrapping the pressure dressing. As the bandage came off, I realized that Raz, who was an excellent machine-gunner but a piss-poor medic, had basically put a tourniquet on my forearm, cutting off the blood supply to my hand. As the feeling returned, Burton reapplied the dressing.

"Thanks for dressing me for school, Dad," I quipped as I prepared to push through the door and head over to the barracks to see if I could find some volunteers for this mission. "I promise I'll be good."

Just before heading out, however, there was one last detail I needed to take care of—something that connected back to Hardt and his final radio transmission.

ONE OF THE first things we teach young soldiers is that if you think you're going to have to make a run for it and you're gonna leave some gear behind, it's critically important to make sure that your communications aren't compromised. The best way to do that is either by destroying your radio or "zeroing it out," which entails erasing all the data inside it. Thinking back on Hardt's final words, I realized that it was doubtful he'd had the time to take care of his radio.

I also knew that the men who had taken out Hardt had come through the front gate, where there was a second radio up in the guard tower—one that Davidson, the last guy who was manning that post, may not have managed to bring with him when he fled.

Finally, I knew one other thing, which was that the guys who were doing their best to annihilate us had demonstrated intelligence at every stage of their attack. They had put together a complex and carefully choreographed assault. They had exploited every one of our weaknesses. They had exercised discipline and sound tactics. If they were smart enough to have done all of those things, they were certainly smart enough to grab hold of a radio and start monitoring the traffic in order to figure out what we were doing as we coordinated our next move. So we needed to cut them out of the communications loop—and the fastest way to do that was by calling for a net switch.

When you transmit a net-switch call, everyone who is listening immediately changes frequencies by jumping to a different channel. Anyone who is trying to eavesdrop but fails to make the jump is dropped from the network. It's an effective move, but it features one drawback.

At this point, we had at least three separate groups of soldiers whose exact location and condition were unknown. Gallegos and his team were—I assumed—somewhere in the vicinity of their gun truck. Breeding's team was probably still up at the mortar pit, although we'd heard nothing from them for almost an hour. And then there was Hardt and Griffin, about whom we also knew nothing.

In total, there were almost a dozen of our comrades out there, and unless they were monitoring their radios carefully, they would have no way of knowing about the net switch—and once it had taken place, they'd be cut off. (We had never agreed on a prearranged frequency to jump to.)

In other words, having failed to rescue these men, we would be severing their last line of connection to us.

That sounds pretty brutal. But the possibility that the enemy might be able to listen to our plans and use that information against us was no less appealing. Plus, I reminded myself, any concerns about those guys getting booted off the net were negated by the fact that most of them were probably dead or in the process of dying.

The choice was unpleasant but clear.

"You need to call a net switch," I told Bundermann.

He did so without hesitating. And with that, we cut them off.

Then Bundermann gave me a crisp nod that said, in effect, *Go make something happen.*

WHEN I LOOK back on this part of our story now, I'm struck by two things, the first of which is the harshness of some of the choices that confronted us, along with the speed and the cold sense of detachment with which we made them.

It also gives me pause to take stock of the ferocity of our resolve during those moments. Odd as it may sound, I don't remember being scared or worried about dying—or even, for that matter, contemplating those things as possibilities. What I do recall is a sense of pure and absolute focus—a kind of hypercompressed fixation on a single aim, which was putting together a set of specific moves, a running combination of plays, that would enable us to regain the ground we'd lost and take back our fucking house.

I remember something else too, which was a sense that amid all the pandemonium and the confusion and the noise, it felt as if ten years of training and practice had fused together and coalesced into a single, laser-like sense of purpose.

Finally, I had one other thought, a rogue idea hovering on the periphery of my mind, which was the notion that although we were girding to do what needed to be done all by ourselves, it sure would have been nice to have some help. More than anything else, it seemed to me, what we needed right now was an assist from the helicopter pilots in Jalalabad—the very same guys to whom, just a couple of weeks earlier, we'd been planning to mail out a giant consignment of elephant shit.

I suppose it's one of those poetic twists of fate that, as we were about to discover, they were doing everything possible to get to us. And, by God, they were almost there.

THE FIRST DISTRESS call from Keating had reached the command post of the 101st Airborne's Task Force Pale Horse at the Jalalabad Airfield at 6:20 a.m. just as a group of Colonel Jimmy Blackwell's Apache pilots were sitting down to breakfast in the chow hall. They had already completed their early-morning preflight briefing, and Ross Lewallen had a spoonful of biscuits and gravy in his fist when the alert came through on a handheld radio that he carried with him. With that, everyone dumped their trays and headed for the door.

There were four of them, and what was unusual was that each was a senior pilot with some very heavy combat experience under his belt. Lewallen was a redheaded bear of a man who combined off-duty jollity with a sense of unflappable cool in combat. He was currently on his third deployment, having arrived at the 101st just before Pale Horse deployed to Afghanistan, and he served as the task force's master gunner. Together with his copilot, Chad Bardwell, Lewallen had been in almost every major air engagement since they'd arrived in Afghanistan. As impressive as that was, however, Randy Huff and Chris Wright, the other two-man team, had actually been in *all* of those battles.

Under normal circumstances, you'd never have a foursome of the most seasoned pilots all working the same shift. But they had all just returned from the States (late summer being the time when the older men in the task force who had families preferred to take their one-month leaves), and they'd decided to give a break to their junior colleagues, who had been working nonstop in their absence.

That morning, the weather in the skies above Keating seemed perfect. But at Jalalabad, a different picture was emerging on the radar screens inside the command post, where Blackmon and his team could see multiple fronts moving in from the west that would, over the next eight hours, usher thunderstorms, lightning, and a dense ceiling of low-hanging cloud cover into the surrounding mountains—first around Jalalabad, then at Lowell and Bostick, and finally over Keating itself.

Their sortie consisted of two AH-64 Apaches. In an Apache, the senior pilot typically takes the backseat and is responsible for flying the aircraft, while his junior partner in the front seat is responsible for weapons and communications. (This is generally the arrangement, although these roles can—and often do—reverse: the front-seat man has a full set of flight controls, while the pilot in the backseat has complete access to the radio and the guns.) Lewallen would be piloting the first aircraft with Bardwell in the front seat; Huff would fly the second with Wright handling his weapons and radios.

The plan was for them to head to Bostick first in order to refuel, and proceed from there to Keating. But as they lifted off and started pushing their choppers up through the Kunar Valley, the radio updates they received on the developments at Keating made it clear to the pilots that things were rapidly getting worse.

"The perimeter's been breached," Colonel Brown radioed to Wright from the command post at Bostick about ten minutes later. "They've fired their final protective fire. You can expect to see enemy fighters intermixed with our guys on the outpost."

With this news, the pilots decided on the spot that they would bypass Bostick and proceed directly to Keating by cutting straight over a series of high ridgelines to the southeast, which would bring them in on the back side of the outpost. The loss of their refueling stop would mean that they'd have less time to spend in the air once they arrived. But if they pushed their birds as fast as possible, this direct line would enable them to shave several minutes off of their flight time and get there sooner. As an added bonus, because this approach was outside their normal flight route, it might enable them to avoid the Taliban's early-warning detection system (which consisted of spotters with cell phones on the valley floor) and perhaps surprise the attackers before they knew what hit them.

At 7:06 a.m., Wright contacted Brown for another update and was told that the Taliban were inside the camp.

"Anyone outside the wire is hostile," Brown said. "You are clear to engage."

THROUGHOUT THE FLIGHT, Bardwell—who was in charge of communicating with the American forces on the ground—was making repeated radio calls to Keating, and failing to raise a response. As frustrating as this was, it was nothing compared with the feeling he experienced when the Apaches cleared the final ridgeline at 7:10 a.m., and they saw the outpost splayed below.

"Oh, shit," said Bardwell. "It's burning."

The bottom of the valley was obscured by dense, black smoke, while the outpost itself was in flames. From the air, the fire appeared so massive that it looked as if everything was burning.

As the Apaches circled above, Bardwell repeated his radio calls at five-second intervals while wondering if it was possible that Keating had already been overrun and that none of the defenders had survived. He and Lewallen both had a sinking feeling that they may have arrived too late.

Roughly ninety seconds later—an interval that Bardwell would later claim was one of the longest minutes (and a half) of his life—he finally got a response from Bundermann, who had just finished up his powwow with me and Hill over how to retake the ammo supply point and the Shura Building.

"Guns cold," declared Bundermann, letting the pilots know that Keating's artillery was still down. "Anyone outside the wire is hostile. We're down to about two to three buildings. We have enemy inside the wire. We need you guys to work on taking care of people outside, and we'll kill everybody inside."

Layered over the sound of Bundermann's voice, Bardwell could hear the roar of continuous gunfire. He was impressed by how calm Bundermann sounded.

"We need to know what building you're in," replied Bardwell.

"Can you recognize the front gate from where you are?" asked Bundermann.

At this point, the smoke from our fires was so thick that it obscured pretty much everything.

"Negative," replied Bardwell, who was peering through a screen connected to the target-acquisition sensor mounted in the nose of his Apache. This device was essentially a black-and-white video feed, dubbed "Day TV," that the pilots use to scan their targets on the ground. (The system can be switched to heat-sensing infrared at night.)

"Hey, we're not shooting inside the COP," barked Lewallen, breaking into the same channel. "We can't see well enough, and I don't know where they're at."

No sooner had Lewallen completed that sentence than Bardwell caught sight of movement on his Day TV video feed along the far eastern side of the outpost, just beyond the Afghan National Army barracks at the edge of camp.

A line of more than thirty fighters was winding down the trail that descended from the Diving Board. They were clad in man-jams, and they were heavily armed with RPGs, AK-47s, and PKM machine guns. It was clear that the entire force was heading toward the breach in the wire where the Afghan Army had abandoned their positions and left the camp wide-open to attack.

When the Apaches dropped down a bit lower, most of the insurgents halted in their tracks. Then, realizing they were caught, the bulk of them began running toward the outpost while a handful of others turned around and fled back in the direction they'd come.

"Hey, I got a full platoon-sized element moving toward your location," said Bardwell, a bit stunned by how many Afghans he could see down there. He had never observed that many insurgents at one time on his screen. In fact, over the course of three deployments he'd never once seen such a large force attacking a single, static position. This wasn't the way that the Taliban would normally hit a compound, and he wanted to be absolutely certain that these men weren't Afghan allies who were helping to buttress Keating's defense.

"Do you have any ANA out there?" asked Bardwell.

"No," replied Bundermann. "Anyone outside the wire is hostile. Light 'em up."

AN APACHE'S 30-MM CANNON has two handgrips: one that operates the trigger for a laser, and the other connected to an M230 chain gun that is mounted directly underneath the nose of the aircraft and moved by hydraulic actuators. It is a fearsome machine that can fire at a rate of 625 rounds per minute. Those rounds, each of which is almost half the length of a man's forearm and twice as thick as his thumb, explode on impact, creating a lethal killing radius of more than ten feet. A single ten-round burst from the gun can cut down mature trees. Human beings don't stand a chance. Flesh shreds. Limbs are torn off. Torsos, heads, and bits of unidentifiable remains are hurled into the air and thrown a long, long way.

At this point, both helicopters were circling the outpost in a left orbit, and separated by a lateral distance of about three thousand yards. Lewallen and Bardwell were flying roughly twelve hundred feet off the ground, while Huff and Wright were five hundred vertical feet above them.

Under normal conditions, Bardwell and Wright would have had a quick discussion about how to coordinate their respective sectors of fire—something along the lines of *Chad, you start on the south side, I'll start on the north, and we'll meet in the middle.* At that moment, however, there were so many enemy, and they were so close to the wire, that both gunners had the same thought, which was to obliterate them as quickly as possible, starting at the bottom with the fighters who were closest to the perimeter and methodically working up the side of the mountain to take out the rest. So Bardwell and Wright seized the handles of their 30-mm cannons and sent a series of bursts directly into the insurgents.

From their aircraft, neither gunner could discern what was happening, aside from seeing fist-sized clouds of dust erupting everywhere. But they could hear and feel the power of the chain guns, which were mounted directly underneath them, and which made their seats shake.

Some eighteen hundred feet down below, the effect was brutal and exceedingly violent. Men who moments earlier had cohesion and purpose were reduced to bits of meat and ragged strips of cloth.

There wasn't a man left standing.

Each helicopter was carrying three hundred rounds, and at the end of half a dozen trigger pulls, they weren't even close to going "Winchester," which would mean they were black on ammo. Moreover, each chopper still had several 2.75-inch rockets packed with flechettes, along with its Hellfire missiles. So the pilots continued their orbits and scanned the ridge along the spur that ran from Fritsche to Keating, looking for muzzle flashes and tracer fire.

Spotting somewhere between forty and fifty separate locations with two or three enemy fighters, they got to work targeting as many of those pockets as possible before they ran low on fuel and had to return to Bostick. But they had already accomplished perhaps their most effective stroke of the entire day. If those four pilots had arrived five minutes later, the second wave of fighters preparing to storm the eastern side of camp would almost certainly have overwhelmed us, and nobody would have survived.

Thanks to their ability to fly low and, when necessary, take a ferocious beating, the Apaches offer a level of support unequaled by any other aircraft. This would be the first of several times when they would save our bacon that day. But despite their marvelous advantages, the choppers were not capable of weeding out and eliminating the fighters who were already inside our wire. That task needed to be tackled by men who had their boots on the ground and were willing to engage in a direct, eyeball-to-eyeball gunfight, inch by inch and shot by shot, for this contested piece of dirt.

On that score, we were still very much on our own.

BY NOW, many members of Red Platoon who were not actively fighting on the perimeter or dead had holed up inside our barracks, where they were joined by some guys from Blue and HQ Platoons, plus a handful of extremely confused and frightened Afghan soldiers. It was an eclectic mix that included a number of our youngest and most traumatized soldiers, like Justin Gregory and Nicholas Davidson, along with some experienced hands like Kenny Daise and Jim Stanley, the staff sergeant from Red who had taken over as sergeant of the guard just before the attack kicked off. There were some aggressive badasses like Jones and Raz, and there were some guys like Kyle Knight, who fell closer to the timid end of the spectrum. Finally, there were also a few guys like Matthew Miller—a sergeant with Headquarters Platoon who had arrived at Keating less than forty-eight hours earlier—who were simply wondering how in the hell they'd gotten themselves into this fix.

For the last ten or fifteen minutes, these men had been trickling through the door from every direction, driven inside by the knowledge that our defenses were breached and that our perimeter could no longer hold. Some were clearly freaked out—stricken with fear or shuddering on the verge of all-out panic. All of them knew that things were getting worse, not better. And not one of them, if you'd asked at that moment, would have told you that he expected to live beyond the next thirty minutes.

"It's pretty bad out there right now," Raz said to Armando Avalos, one of our forward observers. "If you go out, you're just gonna die."

Most of these guys were lying on floor with either a machine gun or their carbines, and when I burst through the door, they all looked up at the same time.

Part of what defines an effective leader at the level of an infantry platoon is knowing that in difficult situations, actions carry greater weight than words. In that moment, I could not have asked these men to participate in a counterattack unless I demonstrated that I was willing to take part in it myself and run the show.

"We're taking this bitch back," I announced. "I need a group of volunteers. Who's with me?"

During the pause that followed—the silent interval when the guys in that room stared up and took in what I'd just said—I'm pretty sure that each of them was convinced that I'd lost my marbles. Judging by the looks on their faces, their collective response seemed to amount to a single question:

Are you frickin' kidding?

Then Raz, the former meth addict who had never finished high school and who had lived in people's basements until he joined the army, stood up—all six and a half feet of him.

Half a second later, Dannelley, Jones, and Miller, the new arrival, rose as well. They were joined by Mark Dulaney, a short young guy who was known for being fast and light on his feet.

"We'll follow you anywhere," declared Raz. "What are we doing?"

Five guys. I had my team.

I gave them a quick sketch of the plan and where we'd be heading—the ammunition depot, the Shura Building, the front gate—and I explained that we'd have some crossfire cover from Hill's machine-gun team.

"Any questions?" I asked.

"Uh . . . just one," said Jones, who had no idea that the locks had already been ripped off the ammo supply point. "Do we need a key to get into the ammo shed?"

"Stupid question, Jonesie," I replied, giving him the *if you expect an answer, don't ask me a dumb question* glare that I reserved for my junior enlisted guys.

No more hands were raised, so we moved on to the business of gearing up.

By this point, we were out of ammo for the big machine guns, so most of us were down to our personal weapons. I'd handed the Dragunov off to Hill when I was inside the command post and now had an M4, which was what Jones, Dannelley, Miller, and Raz had, too—although Raz also had a .203 grenade launcher attached to his carbine.

The only person with anything bigger was Dulaney, who was holding a squad automatic weapon, whose chief advantage is its shockingly high rate of fire. (Touch the trigger and a SAW will send out such a dense torrent of rounds it feels like you've broken open the gate valve on a water main.)

Five M4s plus a SAW would be a normal load-out for a standard six-man fire team. But for this job, it was way too light. If I'd had my way, every man on the squad would have been carrying a machine gun. Lacking that, I wanted at least one more heavy weapon. And at the moment, the only other guy in the barracks who had a SAW was Gregory, who was sitting near the west door.

"Hey, Greg, we need an assault gunner," said Raz, who'd read my thoughts. "You up for this?"

"Honestly? No," replied Gregory, who seemed to be in a state of shock from the ordeals he had already endured. "I don't know if I can do it."

Then Jones stepped over to Gregory.

"Hey, dude—no worries at all," he said softly. "Just swap out with me and we're cool, okay?"

So Gregory and Jones traded weapons.

"One last thing, guys," I said, pointing to the west door, where we'd make our exit. "There are no friendlies on the other side. Even if they're wearing an American uniform, do *not* hesitate to shoot first. Anybody you see in front of you is hostile. Roger that?"

I got five nods in response.

"All right, then—let's roll."

As I moved toward the door, there was one thing left unsaid—a part of this mission that I hadn't bothered to mention in the briefing I'd just given.

We were launching a counterattack for a range of reasons. To regain our ammo supply. To seal off our front gate. To push the Taliban back beyond the wire. To take back our house, and to unleash some intensely violent payback on the men who had slaughtered our comrades. But there was another objective as well—one that, in some ways, transcended everything else.

It was well known that the Taliban placed great value on American bodies, which they removed from the battlefield and filmed, then posted the resulting videos on the Internet. If that happened with Larson or any of the rest of my team, those of us who survived would spend the rest of our lives trying to get those YouTube images out of our heads.

For these reasons, we had to get our dead back too—even if the effort to retrieve them might entail losing more guys, me included. Given what we stood for and what we believed in, we really had no other choice.

PART IV

★ ★ ★

Taking the Bitch Back

CHAPTER FIFTEEN

Launch Out

IT WAS PROBABLY somewhere just before eight a.m. when we stacked up at the east end of Red barracks, just behind the door facing the command post, and prepared to launch our counterattack. The battle was now nearly two hours old, and half a dozen of our men were dead, with another six still unaccounted for.

By this point, the entire eastern side of the outpost was burning furiously, generating dense streams of black smoke that would help to conceal us as we made our run. My plan was for us to roll in a tightly packed mass, moving with an emphasis on speed rather than shooting accuracy. The order of the men—who was where and carrying which weapon inside the formation— was less important than violently closing the distance with the enemy and bull-charging them off of the ammo supply wall.

The only nuance to this strategy was to make sure that Raz would be the first person through the door. The reason I wanted him on point—and he knew it—was that if we were hit by a stream of fire, his massive frame would serve as a shield and hopefully enable the men behind him to stay alive long enough to complete this phase of the assault.

Here we go—doing it, Jones muttered to himself just before we pushed out. *Lesseewhathappens . . .*

If this were a battle drill, we would have either been bounding in teams or performing a move called a rolling cover fire, which entails shooting and running at the same time. Since this was not a drill, and thanks to the fact that we had to pull this move off by ourselves with no support by fire, there was nothing to do except charge en masse, which was pretty much the crudest and the least tactical maneuver one would care to imagine. To the extent that we even had a strategy, the theory was that if we encountered resistance, Raz would soak up most of the rounds, and as he died, the rest of us would throw his body into whoever was doing the shooting, then beat them to death with our carbines. From that standpoint, what we were doing wasn't really a military move as much as a gangster-style football play.

It was also kind of awesome.

Instantly, we started taking heavy fire from the Switchbacks and the Diving Board. But the smoke, along with our speed, made it tough for those shooters to get a bead on us as we charged across the open area toward the Hescos that cut the camp in half along the edge of the ammo supply depot. When we hit that wall of Hescos, we banged a sharp right and followed the wall north until we got to the far corner, where we pulled up short.

At the end of the Hescos was the Haji Shop, the small five-by-eight-foot room that doubled as both the living quarters for John Deere, the commander of Keating's Afghan Security Guards, and also the place where he sold cigarettes, chewing tobacco, pirated DVDs, and other items. As we got to the corner, I peered around and saw that the plywood door to the shop was closed.

That wasn't good.

If anyone was in the room, they would be able to shoot all six of us in the back as we were setting up our security. That threat had to be eliminated.

The best tool for the job, by far, was hand grenades. Unfortunately, we'd used up all of ours, and the only way to get more was by reaching the ammo depot. So the Haji Shop would have to be neutralized by hand—a task that fell to me and Dulaney.

Though I couldn't see inside, I was familiar with the interior layout. I knew that the ceiling was low and made of plywood, and that the walls were covered with blankets. I also knew that John's bed was on the right side of the room, and that most of his stock was on a set of shelves to left, along with his TV set, which sat in the corner. Finally, I knew there was a cubbyhole directly behind the bed with a couch inside it. That cubbyhole was my biggest concern. As Dannelley and I posted up on either side of the door, I gave him the plan.

"Look, I don't want to see any fancy double-tap stuff," I said. "Raz is gonna take care of the door, then you and me are gonna *spray* and *clear*. We both start in the center. Keep your M-4 on a three-round burst and work to your right while I go left. Anybody who's inside dies. Got it?"

He nodded.

With that, Raz kicked in the door, then me and Dannelley entered and dropped to waist level, kneeling shoulder-to-shoulder.

I took the center left, he took the center right. We opened up and took the room apart with our guns, destroying everything, including the TV.

There was no one inside.

"*Clear!*" yelled Dannelley.

Phase one of our assault was in the bag.

BEFORE TURNING to phase two, we needed to set up a security team by placing our two machine-gunners in positions that would enable them to cover as many sectors of fire as possible.

I immediately put Dulaney on the corner of the Hescos that made up the west wall of the Haji Shop. By kneeling down on one leg and using the corner of that wall to steady his SAW, he could fire uphill toward the mechanics' bay, the laundry trailer, the Waterfall area, part of the Switchbacks, and, off to his far right, a portion of the trench that led to the east door of the Shura Building. This would enable him to shoot anybody who tried to move through the open area in the western side of the outpost.

Directly behind Dulaney, less than ten feet away, there was an eight-by-eight-foot window in the Hesco wall that formed the northern perimeter of the outpost. This opening, which offered just enough room for a machine-gunner and his assistant, and which was normally manned by the Afghan Security Guards, was known as the Northern Fighting Position. It commanded a view that included our helicopter landing zone, the rickety footbridge leading to the shoreline at the bottom of the North Face, part of the Afghan Security Guards' checkpoint, and a good stretch of the road leading to Urmul, along with the north side of the Putting Green. That's where I ordered Jones to set up.

Jones and Dulaney were now posted back-to-back and facing in opposite directions so that their combined sectors of fire covered both the north and the south. When they were in position and ready to fire, they both called, "*Set!*" That was the signal for me and the rest of the guys to secure the ammo supply depot, just ten feet away.

The doors to the ASP were partly open, and one of them still had a lock dangling from a broken clasp. Miller seized hold of the closest door and swung it all the way open, enabling me to step in with my weapon raised and ensure that no one was inside.

"Clear!" I said.

Time to reload.

We started by plucking out a crate of fragmentation grenades and setting it beside Jones. Then we started grabbing whatever we thought we needed in order to beef up for our next move. This included linked machine-gun ammo for the 240s, the Mark 48s, and the SAWs, as well as loose rounds for the assault rifles, snub-nosed .203 rounds for the grenade launchers, linked grenades for the Mark 19, and a bunch of claymore mines, plus a couple of choice items like a pair of AT4s, which Raz eagerly seized—and which would come in handy shortly.

As we were getting our stash together, a line of guys from all three platoons suddenly showed up—courtesy of Bundermann, who had ordered everyone to hustle out of their barracks—and we started handing bullets and ordnance out in bulk:

Here's two thousand rounds of 7.62 for the Mark 48 machine gun . . .
Here's a crate of linked 5.56 to the SAWs . . .

Here's a case of Mark 19 ammo. Get this to Koppes now!

They disappeared into the enemy fire to make their deliveries, then swiftly came back for more. On his return trip, one of the ammo runners brought up a 240B machine gun, which we immediately swapped out for Jones's SAW.

Within a few minutes, we were feeling pretty solid. We had a medium-range light machine gun and a long-range heavy machine gun. We had as much ammo as we could possibly wish for, along with a couple of other items that could wreak some serious havoc. All we needed now was for Hill to finish getting his machine gun team in place up by the chow hall, and we'd be ready to make our next move.

Suddenly, we heard a burst of fire followed by a warning shout:

"We got guys! *WE GOT GUYS!*" yelled Dulaney as he opened up with the SAW.

Three Taliban carrying AK-47s were making a rush from the area where the front gate was located—a kill zone that was invisible to us, but from which they should have been destroyed by Hill's machine-gun team—and racing toward the mechanics' bay.

They ran as fast as they could while Dulaney chased them with the tracer rounds from his gun. As the trio of gunmen disappeared behind the building, which was basically a large garage made of plywood, four more insurgents popped up from behind the laundry trailer and the latrines, which was another area that should have been covered by Hill's team. It was clear that they were intending to set up their own support by fire so that their comrades would be able to assault directly into us.

My gaze snapped back to the mechanics' bay, where I could now see two of the three gunmen peeking their heads around the corner. Just then, Lakis, the Latvian first sergeant, showed up to see if there was anything he could do to lend us a hand. Once again, he was carrying his grenade launcher.

"Lakis, it's just plywood," I barked. "Hit 'em with your .203!"

Without hesitating, he launched the first in a series of grenades into the mechanics' bay. He didn't bother taking careful aim, preferring instead to start blowing holes through the walls. As each grenade penetrated the cheap plywood sheeting, we could hear the explosions inside.

Pffft . . . buh-wham!
Pffft . . . buh-wham!
Pffft . . . buh-wham!

While Lakis sent out one grenade after another, Dulaney started stitching a ragged line down the entire length of the building at waist height with his SAW.

The combined fire was so murderous that the insurgents on the other side of the structure flung themselves inside a pickup truck parked behind the building, but it did them no good. Although the truck was invisible to Lakis and Dulaney, the rounds they were putting out went straight through the mechanics' bay and shot the truck to pieces. Later on, we would discover the interior and the sides of the truck smeared thickly with blood.

All of this should have been satisfying, but I was appalled that the enemy was moving so freely through the sectors of camp that were invisible to us. The crossfire that should have cut them to ribbons, hadn't materialized.

Where the hell was Hill's team?

AS IT TURNED OUT, instead of getting his machine gun in place up by the chow hall to cover our assault, Hill had been focusing most of his attention on securing the eastern side of the outpost.

In some ways, this made sense. The Afghan National Army compound was now a raging inferno, and if that fire was not brought under control, it threatened to breach our final defensive perimeter and engulf the buildings inside the Alamo Position. Hill was also concerned that Taliban fighters might be moving into that side of camp by using the smoke and flames as cover. Finally, he was worried that the Afghan Army's ammunition stash, which abutted two of our barracks buildings, would cook off and blow up.

To deal with all of this, Hill had sent Sergeant Eric Harder and a handful of Blue Platoon's senior-ranking soldiers toward the eastern part of camp with orders to fight the flames and shoot any Taliban fighters they might see. Unfortunately, that plan had started to unravel when Harder and his team opened the door to the first building they needed to clear—the barracks for HQ Platoon—and were greeted with thick clouds of smoke indicating that the structure was already on fire.

Finding no one inside, they'd moved through a narrow alleyway to the northeast, where they'd posted up and started shooting at shadowy figures inside the burning Afghan barracks, whom they'd assumed to be enemy fighters. When the flames became too intense, they rushed over to the adjacent building, where they feverishly gathered up whatever material they could get their hands on—bullets, radios, first-aid supplies—and began ferrying those items back toward the center of camp.

This might have been a good strategy if me and my guys weren't attempting to launch a counterattack in the opposite direction, the success or failure of which would determine whether we were able to retake Keating or got wiped out. Under the circumstances, however, putting out flames and preventing our valuables from getting torched was of secondary importance—a fact that Harder fully grasped, even if his boss didn't.

"Hey, let me get that machine gun in place for Ro and his team," Harder was now radioing to Hill. "We need to move up to the chow hall!"

Each request was met by the same reply from Hill: "No, you need to stay where you're at."

Harder was clearly frustrated. He knew that we desperately needed some machine-gun support to complete the next phase of our assault. Without effective cover fire from the chow hall, my own team would be dangerously exposed as we made our run toward the Shura Building. Getting that gun in place was absolutely critical, and in Harder's view, the breakdown in communication between himself and Hill had now put me and my squad in peril.

As if to underscore Harder's assessment, a group of Taliban attackers just outside Keating's northern perimeter were already running past the Afghan Security Guard checkpoint toward the front gate with the clear intention of setting up a flanking maneuver that would destroy any attempt we made to retake the Shura Building.

Unfortunately for those enemy fighters, however, Jones had spotted their move and knew exactly what they were trying to do.

BY NOW, JONES had his machine gun poised inside the window that looked out from the Northern Fighting Position. Scanning down the barrel of the Mark M240B, he had a commanding view of the entire North Face, our helicopter landing zone at the confluence of the Landay-Sin and Darreh-ye Kushtāz Rivers, and the Afghan National Police station. He couldn't see the front gate or the village of Urmul, which were both blocked by the Shura Building. But he was in a superb position to observe the open ground that the enemy fighters would have to cover if they wanted to send reinforcements through our front gate. So when he realized that a cluster of insurgents lay partially concealed in a variety of spots spread across his sector of fire, he started laying down the law.

At the base of the Putting Green, roughly two hundred yards away, was a large egg-shaped rock, behind which five enemy fighters were attempting to hide. When they realized that Jones had them in his sights, they broke cover and tried to sprint over a low hill that was strewn with small bits of shale in order to take shelter inside Urmul.

Showing no mercy whatsoever, Jones ruthlessly picked those men off, directing an accurate five-round burst into each fighter before moving on to the next, and dropping all of them in their tracks. It was impressive and devastating to watch—although the spectacle wound up creating an unexpected problem.

In the process of getting Jones set up inside his Hesco window, I had ordered Dannelley to drop down beside Jones's shoulder and serve as his assistant gunner, which meant that he'd be feeding belts of ammo into the M240 to ensure that the gun didn't jam. Even more important, Dannelley was also supposed to be compensating for the fact that Jones had a dangerous blind spot.

Thanks to the thickness and height of the Hesco barrier on which his gun was set up, Jones could see only the far side of the road directly below him. The near side of that road, which ran along the outside of Keating, was invisible to Jones. Thanks to this dead space, any enemy fighters who skirted along the Hescos could sneak up directly beneath the window where Jones was set up and kill him. So Dannelley's primary duty was to prevent that from happening by peering over the edge and monitoring the dead space.

Unfortunately, Dannelley quickly forgot all about this part of his job because it was so much more exciting to watch Jones's shooting and act as his cheerleader.

"Oh yeah, dude, get them fuckers!" he exclaimed as Jones started obliterating the insurgents. "Right on—open that shit *up!*"

Jones, who was focused on shooting, had no idea that his assistant was paying zero attention to the dead space directly below him. *Cool—me and Dannelley got a pretty good thing going right now,* he thought to himself as he finished off the last fighter, scanned for another target, and caught sight of another Taliban team attempting to work its way toward the front gate.

That comradely vibe was rudely shattered when Dannelley abruptly started calling out in a high-pitched voice, "Hey, you there—stop!" he cried. "Stop *right there!*"

What the fuck is he talking about? Jones wondered as he squeezed the trigger and started hammering down on the men in the distance.

Jones wasn't the only one baffled that Dannelley, in the middle of a firefight, had suddenly started sounding like a security guard at a Costco parking lot. Right along the edge of the Hescos, where we were kneeling next to the doorway to John Deere's room, Raz and I shot each other a look of total bewilderment—and then we both rushed over and peered down into the dead space.

Less than ten feet away, a Taliban fighter wearing a camouflage uniform was staring straight up at Jones with a wolfish grin as he unslung his AK-47 and took aim.

"KILL HIM—KILL HIM—KILL HIM—KILL HIM—KILL HIM!!!!!!" Raz and I screamed at the top of our lungs as Jones, who now realized what was happening, struggled to muscle his machine gun over the edge of the

parapet and lower the barrel far enough to shoot the man below while yelling at Dannelley to get out of the way.

Meanwhile, Dannelley, who should have spotted this dude long before he'd gotten in position to waste Jones but was still in the best spot to take care of the problem, stood up, aimed, pulled the trigger—and realized, too late, that he still had his safety engaged.

In the half second that it took for Dannelley to click the safety off, the Taliban flicked his eyes away from Jones and snapped off a crisp burst. One of his bullets drilled Dannelley in the left arm, splitting open his triceps and shoulder like a ripe tomato, while another buried itself in Jones's helmet and snapped the Kevlar band on which his blood type and roster number were displayed.

As Dannelley dropped to the ground crying, "I'm shot—I'm shot!" Raz and I both reached into our racks, pulled out a grenade, and pulled the pin. Without needing to say a word, Raz dropped his straight over the wall. I tossed mine slightly farther out.

Two seconds later, when they both detonated at virtually the same instant, shreds of camouflage clothing flew into the air, surrounded by a pinkish mist.

"Holy crap, did that just happen?!" exclaimed Raz.

We looked at each other in astonishment—and then we both started laughing.

By this point, Jones had confirmed that his head hadn't been blown off, but Dannelley was writhing with pain and covered with blood. Crouching next to him, I unzipped his aid pouch and reached in to pull out a pressure dressing that would stop the bleeding, but my fingers closed around something crinkly.

When I withdrew my hand, I was looking at a packet of peanut butter crackers.

In further confirmation of the fact that Dannelley was not our platoon's number one draft pick, he'd discarded his first-aid kit to make room for snacks to munch on when he was on guard duty.

It was one thing to pull this kind of stunt in training back in Colorado. It was something else entirely to do it in a war zone. Yanking a spare pressure dressing from my own pouch, I bound it tightly around his arm without caring how much it hurt, then stood him up and gave him a hard stare. He'd come within a frog's hair of getting Jones killed. Almost as bad, he'd allowed himself to get shot.

"See the aid station over there?" I said, pointing east and giving him a shove. "Get moving."

Then, out of sheer disgust, I planted my boot as far up his backside as I could before turning around to deal with the business at hand.

DESPITE DANNELLEY'S INCOMPETENCY, we seemed to be holding our own, at least for the moment. Dulaney and Lakis were still going to town on the plywood-sided mechanics' bay, while Jones was now back on his machine gun and concentrating on a pair of fighters whom he had driven from their cover near the Afghan Police checkpoint, almost two hundred yards away, and were now racing up the road to the north.

Those guys had to cover about five hundred yards before the road started to bend with the river and curved out of sight. Jones smoked the second runner in his tracks, but the fighter in the lead was quite a bit faster. He was just a few steps from getting away, running at a dead sprint, when Raz got him in the crosshairs of the scope on his M4.

He shot once and saw the bullet kick up a puff of dust at the man's feet, adjusted, then fired a second time and dropped the runner like a sack of goat shit.

It was probably the finest shot Raz had ever made.

Meanwhile, Jones was taking a harder look at the police checkpoint where the two insurgents had been hiding before they broke cover. The checkpoint was a stone-and-concrete cube with a flat roof, and it sat on flat ground and was backed by a sheer cliff that rose all the way to the top of the Putting Green. Just behind the building, the Taliban had set up a machine-gun team.

That team had a clear line of fire along the entire front gate area, including the guard tower on top of the Shura Building—and thanks to the height of our Hescos, Jones couldn't get a clear shot at any of them. He had them pinned down but no way of eliminating them. The best he could do was lay a barrage of raking fire over their heads.

"Hey, Sergeant Ro?" Jones called out.

"What's going on?" I asked, kneeling down next to him.

"I got some dudes pinned down behind the checkpoint building, right underneath the tree next to that blue tarp."

This was another example of how you really had to give the Taliban credit. Their gun emplacement reflected some careful planning, as well as a shrewd command of small-unit tactics. Until we figured out a way to get rid of them, they would be able to put fire directly on the front gate.

I turned to Raz, who was just behind me and Jones.

"Do you have any smokers for your 203?" I asked.

"Hell yeah I do."

"Okay, find out if you can put one on that gun, and then we'll see what the Apaches can do."

After eliminating the thirty fighters with their chain guns, the Apache pilots had spent the past half hour orbiting the skies above Keating, staying high enough to avoid small-arms fire from the ridgelines, then making selective gun runs on whatever targets they could spot. But unlike the large group of fighters they had eliminated on the eastern side of camp, the roof of the police checkpoint and the machine gun concealed beneath the tree were extremely hard to spot from the air. To solve that problem, I had in mind something called "shifting from a known point."

If Raz could put a smoke grenade within a few feet of the target, the bright-colored smoke spewing from the canister—green, purple, pink, or yellow—would offer everyone a hard point of reference. That, in turn, would allow us to walk the pilots directly onto the target via radio.

It's an effective technique, in theory. But we quickly ran up against two problems. First, in order to reach the checkpoint, Raz would have to lean far out over the edge of the Hesco wall while firing through the branches of a tree that loomed directly above us. And second, it was taking too long to get the directions to the pilots because the information had to be relayed from me to the command post, where Bundermann passed the instructions to at least one other radio operator until the message reached one of the two Apache gunners.

"Tell the pilot that where that green smoke is off to the southwest at four hundred meters, there's a group of guys under the tree behind the rocks," I radioed Bundermann.

By the time this information got to the Apaches, the grenade had burned off and the smoke had already begun to dissipate. It also didn't help that the Apaches couldn't stay in one place: Ross Lewallen and Randy Huff, the pilots, had to switch direction continuously in order to avoid the ground fire that was being directed at them from the ridgelines. Bundermann, who was monitoring the traffic on the Fires net, could hear how challenging this was for the pilots:

> *We don't see the smoke . . . Fire another grenade.*

> *We cannot identify your target . . . Fire again.*

Realizing that our system wasn't working, Bundermann decided to cut himself out of the loop.

"Ro, I want you to switch to the Fires net frequency," he ordered.

I turned the knob on the top of my radio to the number six position, which was preset to the Fires net. Next thing I knew, Bardwell's voice was coming directly into my earpiece. I was now in control of a four-blade, twin-turboshaft AH64 attack helicopter armed with a 30-mm chain gun.

As that handoff took place, Raz was doing his best to get a smoker closer to the target. Knowing he was working at the extreme end of his 203's range, he aimed his barrel high in the air.

"We're about to fire again," I informed Bardwell.

Raz squeezed off the shot, and we watched as the grenade sailed through the air and landed two hundred yards away from the tree that was concealing the gun crew.

"Yellow, two hundred yards south," I said.

"All right, we see it."

Bardwell's bird was almost directly above us when he opened up with his cannon. Jones, who had his eyes locked on the target, was shocked as he watched the explosive-tipped 30-mm rounds obliterate not simply the fighters and their weapon but the entire tree under which they were sheltering. The destructive fury was heightened by the chain gun's metallic whir, which made it sounded as if the air was being chewed apart by a high-speed circular saw. Equally impressive was the deluge of several hundred brass cartridges that rained down from the sky and landed, hot and shimmering, on the ground around us.

Damn, Jones thought to himself, *that was completely insane.*

Raz too was impressed.

"Hey, Ro?" he asked, turning to me. "Do you think this is anything like what it was like in World War II?"

"Nope," I replied, shaking my head. "This is probably just a small taste of what it was like back then, brother."

That was true. What was also true—and what I didn't say to Raz—was that regardless of how impressive that demonstration of airpower might have been, the picture on the ground wasn't looking nearly as good.

Despite the progress we'd made, our counterattack had completely stalled out.

AS THE APACHES continued to orbit above Keating and scan the ridgelines for targets, the enemy on the other side of the river was keeping a low profile. But the larger picture in terms of where me and my team were—and where we needed to be—was disturbing.

Hill's failure to get his machine gun in place meant that we'd lost not only our momentum but also our "violence of action," which is the physical and psychological drive that speed, surprise, and aggression can achieve. By this point, the enemy knew exactly where we were, and precisely what our next move would be. The longer we continued to delay that move—which would involve attempting to retake the Shura building and the front gate—the better their chances of stopping us.

By now, my anger and frustration were starting to boil over. Each request I radioed for our missing support by fire met with the same response: Hill's team was still too busy battling the flames on the eastern side of camp to get his machine gun set up. I could even hear members of Hill's team calling over the Force Pro net for fire extinguishers so that they could try to save Blue Platoon's barracks before it was fully engulfed.

From my perspective, this made no sense. If my squad failed to move within the next few minutes, the enemy gunners on the ridgelines would pin us down and we would be immobilized. And if that happened, it wouldn't matter whether our buildings burned down or not.

"Let the barracks burn—they're just *barracks*," I yelled into the radio. "What the fuck happened to my machine gun? We can't move without it. If you don't get that goddamn thing in place, you're going to get me and everybody with me killed."

"The fire is a threat that needs to be taken care of," replied someone.

At this point, what I most wanted to do was scream into the radio that if that machine gun wasn't in place within one minute I would grab my gun, head over to the center of camp, and personally shoot anyone who had an extinguisher in his hand. What was becoming clear, however, was that the fire wasn't really the problem. Instead, the delay was rooted in the fact that Hill had not irrevocably committed himself, regardless of what it might cost, to securing the chow hall and getting his machine gun to where it needed to be.

In 1958, a soldier named J. Glenn Gray wrote a book about soldiers in combat called *The Warriors: Reflections on Men in Battle*. Gray, who was drafted into the army as a private in May 1941, was discharged as a second lieutenant in October 1945 after having seen fighting in North Africa, Italy, France, and Germany. His book, which is both obscure and revered, touches on something that would later strike me as relevant to what was now unfolding at Keating as our counterassault came in danger of unraveling.

Gray wrote with elegance and precision about how the essence of combat basically boils down to an exchange of trust between two men—or two groups of men—each of whom are providing support by fire for the other. This simple agreement—you will move while I shoot at the guys who are trying to kill you, then I will move while you shoot at the guys who are trying to kill me—depends on a willingness to place one's life into the hands of someone else while in turn taking responsibility for that person's life in your own hands. When this pact is executed well, it is not only extraordinarily effective but also tends to create a bond between the men who enter into it that may stand as the most powerful connection they will ever experience to another human being.

There is, however, one thing that Gray doesn't explore in his book, which is what can happen when one of the two parties who are supposed to be working in tandem fails—for whatever reason, legitimate or not—to keep his end of the deal. That was what appeared to be taking place right then with Hill's machine-gun team.

The south side of camp, including the area around the chow hall, was being targeted by relentless fire from the North Face, the Putting Green, the Switchbacks, the Waterfall, and the Diving Board. Stepping into that zone and laying down cover fire would have required a depth of resolve that blurred the line between flirting with suicide and having a full-on death wish. On the other hand, however, the five guys on my team had already demonstrated exactly that resolve.

J. Glenn Gray didn't have anything to say about this kind of situation. But based on my own experience, I can state that when a support-by-fire pact is not upheld on the battlefield, it can generate the opposite of an unbreakable bond between men. What it triggers instead is a sense of rage and betrayal while—oddly enough—instilling an implacable determination to do whatever it takes to get the job done.

Well, our machine gun just isn't coming, I thought to myself as I listened to the continuing radio chatter about fire extinguishers. *I guess we're gonna have to make this happen on our own.*

I DON'T RECALL being especially disheartened as I scurried over to Jones, who was now paired up with Ryan Schulz, a sergeant with HQ Platoon who Bundermann had sent out to replace Dannelley. My mind was already focused on what we needed to happen next.

"You doing okay?" I asked Jones.

"Just tell me what's going on," he replied.

"We're done waiting," I said. "You and Schulz are gonna hold your position and give us as much cover fire as you can while the rest of us push for the Shura Building. Got it?"

They both nodded.

"One other thing," I added as Raz brought over the first of three boxes of grenades that we'd fished out of the ammo depot.

"There are guys right on the other side of this wall, so every coupla minutes, I want you to pull the pin on one of these and just throw it down the street. That'll keep them from sneaking up on you."

Then I turned to Raz, Dulaney, and Miller.

"We're moving out, so grab as much ammo as you can carry," I said. "It's time for us to retake the Shura Building and the front gate."

Lastly, I keyed my radio and took care of one final piece of business.

"One, this is Two," I said, radioing Bundermann but skipping our official call signs in an effort to keep the transmission short. Then I invoked the expression we used when we needed to continue a mission: "We need to Charlie Mike. The enemy is pinpointing us, and soon we'll be sitting ducks."

I paused for a second to allow Bundermann to absorb this before continuing.

"I'm tired of sitting here waiting. We're movin'."

"Negative, Red Two," spat Bundermann. "Stand down—do *not* move."

It was pointless to argue, so I pulled one of the oldest (and cheapest) tricks in the book.

"Say again," I replied. "You are coming in weak and unreadable . . ."

Bundermann repeated his order, and I deployed the same gambit. Then I reached down to my right hip, where my radio was attached to my vest, and rotated the volume knob to "off."

It was a bogus play and, to be honest, not a cool thing for me to pull on someone I respected as much as Bundermann. But it had to be done. There was no point in waiting any longer for a support by fire that simply wasn't going to come. The Shura Building had to be stormed, and the only way that was going to happen while we still had the ability to maneuver freely was for the four of us to launch out and get it done.

As we got ready to make our run, Schulz turned to Jones and asked, "What are we shooting at?"

"What are we shooting at?" replied Jones. "Any *fucking* thing I see, Schulz, that looks like it's moving and that looks like it wants to kill Ro and his guys. That's what we're shooting at."

CHAPTER SIXTEEN

Not Gonna Make It

THE DISTANCE from where we stood to the Shura Building was no more than about twenty steps, but getting there would be tricky. First we'd have to stack up on the southeast corner of the ammo supply depot, and then we'd race down a narrow alleyway between the wall of Hescos on our right and a row of sandbags stacked three feet high on our left. At the far end of that alley was a door made of three-quarter-inch plywood that opened into the east side of the Shura Building. It was our only way in.

From the perspective of anyone who might be trying to defend the building from the inside, this alley served as a huge kill zone—the kind of choke point known as a "fatal funnel," where a team of assaulters are forced through a narrow passage as they are silhouetted against their entry point. So one of the key questions we faced was whether there was anyone on the opposite side of that door.

As I peeked my head around the corner, I could see that it was cracked open about six inches—just enough to allow a team of defenders to see if someone was moving down the alley toward them while still keeping the interior hidden to anyone looking from the outside.

"This could get bad," I said to the three men huddled in back of me on the near side of the corner. "You guys trust me, right?"

"We're with you all the way," said Raz.

Dulaney and Miller both nodded.

I knew that aside from a handful of eight-by-eight posts that supported the roof, the space inside the Shura Building was relatively open but also strewn with a few significant obstacles. There were a dozen or so benches that were used for meetings with local Afghan dignitaries. Off in one corner, there was a treadmill and an elliptical machine that had been salvaged from the gym and were awaiting transport to Bostick as part of our pullout. If the number of fighters inside that space were equal to or greater in number than us, the close quarters combat that would unfold inside that space would be savage and deadly. A four-on-four gunfight in a room the size of a one-car garage never ends well.

Worse, if they had a machine-gun pointed at that door, they would probably annihilate all four of us before we even set foot inside.

There was only one way to find out what we were up against.

"Okay, listen up," I said. "Here's how this is gonna work."

The basic plan was to nail the door with the grenade launcher and follow up with the machine gun. But the key to the whole deal lay in how we choreographed our move, and the level of violence we achieved.

"Dulaney, you've got the SAW, so you're number one," I said, looking at my assault gunner. "When we go through that door, you're gonna be the first guy in the room. I'm gonna be right behind you, and I'm gonna push you in the back to make sure you get all the way in. All I want you to concentrate on is clearing the inside and killing anybody that's in there. Put your gun on full auto. Start left and sweep all the way to the right, and just machine-gun it all. Got it?"

He nodded.

"Miller," I said, turning to our new guy. "You're gonna be number three, which means you'll stack up right behind me. We will sweep up after Dulaney—I'll move right and you'll move left."

Finally, I looked up at Raz.

With his massive height, he towered a full foot above me. He was at least eight inches taller than Miller and Dulaney too. That was a key element for what I had in mind, because I needed Raz to be able, if necessary, to shoot directly over our heads.

"You're the last guy in line on this one, Raz, but what's gonna kick off this move is that you're gonna peel around the corner first and put a grenade straight through that door with your 203."

He nodded.

"While you do that, Dulaney's gonna lead out with me and Miller right behind. The three of us will enter, and then you'll pull rear security."

"Roger that," said Raz.

As this entire exchange was taking place, I knew Bundermann would be on the radio, still trying to get me to stop.

"Okay, can I hit 'em with the 203 now?" asked Raz.

"Do it."

With his gun raised, he leaned around the corner and punched a grenade through the middle of the door.

As the plywood exploded and the room beyond it filled with a ball of fire, Dulaney hurled himself down the alley with me and Miller in tow. What happened next wasn't the sort of thing you'd find in a military textbook, because it was more of a rugby play, except with guns.

We rolled in a tightly linked mass, back-to-back and stride for stride. I had the rear handle of Dulaney's body armor firmly in my left hand and was resting the barrel of my assault rifle on his right shoulder so that I could spray to the right as soon as I entered. Directly behind me, Miller was doing the same thing, but his weapon was resting on my left shoulder so that he could sweep in the opposite direction.

The second Dulaney cleared the door frame, he started his sweep, and by the time he'd completed his rotation, he'd emptied an entire drum of ammo—two hundred rounds—into the room. Miller and I joined in as soon as we were inside. The noise we generated was defeaning, which was disorienting enough. But as we fired, the room filled up with a mysterious white smoke.

We hadn't anticipated the smoke.

It was horrible stuff—blinding, impossible to breathe, harsh enough to make it feel as if we'd stormed into a factory that made pepper spray. By our second or third inhalation, it felt like our lungs had quit working. But we were fully committed and had no choice except to push through while we sputtered and gagged.

"Keeping moving—KEEP MOVING!" I screamed at Dulaney as I shoved him from behind.

"Can't breathe," gasped Dulaney. Can't even *see!*"

"I don't care," I yelled back. "Keep going till you hit the wall or someone shoots you. *Move!*"

Finally, we made it to the west door at the far end of the room.

There, just outside the door and less than an arm's length away, a pair of AK-47s and a PKM heavy machine gun lay in the dirt. They had been abandoned just seconds earlier. The barrel of the machine gun, still cradled in its tripod, was pointed directly at the door we'd just come through.

While Dulaney and Miller dragged the weapons inside, I marched back across the room, where Raz was supposed to have posted up with his gun leveled into the alleyway we'd just run through to ensure that nobody snuck up and took us out from behind. Instead, he was crouched with his hands over his knees and vomiting on the toes of his boots.

"You mother*fucker,*" I yelled. "Did you fire a CS grenade through that door?!" (A CS grenade contains tear gas.)

"No way—it was HE, guaranteed!" he yelled back, using the term for a high-explosive grenade, which was exactly what he was supposed to have used.

By this point, the room was starting to clear out and we spotted the source of the smoke.

By some weird combination of skill and dumb luck, Raz had managed not only to put his grenade through the door itself but to send the thing all the way to the far wall, where it had center-plugged a twenty-pound fire extinguisher that had been sitting just to the left of the west door.

The secondary explosion from the extinguisher, and the acrid waves of smoke that it generated, must have been a nasty surprise to the insurgents inside that room, supplying the extra kick that drove them from the building.

I paused just long enough to glance at the destroyed extinguisher and the PKM machine gun that was now lying next to it. If those fighters had chosen to hold their ground and turned the full force of that gun on my squad instead of fleeing, they would have cut us to pieces.

Raz had just saved all of our lives.

We didn't have a chance to thank him, though, because the Taliban were about to turn things up another notch.

ENRAGED OVER HAVING been forced to give up such a key position, the insurgents now gave vent to their anger by shooting at the Shura Building with everything they had. As the four of us set up points of domination at the entryways—two men to a door—bullets began thudding off the outside walls with dull slaps while the entire structure shivered from the impact of dozens of exploding rockets. The intensity of this renewed engagement resembled the first few minutes of the initial attack. Crouched inside, it seemed as if the building was hit with some form of explosive every three seconds.

It was dark inside that room—the wooden covers on the three windows on the north side of the building were fastened shut—and the air was thick with dust from the walls and the remnants of the smoke from the fire extinguisher. But as we huddled against the walls, holes began appearing as the plywood roof was shot to pieces. And with each new bullet hole, another pencil beam of sunlight appeared, cutting a line from the ceiling to the floor and illuminating the swirling dust particles that were suspended in the air and vibrating with each new shock wave.

The room took on the appearance of a grotesque dance club whose walls and floor coruscated with the light of a devil's disco ball. But even more striking—the thing that overrode both sight and sound—was the overpowering smell. It was an odor I'd never before encountered, an olfactory assault composed of several layers. There was the sulfuric tang of gunpowder from the exploding rockets. There was the chalky odor of the chemicals in the fire extinguisher. And there was the smell of Kirk's blood, which had spread to form a dark and sticky pool on the plywood floor just inside the entryway of the west door. I could taste that combination of sulfur and chalk and copper on my tongue. It was sharp and heavy, and it grabbed the back of my jaws in a way that made me feel like I was about to gag. The pungency seemed to underscore how tenuous and uncertain our grip on the building was.

At this point, we were *extremely* vulnerable. With the west door that led to the front gate wide-open, our standoff—the open stretch of ground in which we would be able to spot any attackers who were trying to rush us—was no more than fifteen feet. If the enemy decided to come at us with a dozen or more guys in a full-on sprint from the ASG checkpoint, just twenty feet away, they would be on top of us before we could react.

In the hopes of slowing them down, we started tearing the room apart. The wooden benches, the chairs and tables, the raised area where the elders sat during our meetings with locals—we ripped all of it up with our bare hands and flung the scraps through the door into the open space leading to the front gate to create a makeshift barricade. At the corner of the gate, we also set up two claymores that we had brought from the ammunition depot: one facing toward the police checkpoint, the other pointing back up the road leading to the concrete bridge over the river.

While the rest of the team finished strewing obstacles, I climbed the ladder to get a sense of what shape the tower was in, and see if I could get eyes on the front gate. The turret was pretty banged up—the armor was pitted and grooved from the intense fire, the wooden shade structure had been blown to pieces, and there were hundreds of empty shell casings strewn in all directions. But the M240 that Davidson had abandoned seemed in good order, and there was even a bit of ammo left, totaling roughly seventy rounds.

I peeked over the turret shield. Off in the distance, I could see muzzle flashes inside Urmul and all across the Putting Green. On the road nearby were several trucks that had belonged to the police. All of them were burning. There were also a number of bodies lying along the road by the bridge.

My main concern was making sure that none of the militants were moving through the front gate. I didn't spot any live targets, but it was impossible to see if the enemy had stacked up along the wall directly beneath me without leaning out and exposing myself. Instead, I dropped a couple of grenades over the edge, then let off a quick burst with the M240 to confirm that it was still firing.

Just before heading back down the ladder, I keyed my radio and called up Bundermann.

"So, hey, we're here at the front gate, and we got it closed down," I reported. "I can't do anything else until I get some additional personnel out here."

"Roger that, Two," he replied.

Bundermann may not have been pleased by my behavior, which qualified as reckless and insubordinate. But he certainly wasn't upset with the results. We had access to our ammo. We'd locked down the front entrance. And thanks to the west doorway of the Shura Building, which looked directly through the front gate and across the river, we now had a new and effective position from which to observe one of the enemy's primary strongholds.

By leaving that door open and standing back in the recessed shadows within the Shura Building, where the enemy could not see me, I could survey the entire Putting Green, and even more important, Urmul itself, where the Taliban had firmly dug themselves into the houses and were still using this vantage to devastating effect.

From almost every window of every structure in the village, I could see the muzzle flashes from AK-47s and machine guns. Between those buildings, men were continuously darting in all directions as they delivered ammunition or scouted for a more effective angle of fire. There was so much activity that I found myself half-convinced that they were massing for an imminent assault on our western wall. But what made our present position so advantageous—and therefore part of the reason why the enemy was so furious—was that we could now provide grid coordinates for precise locations within the village, as well as additional feedback that would enable Bundermann to lay any form of ordnance directly on target.

Given the intensity of the fire that was pouring out of Urmul, it was clear that there was only one way to handle the situation. Pulling out my map of the area, I noted the six-digit coordinates for the mosque and the mayor's house, then relayed them to Bundermann.

"Those grids are both located in the center of the village," I said. "I need for you to level Urmul."

Under normal circumstances, a request like that would have provoked a heavy pause, followed by a barrage of questions. Nobody authorizes a direct strike on a population center without at least demanding confirmation that there are no civilians inside the drop zone.

Bundermann didn't even blink.

"Roger," he replied.

Once again, it was time to call in the Apaches.

IT WAS NOW almost ten a.m., and for the better part of the past hour, the pilots and gunners of the attack helicopters had been busy. Shortly after eliminating the machine-gun nest near the Afghan National Police checkpoint, Ross Lewallen had called "bingo"—meaning that he had barely enough fuel to return to base—and both pilots had turned their aircraft back down the valley in the direction of Bostick.

While their birds were being refueled, Lewallen and Randy Huff had raced into the command post to brief Colonel Brown and the rest of the operations team on what they'd seen from the air. Meanwhile, Chad Bardwell and Chris Wright helped the ground crew reload their chain guns with seventy-pound boxes of 30-mm ammo and affix another suite of Hellfire missiles to the rails of each helicopter.

The moment everything was on board, the two choppers were in the air and on their way back to Keating.

Both aircraft were once again orbiting overhead, with Bardwell and Wright scanning the ridgelines and the main road for targets, when they received Bundermann's request to put a couple of Hellfires into the mosque and destroy it. They spent several minutes circling while they made certain that they had identified the target and determined how best to engage the structure. It would not be easy.

Given the mosque's location inside the narrow valley, the only way for the helicopters to get a clean shot was to make an east-to-west run, which would expose them to one of the biggest threats in the entire area.

Somewhere along the high ground between Fritsche and Keating, the Taliban had placed a Soviet heavy machine gun known as a DShK. Nicknamed the *dishka*, the gun throws out 12.7-mm rounds at such a high rate that it can serve as an effective antiaircraft weapon. It's more than enough to seriously mess up an Apache.

Suspecting that they might actually be dealing with more than one *dishka*, but unable to figure out exactly where the weapons were located and eliminate them, Lewallen and his team tried in vain to come up with an alternate plan. When they finally realized there was no other way to get the job done, they set up by flying more than two miles to the east, then spun their birds around and embarked on a long, straight run that would take them down the valley, directly over Keating, and enable them to send several missiles directly through the east side of the mosque.

Lewallen's ship led the strike, and Bardwell, his gunner, would put the first missile on the mosque.

As the Apache drew near the village, Bardwell spotted muzzle flashes sparking from virtually every window and doorway in the building.

"We're inbound with Hellfire missiles," Bardwell radioed to Bundermann. "We see the mosque and see the enemy fire."

Huff was following directly behind, flying at a slightly higher altitude, and Wright, his gunner, was scanning for smoke from Bardwell's missile strike when he heard Lewallen's voice on his radio:

"I got a Hellfire malfunction," Lewallen reported over the team's internal radio. "I can't get my missile off the rail."

Both pilots reacted instantly. While Lewallen broke sharply to the left, Huff lined up so that Wright could take the shot. The bird was slightly less than two thousand yards away when Wright got the mosque squarely in his sights and squeezed the trigger. As the missile released, Huff pulled back on his run and held the profile of the mosque so that Wright could keep his laser range finder locked on the mosque and guide the missile into the target.

When viewed through the sensors in the gunner's seat of an Apache, a Hellfire strike is not especially dramatic. As the missile plowed into the east wall of the mosque, the only thing that Wright could discern was a small puff of white smoke. Far more impressive was the *dishka* round that, at the very same moment, slammed into the bottom of their Apache.

The bullet struck directly under the pilot's seat, where it penetrated the forward avionics bay, severing a bundle of wires and destroying the bird's environmental control systems condenser. Inside the cockpit, Huff suddenly found himself staring at a bank of warning lights. He had multiple electrical system failures, and the Apache's automatic stabilator had quit.

"We're hit," Huff announced over the radio.

Lewallen moved his aircraft closer to Huff's to see if he could help assess the damage. In the meantime Bardwell, who was still scanning the mosque, noted that the structure had not been completely destroyed and could, in theory, still be used as a fighting position. Eliminating the threat completely would require another Hellfire.

After radioing back and forth about the damage, both pilots agreed that Huff's stricken bird could remain airborne while Lewallen took another shot with his second Hellfire. Then Lewallen would follow Huff back to Bostick for battle-damage assessment and repairs.

While Huff peeled away, Lewallen lined up to enable Bardwell to take aim and fire.

This time the Hellfire got off the rail. With Bardwell guiding the missile in via his laser, it punched through the southern wall and demolished the mosque.

As Bardwell confirmed the hit, Lewallen was moving his bird behind Huff's so that he could cover Huff during the flight back to Bostick. In that moment, Lewallen suddenly noticed a vibration in his pedals. A second or two later, his master warning system activated. The Apache was losing its utility hydraulics.

Unbeknownst to Lewallen, his bird had been hit by the very same *dishka* that had already nailed Huff. One bullet had passed through a tail rotor blade, while a second had drilled into the driveshaft cover, severing one of his hydraulic lines.

Both of the damaged aircraft now had to beeline for Bostick.

As they headed out of the valley, Lewallen's thoughts stayed with the *dishka* that had come close to taking out both Apaches. He wasn't sure exactly where that gun was, but he could see that the general area did not afford a direct line of sight down into Keating. This meant that the *dishka* had been emplaced not with the aim of shooting at Keating's defenders, but instead to ambush any helicopters rushing in to the aid of the outpost.

That machine gun, Lewallen realized with a chill, was also perfectly positioned to shoot down a medevac. There would be no way to get a chopper into Keating to extract the wounded, Lewallen realized, until they located and destroyed the *dishka*.

While Lewallen mulled this over, Wright was on the radio advising the command post at Bostick that they were returning to base with two damaged airframes: one that no longer had any hydraulics, and another that was experiencing multiple electrical system failures. He requested that a repair team and two replacement helicopters be dispatched from Jalalabad to Bostick immediately.

Several minutes later, both Apaches landed safely at Bostick. But it would be more than an hour before Lewallen and his team could get back in the air.

INSIDE THE SHURA BUILDING, my team and I weren't privy to the drama that the helicopter pilots and their gunners had just endured. All we knew was that they were leaving.

"The Apaches had to check off station again," Bundermann informed me by radio. "I'm not sure when they'll be back."

This news was not well received. Every time the Apaches showed up, it felt as if our guardian angels had arrived and perhaps the tide was about to turn in this fight. But the moment they peeled away, we couldn't help but feel abandoned and vulnerable. Absent the reassuring sound of their guns, the same set of urgent questions flooded back into our minds:

Why did they leave?

Where are they going?

When will they be back?

As I wrestled with those unknowns from my position just inside the west door, I happened to glance over at Miller, who was slouched by the other doorway with his weapon in his lap, staring listlessly at the floor. He'd handled the stress of battle well up to this point. But judging by his body language and his demeanor, it was clear that he'd now exceeded his tolerance for combat.

"Miller is one hundred percent checked out—I need a replacement," I radioed to Bundermann. "And whoever you send, have him bring an IV with him. We need to get Miller rehydrated."

A minute or two later, Raz crouched down next to me. We were no longer taking direct fire from the mosque, but we were still getting hit from every other direction. The walls continued to shake, and every minute or two another bullet drilled through the ceiling and buried itself in the floor, creating yet another pencil-sized beam of light.

"We're not gonna make it outta here, are we?" asked Raz, looking me straight in the face.

I met his stare.

"We're doin' all right," I replied.

To be honest, I'm not sure that I believed that, but it seemed like the right thing to say. And perhaps it was, because right about then the east door swung open and Miller's replacement burst inside carrying an IV bag, along with a radio strapped to his back, a notebook in his hand, and sticking out of the breast pocket on his uniform, a fistful of colored pens.

Bundermann had just done us a solid.

Armando Avalos, who we called "Red Bull," was our best forward observer. Nobody at Keating was better at identifying target grids, running the necessary calculations, and calling in artillery and air strikes where we most needed them.

Avalos lost no time in getting down to business. Taking my position along the far wall with its view through the west door, he spread out his maps, keyed up his radio, and swiftly called in a fire mission from Fritsche, were the gun crew had finally secured access to their mortar pit and was now ready to start laying 120-mm rounds anywhere we needed.

Unfortunately, that didn't last long.

Armando Avalos on the Putting Green

During the initial attack on Fritsche, the ballistics computer in its mortar pit had been knocked out. After regaining control of the pit, the gun crew had attempted to jury-rig a fix to that problem. But the very first round that Avalos called in missed its intended target—the village of Urmul—by such a huge margin that Avalos wasn't even certain the shell had come from Fritsche. It landed less than thirty yards in front of the Shura Building.

"Repeat," he said, calling for another round.

When the second round exploded in exactly the same spot, he concluded that it was too dangerous to keep calling in fire missions from Fritsche: the odds of a mortar round landing on top of us were simply too high. So Avalos—who had unzipped his pants and was now attending to some important personal business by squatting on top of an empty box of .50-caliber machine-gun ammo while continuing to work his radio—turned to a weapons system that was quite a bit more complicated than a single 120-mm mortar tube, but potentially far more devastating.

Ever since the start of the attack on Keating, army and air force aviation units at Jalalabad, Kandahar, and Bagram had been scrambling to respond. Over the past several hours, the commanders of those units had been assembling an airborne armada in the skies high above Keating—a dizzying array of fixed-wing attack and surveillance planes, each carrying an assortment of either weapons and bombs or cameras, video feeds, and electronic-jamming technology.

The sheer range and number of aircraft up there was matched only by the complexity of coordinating this mess and keeping its moving parts from smashing into one another. That task, which would directly affect whether we could continue holding out, was now being performed by a twin-tailed fighter jet that was never intended to serve as a flying air-traffic control tower—and which was being flown by two guys whose nicknames were Ox and Finch.

CHAPTER SEVENTEEN

Ox and Finch

AT SIX FIFTEEN THAT MORNING, a pair of F-15E fighter jets on the tarmac at Bagram Airfield, just outside of Kabul, were ordered to get into the air and fly to the relief of Keating. In the cockpit of one of those planes was a captain named Michal Polidor, whose call sign was "Ox." Sitting directly behind Polidor and serving as the plane's weapons systems officer or WSO (pronounced "wizzo") was first lieutenant Aaron Dove, whose call sign was "Finch." He was responsible for navigation and targeting from the back seat of the jet's cockpit. Their aircraft, which was identified as "Dude 01," was armed with a 20-mm machine gun and five five-hundred-pound smart bombs (two laser-guided and three GPS-guided), plus one two-thousand-pound bomb, all of which could be guided onto their targets from up to ten miles away.

When Dude 01 reached Keating, Polidor and his wingman—Captain Justin Elliot, who was piloting the second F-15—were briefed by the pilots of another pair of F-15s who were already in the air and just coming off of a night mission when they'd been summoned to Keating. Having arrived a few minutes earlier, those two planes had already dropped most of their smart bombs along the Switchbacks. Running low on fuel, they returned to Bagram while Polidor and Elliot saturated the Switchbacks with additional bombs and conducted strafing runs with their cannons.

As Elliot was dropping his first bomb, his fighter experienced a severe hydraulic failure, which meant that he too was forced to return to base. It was then that Ox and Finch began to grasp the magnitude and severity of the assault on Keating.

From his position in the rear of the cockpit, Dove stared into his targeting pod and counted as many as eight separate fires burning inside the compound, as well as dozens of rocket explosions. Along the surrounding hillsides and ridgelines there were too many muzzle flashes for him to tally, but they formed a 360-degree ring of fire around the outpost. From Polidor's vantage in the front of the aircraft, it looked like the Fourth of July.

As bad as the situation appeared to be on the ground, the two pilots were no less struck by the confusion in the air around them. On the cockpit's radio, operators were simultaneously flooding them with information, questions, and requests on three separate channels.

Meanwhile, additional aircraft were approaching from all directions. Lewallen and his team of Apache pilots were on their way from Jalalabad. Taking off from Kandahar were several A-10 Thunderbolts, a relatively slow-flying, twin-engine fighter known as a "Warthog" that is designed to provide close air support against tanks and other armored vehicles. More F-15s would soon be joining the fight from Bagram, along with a hodge-podge of drones and other aircraft. In short, a host of planes from the army, the air force, and even the navy was in the sky—and not all of these aviators could speak, either to one another or to their counterparts on the ground. Moreover, there was no one on hand to coordinate their movements.

In the vernacular used by pilots, the section of a battle zone to which the aircraft providing close air support are assigned is known as the "kill box." Inside this box, even minor communications glitches can result in bombs that are dropped in the wrong place, gun runs that target friendly forces, or midair collisions.

The process of choreographing the midair dance within the kill box is called deconflicting the airspace, and that job usually falls to one aircraft that is responsible for operating the airborne warning and control system, or AWACS. That plane, which is larger than a Boeing 707, is readily identified by the distinctive radar dome that is mounted above its fuselage and has a crew that specializes in the complex and potentially deadly task of providing air-traffic control in a combat environment.

Needless to say, this isn't the sort of endeavor that can easily be taken on by the crew of an aircraft that's not specially equipped to coordinate an areal battle scene. A plane like, say, Michal Polidor's F-15 Strike Eagle, which, apart from its avionics and its electronic gadgetry, basically consists of a couple of fuel tanks and some horrifically deadly armaments strapped to a pair of Pratt & Whitney afterburning turbofan jet engines. What's more, stepping into this role on the fly (both literally and figuratively) wasn't something that either Polidor or Dove had specifically trained for.

Nevertheless, someone had to do it—and despite the fact that this sort of thing wasn't exactly in his wheelhouse, there were a few elements that helped to stack the odds in Polidor's favor.

The cockpit of an F-15 features a shockingly complex array of aeronautics sensors that are capable of delivering multiple streams of information about not only the fighter jet itself but also its surrounding environment: enemy aircraft, targets, and weather, along with a host of other variables. Directly in front of both the pilot and the wizzo, and also stacked on both sides, are rows of screens that are aglow with incoming radar signals. Inside their helmets there are three separate radio links, plus an intercom that they use to speak to each other. The multiple streams of data spew out with a speed and density that makes it feel like the informational equivalent of being hit in the face by a fire hydrant. It's far more than most ordinary people have the bandwidth to handle.

As a fighter pilot, Polidor had been trained not only to process this sort of overload but also to channel it into crisp decisions and responses. It also probably helped that while maintaining a 3.9 GPA as a cadet majoring in astronautical engineering at the Air Force Academy, he'd played as starting goaltender on the school's hockey team. But more than anything else, what may have bolstered his resolve to step into an unfamiliar role had less to do with his skills and training and more to do with an idea.

Back at Bagram Airfield, the 335th Fighter Squadron had a little sign hanging next to a door leading out to the flight deck that read as follows:

THE MISSION IS AN EIGHTEEN-YEAR-OLD WITH A RIFLE. EVERYTHING ELSE IS SUPPORT.

Those words, which Polidor and his colleagues had to pass by every time they headed out to the tarmac, reminded them that they were a small—albeit vitally important—piece in an intricate machine. It was also an affirmation of a core principle: the notion that an aviator's sense of purpose lay in serving the soldiers who performed the dirtiest job in the military and who, by dint of that, embodied the purest essence of war. An airman's highest duty lay in doing whatever was necessary to buttress the men with boots on the ground.

That philosophy, more than anything else, helps explain why Polidor, after using up almost every armament and munition on board his fighter to pound the Taliban fighters on the Switchbacks, immediately set about turning his Strike Eagle into a miniature version of an AWACS.

POLIDOR'S FIRST TASK was to start deconflicting the planes that were arriving on station to ensure that none of them were attempting to fly through the same section of sky at the same time. So after setting himself up as a command-and-control nexus for radio communications, he started separating out the aircraft and assigning them to different sectors. The key to this lay in what's called the "stack," a concept best grasped by imagining a massive cyclone spinning in the air near Keating. The top of that vortex was thirty thousand feet high, and each thousand-foot layer or "window" beneath was reserved for a particular type of aircraft.

The highest levels of the stack were slated for the surveillance drones and unmanned aerial vehicles: MQ-9 Reapers and MQ-1 Predators that had started arriving from the airfields at Kandahar and Bagram as early as 7:20 a.m., and which Polidor placed by directing their operations teams, members of which were posted as far away as Creech Air Force Base just north of Las Vegas, Nevada—to establish orbits between twenty-five thousand and twenty-three thousand feet.

Below the drones but roughly fifty miles away from the main stack were three KC-135 Stratotankers and a KC-10 Extender—flying gas stations that would enable the fleet to stay aloft for many hours. Directly inside the stack there was also an RC-135, a plane as large as a tanker whose crew had electronic warfare countermeasures that included the ability to selectively monitor and jam the cell phones that the Taliban were using to communicate.

This hodgepodge, which arrived from airfields as far north as Kyrgyzstan and as far east as Qatar and the United Arab Emirates, would eventually grow to include a U-28A surveillance plane that would later provide reconnaissance for a special forces team that was set to be flown into the area shortly after nightfall, along with an AC-130H Spectre gunship (also known as "Spooky") that was armed with—among many other features—a five-barrel rotary cannon that can fire eighteen hundred rounds per minute.

Underneath all of this were the strikers, the F-15s and the A-10 Warthogs that would conduct strafing runs and bomb drops. Finally, the very bottom layer—anything below three thousand feet—was reserved for rotary: the Apaches that were conducting their gun runs and missile strikes, as well as the Black Hawks that were poised to swoop in to medevac our wounded the moment that we were able to regain control of our LZ.

Communications were so tangled that it was twenty minutes before Polidor and Dove were able to figure out who was talking over the radio, where they were transmitting from, and what they were trying to say. Straightening out the mess and getting the stack sorted took the better part of an hour. (One of the biggest challenges arose because the mountainous terrain blocked radio transmissions from the ground to any aircraft that did not have a direct line of sight with either Keating or Bostick.) But even before they had everything under control, Polidor and Dove were grappling with the second part of their job, which involved coordinating air strikes.

This was every bit as complicated as building and managing the stack, and it involved plugging into the tail end of a jury-rigged chain of communication that started inside Keating's command post, where Bundermann was putting together a running list of targets that needed to be destroyed:

I need for the A-10s to hit the entire North Face . . .

Let's get the Apaches to put a Hellfire into the clinic to the east—here's the grid location . . .

I want bombs on these two TCPs along the Switchbacks . . .

Those air-strike requests, which were based on information that Bundermann was getting mostly from me, Avalos, and Adams (who was Blue Platoon's forward observer), were passed to Cason Shrode, who was with Bundermann inside the command post and whose responsibility included handling all communications concerning air support. The unspoken message from Bundermann that accompanied each here's-what-I-want-and-where-I-want-it request was: *I don't give a shit how you make this work—just figure it out.*

Part of Shrode's training—and a big reason why he was good at his job—had involved mastering a highly specialized system of communicating with the air force operators who assign targets to the pilots conducting air strikes. These operators are known as joint terminal attack controllers, or JTACs, and during the battle for Keating, Shrode was communicating with two of these specialists—Senior Airman Angel Montes and Airman First Class Stephen Kellams—both of whom were inside the command post at Bostick. Once the JTACs received the target coordinates from Shrode, they would relay the information up to Polidor.

What all of this meant was that Polidor's Strike Eagle was now serving as a flying relay station for three different army bases while simultaneously managing a multilayered armada of nineteen separate war planes, each moving into and out of a battle space spread across thirty thousand vertical feet of sky. Working together, Polidor and Dove had to lay out target coordinates and elevations, relay final clearance on air strikes, and set priorities on which planes were assigned to which targets. They had to move aircraft up and down within the stack whenever a new arrival came on station. Each time the Apaches returned to the battle space, they had to lift the floor of the stack and push everything inside it up another three thousand feet in order to allow the helicopters to move directly to their targets. And whenever a two-thousand-pound bomb was dropped from a fixed-wing aircraft inside the stack, the Apaches had to be moved a safe distance away so that they weren't knocked out of the sky by the blasts from those enormous bombs. But there was much more.

They had to make sure that everyone was able to pay a visit to the tankers before running out of fuel, and they had to handle any emergencies that arose within the stack. (One plane's cockpit depressurized, forcing it to return to base.) They had to cope with spotty communications as the radio signals linking them to Bostick and to other aircraft—especially the Apaches—were degraded by the mountainous terrain. They had to monitor the cloud cover (which was getting ever more dense) and the weather, which was rapidly deteriorating as a series of massive thunderstorms began moving east across the Kunar Valley, impairing visibility and eventually causing dangerous levels of ice to build up on the wings of the aircraft at the top of the stack. (For jets that were jockeying to obtain fuel from the air tankers amid the worst parts of these storms, the rain and hail reduced visibility to as little as ten feet.) They had to double-check grid coordinates to confirm that bombs weren't being mistakenly dropped inside Keating's perimeter (Dove discovered two such errors and directed the attacks to be aborted before munitions were released). They had to make sure that none of the bombs that were plummeting through the kill box accidentally struck another American plane. And while they did all of those things, Polidor also had to keep an eye on his altitude, attitude, fuel level, and a litany of other details as he attended, not incidentally, to the business of flying one of the world's most sophisticated jets.

It's almost impossible for someone who hasn't sat inside the cockpit of a fighter to imagine the mind-boggling complexity of what Polidor and Dove were doing. And yet all of this was unfolding without a single soldier down on the ground at Keating—with the possible exception of Cason Shrode—having the faintest clue of what was happening. But what amazes me most is that this superbly calibrated, exquisitely tuned, and unimaginably expensive war machine—this marvel of aeronautic engineering and communications wizardry and weapons technology—was at the beck and call of one man with a radio strapped to his back. A sergeant from Stockton, California, who called himself "Red Bull" and who, right now—more than four hours into the Battle for COP Keating—was calling fire missions through the western door of the Shura Building with his pants around his ankles while he squatted over an empty ammo box and took a dump.

THE AIR STRIKES that Avalos was calling in were impressive. Most of the targets on the Putting Green were more than six hundred yards away, but the bombs that landed on the Switchbacks and Urmul were far closer. About ten seconds before their impact, Avalos would give us a heads-up by yelling, "Splash out!" When the bombs hit, the sound of the concussion and the blast of dirt and pulverized rock were immense.

Those bombs were definitely having an impact—and not just on the Taliban. As the intensity of the air strikes increased, our confidence started to grow too. Granted, we were still in big trouble. Half of the outpost was on fire; we had dead men scattered across a wide area whom we couldn't see or get to; and it still wasn't possible to extract our wounded. But for perhaps the first time since the attack had started, it felt as if we were hitting the enemy at least as hard as they had been hitting us.

With Raz now concentrating on getting an IV line into Miller's arm and Avalos continuing to call in fire, things were under control at the Shura Building. This freed me up for what I needed to do next, which involved dashing back to the other side of camp to put a special request in front of Bundermann.

What I had in mind could have been relayed over the radio. But it was important enough that I wanted to drive the point home in person.

WHEN I WALKED into the command post, I shot Jonathan Hill a harsh look while tossing up my hands in a *what the fuck?!* gesture. Then I let the matter drop. We had more important things to worry about than his missing machine-gun team—starting with the fact that we still had no idea where our lost comrades were.

Seven men were now missing: Gallegos, Larson, Mace, Martin, Carter,

Griffin, and Hardt. Assuming that their bodies were still inside the wire, we had to find and retrieve them before they were taken by the Taliban.

"We need a plan," I said, turning to Bundermann. "We have to figure out how me and my team are going to get those bodies back."

At this point, I explained, there were only three men at the Shura Building on whom I could rely: Raz, Dulaney, and Avalos. In order to generate sufficient cover fire for my next move—which would entail pressing into the exposed sector on the far western end of camp, where I suspected that most of our dead were located—I would have to leave one of those men at the Shura Building with a machine gun. A three-man team wasn't even close to what we needed to find seven dead and carry them back.

"I need more guys," I said to Bundermann. "Who can you give me?"

Before I'd even completed the question, Bundermann was already shaking his head. He understood, probably better than anybody, just how far I'd pushed things by storming the Shura Building without any fire support. He was glad it was done, but he knew that I'd gone well past the bounds of acceptable risk, and that me and my squad were damn lucky to be alive. Sending a tiny group of us even farther into the kill zone beyond the Shura Building would be a bold move. But if we got wiped out and all of our gains were reversed, it would also prove to be a colossally stupid move.

"Get back to the Shura Building and hold your position until we can get a better handle on this situation," he ordered. "I want you and your guys to hang tight and just keep calling fire."

This wasn't the time to argue—and in any case, he was right.

"Roger that," I said, and raced back.

When I arrived, the Warthogs and the F-15s were still conducting bombing runs on the Switchbacks and the Putting Green. With the enemy gunners up there being subjected to such a heavy pounding, my concerns focused on the immediate standoff area surrounding the Shura Building. Our visibility was so limited that it would be a simple matter for a small team of gunmen to move right next to our walls and stack up without us knowing. To ensure that didn't happen, we needed to start getting creative.

The north side of the Shura Building featured three small windows, each no bigger than two feet by two feet. There was no glass in any of these windows—they were simply rectangular holes in the wall, although each was protected by a wooden cover that swung inward and functioned as a kind of portal. Up to this point, we'd kept those shutters firmly latched, but now we started using them as part of a bizarre and deadly game conceived by Raz, Avalos, and me.

We each selected a window and crouched next to it with a pile of the grenades that we'd collected from the ammunition depot. Each grenade had a three- to five-second delay before it exploded. Under normal circumstances, you would pop the spoon and wait one or two seconds before making your throw.

The problem was that if anybody was on the other side of the wall, he'd have a few seconds to grab the grenade and try to hurl it back through the window or onto the roof. So every thirty seconds, one of us would pull the spoon and hold the live grenade in his hand for as long as he dared—three seconds, four seconds, 4.49999 seconds—prior to grabbing the latch, yanking open the shutter, then chucking the grenade through the opening and slamming the shutter closed before the concussion sounded.

We'd each select a window at random. Sometimes we'd open them in sequence. Other times we'd skip one. Occasionally one of us would toss two or even three grenades from the same window before we switched. But in every instance, one thing remained constant: the guy with the live grenade counted down the seconds in the knowledge that if he misjudged and waited too long, it would explode in his hand and kill everybody inside the room.

We called this "grenade chicken," and I honestly can't say how long we kept at it because the intensity robbed us of any sense of time. All I know is that we maintained the same rhythm—a new grenade once every thirty seconds—for what seemed like more than an hour while we waited for Bundermann to let us know that he was sending out some more guys and giving a green light for our body-recovery mission.

Finally, the call came through—and when it arrived, it wasn't what any of us expected.

"Hey, Ro, you're not gonna believe this," Bundermann announced, "but I just heard from Red Dragon out at LRAS2."

I was so stunned that I was at a loss for words.

If what he was saying was true, Brad Larson was within one hundred yards of where we were sitting—and he was still alive.

CHAPTER EIGHTEEN

Alive!

SINCE SHORTLY BEFORE eight a.m., there had been no word from Larson's gun truck. The last anybody had heard from that sector was just prior to the fatal exfil when Gallegos had tried to use the diversion created by Josh Hardt and his rescue team to stage a withdrawal to the Shura Building. As a result, none of us had any clue of what had happened when Gallegos, Martin, and Mace tried to make their break toward the latrines while Larson and Carter laid down cover fire:

We knew nothing about the RPG that had coated Martin in soot and destroyed Mace's legs and abdomen. We knew nothing about how Gallegos had picked Mace up and disappeared behind the laundry trailer—only to come tearing back a few seconds later and get shot to pieces in full view of Carter, who, together with Larson, was trying to provide cover fire for their escape. Nor did we know that Larson had been drilled by a Taliban sniper. All we knew was that there had been no word from anyone on the western side of camp near that gun truck—and from that silence, we had assumed they were all dead.

Not true.

Unbeknownst to the rest of us, several members of that lost squad had managed to hang on, albeit just barely. The details of what they had endured were as dramatic and bloody as anything else that had happened so far, with the added twist that they were still in terrible straits and that one of them had been wounded so badly and in so many places that the mission to try and save him, in the midst of a battle whose final outcome still hung in the balance, would take a commitment by every soldier who was still alive at Keating along with the pilot of every fighter jet, helicopter, and support aircraft who was part of Michal Polidor's stack in the sky above.

How all of this unfolded makes for quite a tale—but that's getting ahead of things.

First, I need to tell you what happened after Larson, whose call sign was "Red Dragon," got shot in the head.

THE BULLET THAT was fired at Larson as he stood behind the Humvee drove into the lip of his helmet, where the Kevlar stopped the thing cold, although it left an indentation just above his left eyebrow and snapped his noggin back as if he'd been clocked in the face with a nine iron.

It was a shockingly close call. Half an inch lower and the round would have blown straight through his left eyeball.

"Get back in the truck!" Larson yelled to Carter.

As both men moved toward the doors, Larson caught sight of a pair of Taliban gunners emerging from behind the generator that was attached to our cold-storage shipping container, no more than twenty feet away. The first man had an RPG balanced on his shoulder, while the second was carrying a PKM machine gun. Neither of them had spotted Larson.

He raised his carbine and shot both insurgents in the face. Then he climbed into the driver's seat of the truck and slammed the door.

"Gallegos was hit," Carter reported as bullets and RPGs continued to slam into the armored Humvee. "I don't know what happened to Mace or Martin."

Larson didn't know what happened to Martin either. But he'd seen Mace absorb much of the blast from the RPG that had landed between the two men, and he'd also watched Gallegos drag Mace to his feet and hustle him behind the latrines. He was in the midst of explaining this when Carter, who was sitting in the tactical commander's seat, spotted something moving on the far side of a pile of rocks less than fifty yards away from the truck.

It was Mace. He was crawling around the corner on his elbows and forearms, dragging his legs.

"I can see Mace—he's still alive," Carter exclaimed. "Let me go get him!"

"No," Larson declared. "You're no good to him dead."

Unlike Carter, Larson had spent enough time in combat to know that one of the best ways to get killed was by rushing out to rescue a wounded comrade or retrieve the body of a buddy who had just gotten smoked. "Dead bodies attract more dead bodies" was one of the many mantras that he and I often traded back and forth during our time in Iraq.

Having seen this phenomenon unfold too many times with his own eyes, Larson had no intention of allowing Carter—whom he outranked—to step outside the truck and offer up another tempting target for the Taliban. Instead, he ordered Carter to make sure that the combat locks on the doors were engaged while he tried to raise Bundermann on the truck radio.

Getting no response, Larson switched to another channel and got nothing there either. He tried yet another channel, then two or three more.

Each attempt yielded the same result: static.

Larson had no way of knowing that while he and Carter had stood outside the truck trying to provide cover fire, the rest of us had jumped to a new frequency in order to ensure that our communications weren't compromised. Having missed the signal to jump, and with no way of knowing the new frequency—which was passed around the Alamo Position by word of mouth—Carter and Larson were now out of the loop.

Baffled that the radio seemed to have stopped working, and realizing that neither he nor Carter had a handheld unit, Larson gave up and turned to their next problem.

The Taliban rockets had played havoc with the gunner's turret above the cab of the Humvee, and the hatch to the turret was now wedged open by a tangled rat's nest of wreckage that included the smashed .50-cal, a jagged piece of the housing that had been blown off of the cold-storage connex's generator, and a bunch of electrical wiring. With RPGs continuing to slam into the wall of sandbags directly in front of the truck, it was imperative that they find a way of getting that hatch closed and locked.

Using Larson's Gerber, Carter cut through the wiring, then put his shoulder to the hatch and managed to force it up just enough to be able to shove aside the machine gun and the wreckage of the generator. That enabled him to slam the hatch closed. The locks refused to turn, so he tied down the lid with nylon parachute cord.

With the hatch shut and the radio still refusing to work, there wasn't much else they could do. They could hear gunfire coming from the center of camp, but they had no idea whether their fellow Americans or the Taliban were doing the shooting. Occasionally they could spot enemy soldiers moving around the Afghan Police guard shack about a hundred yards away, on the far side of the river. But the moment they cracked one of the windows to get off a shot, the snipers in Urmul would start putting rounds through the gap.

Even more worrisome, they were almost out of bullets. By this point, each man was down to less than half a magazine's worth of M4 rounds, about seven shots apiece. Knowing that they needed to conserve the last of those bullets, there was little they could do except settle into their seats and try to take stock of what had happened.

Gallegos, perhaps the only member of Red Platoon whose size, strength, and fury rivaled Josh Kirk's, was dead. Martin had vanished, and Mace lay beyond their reach. No one at the command post had any inkling that they were alive, and Larson had been hit in his right arm and right shoulder, as well as having received wounds to his face and neck. The enemy had them surrounded. And as an added bonus, both men loathed each other because, as it turned out, Larson and Carter had some history between them, and none of it was good.

The problem dated back to just before we'd deployed to Afghanistan when they had attended sniper school together in Fort Benning, Georgia. There, friction had arisen over radically different interpretations of the school's rules and honor code, which Larson felt Carter had violated. The rancor engendered by this clash hadn't been especially problematic during our time at Keating, because with Carter being in Blue Platoon and Larson being in Red, they'd had very little contact. But in light of how much the two men disliked each other, the irony of their current predicament wasn't lost on Larson. If there was one person in the entire outpost, Afghans included, whom he least wanted to be trapped with inside a stricken gun truck that had no radio, no machine gun, and a turret hatch secured with string, it was Carter.

And yet, like it or not, there they were. But to Larson's credit, as much as he might have despised Carter, he would later be the first to acknowledge that his teammate was about to rise above his reputation as an oily, smooth-talking douche bag and find his center as a soldier.

The transformation was swift, and it started when Carter glanced out his window and noticed, to his astonishment, that while they'd been fiddling with the radio and the hatch lid, Mace had somehow managed to drag himself from behind the rocks and was now lying about twenty yards away, close enough that they could actually hear one another. In fact, he was raising his head right now and saying something.

Carter cracked his window just enough to be able to catch the words.

"Help me," cried Mace. "Help me—*please!*"

IN LARSON'S ESTIMATION, there was still no way for Carter to run from the gun truck to the area where Mace lay without getting shot to pieces. With Mace so damnably close, however, it was far harder for Larson to keep denying Carter's repeated requests that he be allowed to at least try.

Things finally shifted when Carter announced that he was hearing something else through the crack in his window. It was the sound of a horn, and from what Carter could tell, it seemed to be coming from Truck 1, the Humvee that Hardt had used in his failed rescue mission, which was still high-centered on the berm of rubble about five yards from the back of the gun truck where he and Larson were sitting.

Was there a wounded man inside that truck—Martin, Hardt, maybe Griffin—who was trying to signal for help? They needed to find out. So when Carter suggested that he step outside and clamber under their gun truck to see if he could spot anything, Larson gave him the nod.

The moment Carter got out, he could see that his idea wasn't going to work. The tires on their Humvee had been riddled with bullets and shrapnel, and were completely flat. There wasn't room for him to squeeze under the chassis.

"Under the truck's no good," he told Larson as he climbed back in. But Truck 1 was only fifteen feet away and its doors were open. Shouldn't he dash back and do a check for survivors?

Larson had no idea that by now me and my team had reached the ammo supply sheds and were working with the Apache pilots to eliminate the enemy machine-gunners on the other side of the Darreh-ye Kushtāz River and inside Urmul. But it was clear that the Apaches had resumed making intermittent gun runs throughout the valley, and that the Taliban's fire died down each time the helicopters conducted another sortie. So he told Carter that he had a green light to go, but that he had to wait for the birds to return.

When they heard one of the Apaches open up with its chain gun, Carter hopped out, dashed back to Truck 1, and jumped inside.

No one was there and the radio—along with most of the cab's interior—had been smashed by an exploding RPG. There was nothing to explain what might have caused the horn to go off, except perhaps a short in the electrical system caused by the damage the truck had sustained. But Carter spotted a pair of items that could come in handy: an M4 and a SAW.

He grabbed both weapons and scurried back.

When he arrived, they opened the drum on the SAW and started delinking rounds. There weren't many left, but they were the same caliber as their own rifles. Along with the bullets in the extra M4, they now had enough rounds to completely fill one magazine.

It wasn't much, but it might be just enough to allow Larson to cover Carter while he retrieved Mace.

"Mace is moving!" Carter exclaimed.

"All right, he's been alive this long," said Larson. "We gotta wait for the Apaches to come in again."

While they waited, they discussed how their next move would work.

First, Carter would need to get to Mace and find out how badly he was hurt. Depending on how things looked, the best option might be for Carter to then drag Mace to a drainage gully that ran down from the mortar pit and tuck him under the concrete bridge that led across the river to the helicopter landing zone, where they would maybe have some cover.

When the Apaches returned and the enemy fire again subsided, Carter got out for a second time and sprinted over to the rock pile where Mace lay. Meanwhile, Larson exited on the driver's side with his carbine. Because he was down to just fourteen rounds, he refrained from shooting and concentrated on scanning Urmul, the Switchbacks, and the Waterfall area through the scope of his M4, looking for anything that might pose a threat.

When Carter reached Mace, he found him lying facedown, with Gallegos's dead body stretched out just a few feet away.

Mace was mumbling and in shock. He had also lost a great deal of blood. When Carter rolled him over, the front of his shredded uniform was crimson-colored from the wounds to his abdomen and legs. His intestines were partially exposed, his legs were covered with bullet holes and shrapnel, and one of his feet had almost been severed at the ankle. In addition, pieces of shrapnel had penetrated his hip, buttock, and flank on the right side of his body, as well as his back and his right arm.

Kneeling beside him, Carter got to work. Mace's left leg had been shattered—he had a compound fracture of both the tibia and fibula—so the first order of business was to get a tourniquet around the leg. Then he used a pressure dressing to pack the wounds in Mace's belly, and rolls of gauze and tape to plug up some of the larger holes in his legs. Finally, he snatched up a stick and used it to splint the damaged ankle.

When he was finished, Carter took a moment to look over the concrete bridge twenty yards to his south. Then he told Mace to hold tight and dashed back to the truck to confer with Larson.

The bridge was no good, Carter explained: too exposed, not enough cover. The only safe place for Mace was inside the gun truck.

"All right," Larson agreed. "But we need to do one thing first."

Grabbing his multitool, Larson prepped the truck using an old trick that he'd learned from me back in Iraq. The seat rest in a Humvee is supported by four bolts—two on each side. If you unscrew the top two bolts, the seat will go all the way down and you can turn it into a recliner, enabling a wounded man to lay almost flat. (We used to call it "riding gangster-style.")

When the seat was ready, Larson again posted up with his M4 to provide cover, and Carter sprinted back to Mace.

Reaching Mace, Carter picked him up and carried him over to a nearby rock ledge. Setting Mace on top of the rocks, he climbed up the ledge and dragged him the rest of the way to the truck. Then he picked Mace up again and lifted him through the front passenger-side door.

When Mace was settled in the reclined seat, Carter scurried around the back of the truck and climbed into the seat behind Larson.

As he slammed the door shut, Mace turned his head and looked over at both of them.

"Say, do one of you guys have a cigarette?" he asked. "I could really use a smoke right now."

IN ADDITION to his sense of humor, the thing that defined Mace was his tolerance for pain. Once, back in the eighth grade, he'd gotten tangled up in a scrum of kids during a football game and was tackled hard enough to break his femur. It was a bad fracture—the orthopedic surgeon would later say that it looked as if he'd been in a car accident going a hundred miles an hour—and to prevent the ends of the bone from severing his femoral artery, the paramedics were forced to set the bone right there on the field without any anesthetics. When Mace was delivered to the hospital, the staff in the emergency room couldn't believe that a thirteen-year-old boy could handle such agony. But he had. Even his mother was astonished by what he'd been able to absorb.

Now that stoicism was about to be tested far beyond the limits of anything Mace had ever endured. He didn't cry out or scream, but Larson could see the torment etched in his features. The skin on his face had taken on a bilious shade of green, and his eyes seemed to swim inside twin pools of pure, undiluted suffering. To Larson, it seemed like the worst pain one could ever imagine, multiplied by a factor of ten. And perhaps the most awful part of it was that neither he nor Carter could provide the one thing that might have given Mace a dollop of relief, the *only* thing he asked for—a cigarette.

"Give me a cigarette, will ya?" he kept pleading, over and over.

It just killed Larson that he hadn't brought any cigarettes or chew with him. But there was no way for him to get that across to Mace, who listened politely each time Larson told him that they were fresh out of tobacco, and then plaintively put forth the same request:

"Please, dude—just *one* cigarette."

Eventually, Larson gave up trying to explain things and fell back on small phrases of encouragement—*You're tough . . . You're good . . . We'll getcha*—while he and Carter tried to figure out their next move.

They continued to hear gunfire coming from the center of camp, but they still had no idea who was doing the shooting. It was quite possible, they reasoned, that some of us—HQ Platoon, plus maybe a few guys from Red and Blue—were still alive and making a final stand. But then again, maybe the Taliban had penetrated to the center of camp and were finishing off the last pockets of survivors. Or perhaps a group of our guys had fled beyond the wire into the hills, and the enemy was now *inside* the camp shooting *out* at them.

Isolated and cut off as they were, each of these scenarios seemed equally likely. And in light of those possibilities, it seemed that perhaps their only viable path of escape lay directly in front of them.

"Can you swim?" asked Carter, staring through the shot-up windshield out toward the river.

Larson was silent for a moment. The answer was an emphatic no: he couldn't swim worth a lick, even when he wasn't wounded in multiple places.

"Enough to survive," he replied.

With that, they hatched a desperate plan in which they would wait until dark, crawl to the edge of the river while dragging Mace, then slip into the current and allow it to carry them more than a dozen miles downstream to Lowell, an American combat outpost carved into a rocky spur beside the river.

Needless to say, that plan had some serious drawbacks, starting with the fact that Mace was almost guaranteed to bleed to death within the first couple of minutes after entering the water. Soon thereafter, Larson would probably drown—a prospect that might sound slightly less unacceptable, he sardonically conceded to himself, if he could have one last dip of chewing tobacco.

Eventually, they agreed that making a Huck Finn–style bid to reach Lowell was an asinine scheme. But they also knew that Mace—who still hadn't stopped campaigning for a cigarette—was suffering from massive internal bleeding and wouldn't last much longer. And so it was around this point that Carter decided that he needed to try to find out what was happening toward the center of camp and determine, once and for all, whether anybody else at Keating was alive.

"I'm going out on a recon," he announced. "If I'm not back in ten minutes, I either made it, or don't worry about it."

With that, he was out of the truck, over the terrace, and running for the rocks by the latrines where he had picked up Mace. He passed Gallegos's body, then turned the corner of the latrines, paused, and scanned what lay before him. The first thing that caught his eye was Mace's M4, which was on the ground next to the laundry connex.

He was about to make a dash for the connex when he glanced behind him and spotted something else.

It was an EFJohnson, lying in the dirt.

An EFJohnson radio is a two-way, handheld, open-channel walkie-talkie that is neither coded nor encrypted. As such, it's not the sort of device you want to be using in combat, because the communications aren't secure. But at Keating, the maintenance crew really liked the EFJohnsons because they offered a simple way of talking to one another.

Keating's chief mechanic, Vernon Martin, had carried one of these radios. Apparently he'd dropped the thing when he, Mace, and Gallegos had tried to make their run for the Shura Building. Although it still wasn't clear what had happened to Martin, Carter had just found that radio—and in so doing, he had stumbled on perhaps the only communications link that had not been affected by the net switch. The critical question was whether anybody was still alive in the center of camp—and if so, whether they were bothering to monitor Martin's frequency on the EFJohnson that was kept inside the chargers on the eastern wall of the command post.

Carter snatched up the radio, keyed it, and heard nothing.

He turned it off, then on again, keyed it a second time, and heard it working.

"This is Blue Four Gulf," he said, giving the call sign that identified him as a member of Blue Platoon. "Is anyone still alive?"

In response, he heard a voice. He couldn't make out who it was or what was being said, but it was enough to send him racing back to the gun truck, where he handed the radio off to Larson.

"This is Red Dragon," said Larson.

"Red Dragon, this is Black Knight Seven," replied First Sergeant Burton. "What is your sitrep?"

CHAPTER NINETEEN

The Bone

INSIDE THE COMMAND POST, Burton handed the EFJohnson off to Bundermann so that Larson could provide a brief situation report that included only the most important details: that Gallegos was dead; that Hardt, Griffin, and Martin were missing; and that Mace was critically wounded and needed to be delivered to the aid station as fast as possible if they were to have any chance of saving his life.

"If I lay down a fuck-ton of fire," asked Bundermann, "can you and Carter get him back here on your own?"

"Hell yeah," replied Larson. "We've got a litter right here. But we need a two-minute window to do it."

"All right, get him on the litter," said Bundermann. "As soon as you hear a boom, start moving."

Picking up an ICOM radio, Bundermann then called Jordan Bellamy up at Fritsche. The mortar crew there was still trying to calibrate their guns so that they could hang rounds accurately, but Bundermann didn't care about that right now.

"I need you to prepare to hit Urmul," he said.

"Which part?" asked Bellamy.

"All of it," said Bundermann, giving him the eight-digit grid for the center of the village and specifying he use incendiary white phosphorus shells, which would cause whatever they hit to burn. "Give me fifteen rounds from the 120 and fifteen from the 60."

"Roger," said Bellamy.

Bundermann's next call was to me at the Shura Building.

"They're gonna try to get Mace outta there," he told me after passing along the astonishing news that Larson was alive—news that lifted my spirits and boosted my confidence in a way that nothing else could.

If Larson is still in this fight, I thought to myself, *we're solid.*

"Can you provide covering fire?" asked Bundermann.

"Yep," I confirmed. "We can set up in the front and the rear of the Shura Building."

"Okay, so what's gonna happen is you're gonna hear a boom and then we're gonna fire the 120s," he said. "That's when I want you and your guys to push out and set your support by fire. Anything your team can shoot at the Putting Green, Urmul, or the North Face, do it. Larson and Carter are gonna grab Mace and run."

"Roger that," I said.

Then Bundermann summoned Hill, who was just outside the command center, and gave him the same orders, but with instructions for Hill's men to direct their fire at the Diving Board and the Switchbacks.

Finally, Bundermann put out a call to anyone listening on the combat net. "If you have any sort of weapons system, it needs to go on target," he declared. "I don't care what it is—I want everything we have ready to fire in one minute."

It was a bold gamble. Every weapon inside Keating would open up at the same time in the hope that a massive barrage of outgoing fire would provide just enough cover for Larson and Carter to pick up Mace and complete an extended sprint over uneven terrain, weaving their way through ammo cans, rocks, and assorted pieces of wreckage, across an unthinkably long distance—almost two hundred yards—from the far end of camp to the aid station, without being picked off.

All of us assumed that the trigger for this move—the "boom" that Bundermann had referred to—would be the 120-mm mortar rounds from Fritsche.

In fact, he had something quite a bit bigger than that in mind.

• • •

ROUGHLY FIVE HOURS prior to the start of the attack on Keating, a captain named Justin Kulish pushed his throttles and started hurtling down a runway at Al Udeid, an air base in Qatar more than thirteen hundred miles southwest of Nuristan, at the controls of a B-1 Lancer.

The Lancer is a supersonic intercontinental bomber whose size and power are enough to boggle the mind. On the ground, the aircraft sits higher than a three-story office building. Its wingspan is almost half the length of a football field. When fully loaded it weighs nearly half a million pounds, and when it gets into the air, the thing can fly more than nine hundred miles an hour. Pilots like Kulish who fly this plane don't call it a Lancer, however. Instead, using a riff that derives from "B-1," they simply refer to it as "the Bone."

The Bone also happens to carry the largest payload of any guided or unguided weapon in the entire air force inventory, which means that it offers an unrivaled bouquet of options for an on-the-ground commander who is calling in an air strike. Air force crews sometimes say that the Bone functions as a kind of airborne Dunkin' Donuts showcase of death where the guys on the ground can browse through a menu of offerings and order up whatever they want. Regardless of whether you need a five-hundred-pound GPS-guided bomb to demolish a building, a wind-corrected cluster bomb to rip the guts out of an armored column, or a standoff missile to take out a surface-to-air missile site from fifty miles away, a pilot like Kulish and his three-man crew (copilot plus two wizzos) have got you covered.

Kulish's bomber, whose call sign was "Bone 21," was conducting a routine patrol and had already been in the air for almost eight hours when the call came through that Keating was in danger of being overrun and needed help. As Kulish swung in the direction of Nuristan, the air force controllers at Bostick asked him how long it would take him to get there.

Thirty minutes, radioed Kulish, if he flew at maximum speed without his afterburners—but far less if he went supersonic. The catch: the Bone would inhale five times as much fuel once it broke the sound barrier, and he would need to refuel pretty much the moment he showed up.

Do it, replied the controllers.

Kicking in his afterburners, Kulish pushed his bomber to 1.2 Mach. Meanwhile, Michal Polidor and Aaron Dove started rearranging the stack to make room for his arrival.

Shortly after ten thirty a.m. as Kulish drew near the target zone, he and his crew started catching the radio traffic, and were a bit stunned to discover how many aircraft were in the area. The airspace above Keating seemed to be packed with jets, so they knew that whatever was taking place on the ground was no ordinary engagement.

When they finally got directly overhead and were able to pick up details of what was unfolding, they had the same reaction as every other pilot who arrived on scene that day. What struck Kulish most forcefully was how much of Keating was on fire. From the air, it looked as if the entire outpost was burning.

The other thing they noted was that the weather was starting to change.

At 10:39 a.m., the controllers at Bostick requested a weather check from any Predator surveillance aircraft orbiting inside the stack. One minute later, a drone with the call sign "Sijan," which was working the airspace five nautical miles southeast of Keating, started receiving icing warnings on its sensors. At the same time, Lemay—the call sign for another drone in the area—recorded that heavy cumulous clouds were gathering everywhere.

An early-winter storm was starting to roll in from the east, pushing a wall of clouds laced with thunderstorms from two hundred feet off the ground all the way up to thirty thousand feet. When the storm kicked in fully, the ground would no longer be visible and any aircraft inside the stack would be able to drop only GPS-guided smart bombs whose sensors were locked on to coordinates provided by forward observers on the ground. As an added difficulty, the storm would force the Stratotankers to move off about a hundred miles away, which would force the smaller jets inside the stack to fly farther in order to refuel.

Fortunately, in addition to all of its other munitions, the Bone was equipped with twenty precision-guided bombs known as JDAMs. Twelve of those smart bombs tipped the scales at five hundred pounds apiece. The other eight were monsters that weighed two thousand pounds each and were as long as a pickup truck. Jammed with high explosives and encased in a metal housing that was designed to fragment into hot shrapnel, those bombs were collectively capable of blowing a sizable hole into the middle of the Taliban's assault—although there was a hitch that needed to be taken into account.

When word reached Keating's command post that a B-1 was on its way, Bundermann told Shrode to break out the Field Artillery manual and pull up the specs on just how close they could drop those bombs without obliterating everybody inside the wire.

The JDAMs on board the Bone were equipped with GPS receivers in their tails, along with small steering mechanisms called "servo motors" that could redirect their flight path. Thanks to that guidance package, the bombs were supposed to be accurate to within fifteen yards. This was an important consideration, because the normal rule of thumb during training is that you want to have a yard of standoff—the distance between the point of detonation and the nearest personnel—for every pound of explosives, because no one who is inside that radius and not under some sort of cover is likely to survive the shock wave and the shrapnel.

This wasn't a training situation, however, so when Shrode pulled up the information, he and Bundermann determined that they were comfortable with calling in an air strike within two hundred yards of the outpost—which they immediately passed along to the air force controllers at Bostick. Then Shrode and Bundermann performed a quick huddle to figure out exactly how far they wanted to push inside the zone of what is called "danger close," the unspoken question between the two of them being: *What's the closest strike we can call in while lowering the odds that any of us will survive by an additional ten percent?*

One minute later, they sent word to Bostick that anything to within one hundred yards of Keating was fair game.

What Bundermann intended to submit was a request that a cluster of smart bombs be dropped between the Putting Green and Urmul. This, he envisioned, would serve as a kind of two-for-one special. In a single stroke, he'd terminate a swath of enemy gunners and RPG teams all along the spur that connected those two hot spots. And if he got extra lucky, those bombs might also take out one or two *dishkas* that the Taliban had placed along those ridgelines overlooking the village. (Although these *dishkas* were in a different location from the heavy machine gun that had just succeeded in damaging Lewallen's and Huff's Apaches, the pilots were also concerned about these weapons systems. Eliminating them before the helicopters returned to the battle space was a priority for Bundermann.)

This entire plan was already in place when the first sergeant handed over the EFJohnson radio and Bundermann learned that Larson, Carter, and Mace were alive. From Bundermann's perspective, the next step—using the Bone's bomb drop as the trigger for a massive barrage of cover fire from Red and Blue Platoons, plus Fritsche's mortars, so that Larson and Carter could make their run with Mace to the aid station—seemed like a no-brainer.

By 10:56 a.m. the air force controllers at Bostick had radioed Kulish and his crew—who by now had topped off their fuel tanks and were ready to drop—to prepare to engage.

One minute later, Kulish announced, "Weapons away," and let loose six of the Bone's smart bombs, all of them targeted at the Putting Green and the spur leading down to Urmul.

As the bombs fell, Bundermann sent out a final warning to anyone who was listening on the combat net:

"Everybody get low," he ordered. "This one's gonna be close."

WHEN YOU'RE LESS than two hundred yards away from a massive bomb drop, the impact is unspeakably violent.

The initial explosion registers as a deafening bolt of sound, but the auditory assault doesn't really matter, because the concussion that follows is so much more powerful. What's more, these two forces—sound plus shock wave—are stacked so closely together that you're barely aware of the distinction. What you feel, mostly, is a kind of vast *pushing* sensation, almost as if an ocean wave has struck you in the solar plexus and, through some strange trick of physics, is now passing through your tissue, your bones, your entire body.

If you haven't experienced it directly, the effect is hard to imagine unless you try to conceive what it might be like to be an especially tiny insect—a type of mite, say—huddled inside the bass drum of a heavy-metal rock band.

Wow, that was close, you say to yourself as first shock registers and passes.

But damn—it was kinda cool too, you think as the last shock recedes.

And then you're struck by a disturbing idea:

Oh my God . . . did I just die and I haven't yet realized it?

As impressive and fearsome as all of this was, however, the thing that truly blew our minds was the visual impact of the Bone's air strike.

When the bombs started falling, Raz and I were crouching on the floor in the middle of the Shura Building, having already moved away from the walls on the theory that if the building collapsed around us we'd have a better change of surviving a hit from the plywood roof than if we were buried beneath the wreckage of the stone walls. This meant that we were staring straight through the west doorway, which neatly framed the Putting Green.

The first bomb sledgehammered the top of the ridge directly above Urmul, blowing chunks of dirt, clouds of pulverized rock, and shredded bits of trees high into the air. The impact created an unearthly sound that was louder and darker and more menacing, by far, than any thunderclap that either of us had ever heard, and as the explosion unfurled like a crimson flower, we realized that we could actually *see* the concussion coming at us in an undulating pulse that was causing the air itself to vibrate.

When the concussion struck the Shura Building, it picked up the entire roof and slammed it back down while seizing all four walls and shaking them as if they were a cluster of dead leaves on a tree branch. The air inside filled with a cloud of deeply agitated dust particles. And as all of this was unfolding, the second and third bombs were now striking the Putting Green, to be followed in turn by the fourth and the fifth and the last.

> *Krak—BOOM*
>> *Krak—BOOM*
>>> *Krak—BOOM*
>>>> *Krak—BOOM*
>>>>> *Krak—BOOM*
>>>>>> *Krak—BOOM*

It was, quite simply, the most awesome thing that Raz and me had ever witnessed in our entire lives—and under any other circumstances, we would both have felt compelled to pause for a moment to breathe in and acknowledge the blunt and feral majesty of that awesomeness. But at that moment, I could also hear Bundermann on my radio giving the count-down to open up:

> *Anyone who can hear this, give fire on three!*
>> *—One . . .*
>>> *—Two . . .*

"Grab your 203 now!" I yelled to Raz. "Get out the back door and unload everything you've got!"

Without missing a beat, Raz dashed through the door, crouched down in the trench with his back to the east side of the Shura Building, and began launching grenades backward over his shoulder in the direction of the North Face. He pumped them out as fast as Miller—who had revived enough to serve as his assistant—handed them to him, not even bothering to look where he was shooting.

Meanwhile, me and Dulaney had sprinted through the west door and set up just outside. While Dulaney let loose with his SAW, vomiting out an entire drum of rounds into the Putting Green with a prolonged, vicious-sounding *braaaaaaaaaaaaaaaaaaaaack*, I was burning through a belt of ammo on the PKM machine gun that had been abandoned by the Taliban, concentrating on the Switchbacks and Urmul.

All across Keating, every man who could stand and shoot was spring-ing from his position and doing exactly the same thing. Koppes was pump-ing grenades into the Diving Board with the Mark 19 on our last remaining gun truck. Hill and the men of Blue Platoon were riddling the sides of the North Face and the Switchbacks with every heavy machine gun and per-sonal weapon they could lay their hands on. Even Big John Breeding and the two surviving members of his gun crew up at the mortar pit, who by some miracle had managed to reestablish radio contact just as Bunder-mann was ordering every weapons system on post to open up, were put-ting out fire. (Only much later would we learn that Breeding and Daniel Rodriguez had managed to retrieve the 60-mm mortar tube from the pit and were now firing it, by hand, into the North Face from *inside* their hooch.) And while all of this was taking place, the gun crew up at Fritsche was hurling mortars into the center of Urmul—accurately this time—as fast as they could load and shoot.

The combined effect of all that outgoing firepower was something to behold. Bullets, grenades, and mortars were flying in all directions. None of us had the faintest idea how accurate we were or what sort of damage we might be inflicting on the enemy. But one thing that I can say for sure is that when Larson and Carter heard the barrage go off, they knew exactly what to do.

Carter had been hoping for a brief lull so that he could prep the stretcher that we kept on the back hatch of the gun truck and clear a path for the first part of their run. But as soon as the last of the smart bombs from the Bone struck above Urmul, Larson was yelling, "Go! Go! Go!"

Jumping out of the truck, Carter kicked a few loose ammo cans out of the way, seized the stretcher, and raced over to the rear door on the pas-senger side, where Larson had the door open for Mace.

"Mace, you need to shift your legs," Larson ordered. "We're gonna throw you on this litter, and then we're gonna run."

As Mace tried to move, they pulled him from the truck and placed him on the stretcher. Larson tucked their weapons next to Mace, then grabbed the handles on the back end while Carter took the front.

They had more than a hundred yards of open ground to cover. The terrain was uneven and would be swept by sniper and machine-gun fire the entire way.

"Mace, this is gonna hurt like a motherfucker," Larson announced. "*Hang on, boy!*"

With that, they started running.

Charging as hard as they possibly could, they tried to keep to a straight line without any weaving or dodging except for when they had to skirt around bomb craters or pieces of wreckage. It was pretty much exactly the same way that the other guys had carried Kirk on his litter three and a half hours earlier, except that there were only two runners instead of four and now they had to cover more than twice the distance.

Neither Larson nor Carter would remember much about that run, except that it was one of the hardest physical things that either of them had ever done—and that they hauled ass the entire way. They jumped straight over at least two dead Taliban soldiers, and somewhere between the piss tubes and the Shura Building, they also encountered the body of an American soldier. It was Chris Griffin, who had given up his life while trying to rescue them. This was as far as he'd gotten when he was gunned down.

They ran straight past him and kept going.

As they peeled by us on the south side of the Shura Building, I caught them out of the corner of my eye. From there, they traced a reverse version of the same route that we had taken when we'd fought our way to the ammo supply point: past Jonesie and his machine gun; past the demolished door to John Deere's room; around the end of the Hesco wall, along the side of Red barracks, and straight through the white plywood door with the red cross painted on it, where Larson and Carter delivered up Mace to the medics by dropping to their knees on the blood-smeared blue linoleum floor of the aid station.

THE MOMENT we got word that the litter team was safe, everybody ceased fire and ducked back inside for cover. As our shooting subsided, a stunned silence descended over Keating and the surrounding ridges.

The fighting would quickly resume. But in the lull, as I crouched inside the Shura Building and surveyed the mud-and-stone walls around me, I keyed my radio and spoke to Bundermann.

"I'm no structural engineer," I said, "but I don't know how much more this building can take."

"Well, do you want me to stop it?" he asked. The Bone had plenty more smart bombs and Bundermann had every intention of using them.

"Nope, keep giving it," I replied. "Let the building collapse around us and we'll figure it out from there."

A minute or two later, I got another call from the command post.

It was my best friend.

"Hey, brother, I just got patched up by the medics and I'm good to go," said Larson. "Where're you at?"

"We're out by the front gate," I told him. "If you can make it here, we've got some more work to do, and we could sure use a hand."

We still had to take back the helicopter landing zone so that we could evacuate our wounded. We also had to find a way to venture out and collect our fallen brothers before the Taliban made off with their bodies. And while we did those things, our medics had to find a way of somehow keeping Mace alive.

On a number of levels, this battle wasn't over yet.

PART V

★ ★ ★

Saving Stephan Mace

CHAPTER TWENTY

"Go Get It Done"

DESPITE THE TWIN HAMMER blows of the B-1 air strike and the barrage of outgoing fire, the Taliban didn't take long to return to the business of trying to wipe Keating off the map. Within a few minutes of Mace's arrival in the aid station, the buildings in the center of camp were once again targeted by enemy gunners. Anyone trying to move outside those structures instantly drew fire from snipers, rocket crews, and machine-gun teams.

From inside the Shura Building, however, it seemed to us that this onslaught was blunted by the increasingly aggressive air support that we were now getting. No sooner did the Bone check off station than the sky above camp was playing host to a gaggle of Warthogs. The snub-nosed A-10 attack jets would appear from out of nowhere, usually in pairs, and hit the ridgelines and mountain sides with long, metallic-sounding bursts from their 30-mm cannon, which fired four or five times faster than even the chain guns on the Apaches. They seemed to concentrate mainly on the Switchbacks and the North Face, homing in on targets that had been relayed from Armando Avalos, who continued to call in coordinates and strike requests.

The helicopters were back too, sweeping through the narrow valley with a vengeance and directing their fire into any cracks and crevices where they thought the enemy might be hiding. And before long—just as soon as Justin

Kulish, the commander of the Bone, was able to refuel his aircraft—Bundermann would be requesting another massive strike, this time using a suite of even larger and more destructive two-thousand-pound smart bombs along the Switchbacks. This furious renewal of the engagement by both sides gave rise to the unstated feeling, which we all shared, that the final outcome of this battle still hung in the balance and had yet to fully swing to one side or the other.

It was amid this atmosphere of uncertainty that Larson showed up at the east door of the Shura Building lugging an M4 that he'd snatched from God only knew where and as much ammunition as he could possibly carry.

When he arrived, I tamped down the elation that arose inside my chest and kept things cool by giving him a quick man-hug (shoulders only). Even so, it was obvious that I was thrilled to have him back.

Then we got down to it.

The most important piece of information Larson had to share was that he'd spotted Griffin's body near the piss tubes as he and Carter had chugged past with Mace. That was less than thirty yards from where we were standing. If we acted fast, we could reclaim the first of our dead.

Larson and Raz immediately volunteered to go get him. They got ready by dropping their ammo, weapons, and anything else that might slow them down. After they'd stripped off everything but their Kevlar body armor, they darted out the west door and sprinted toward Griffin while Dulaney and I stepped outside and opened up on the Putting Green and the Switchbacks with our machine guns.

When they reached Griffin's body, they discovered that rigor already set in and he was as stiff as a board. While Larson picked up his legs—one of which had been badly broken and was now bent at an impossible angle—Raz seized his head and neck. As Raz started to lift, something shifted inside Griffin and a gob of blackish-looking goo, as thick as molasses, erupted from Griffin's mouth and sprayed over Raz's face and arms.

This was the first of several encounters over the next hour in which the members of my team would find themselves literally and figuratively touched by death and its aftermath in a way that was visceral, direct, and ugly enough to stay with us for the rest of our lives. In that moment, however, neither Raz nor Larson could afford to think about what was happening: they were too busy stumbling back to the Shura Building while half carrying, half dragging Griffin's body between them.

When they arrived, we all retreated inside and laid Griffin out on the floor. The damage that the bullets had done to him—the wounds in his cheek, the side of his skull, and his neck; the large-caliber holes in his thigh—was horrific and hard to take in. A few minutes later, Sergeant Jim Stanley and Damien Grissette, a specialist from HQ Platoon who was in charge of Keating's water supply, showed up with a stretcher to take him back to the aid station.

Before leaving, Stanley and Grissette delivered some news: the fire that had started on the Afghan National Army side of camp had now spread to the point where Blue Platoon's barracks was about to go up in flames. Only the command post separated Blue's barracks from Red Platoon's barracks, which meant that there was a good chance that everything we'd brought from the States to sustain us during our year in Afghanistan might be on the verge of turning to ashes.

"Hey, Ro," Larson said softly, "mind if I run back and get my chew before it all burns up?"

Given that we were in the midst of battle, it's hard to imagine a more inappropriate request. But it's a testament to the peculiar chemistry of combat—the surreal and irrational way that it can blend high seriousness with the irredeemably banal—that I didn't blink an eye when he popped the question.

"All right, see you back here in a bit," I replied. "And while you're there, see if you can grab me a can of Dr Pepper, okay?"

LESS THAN FIVE minutes later, Larson was back, with a can of Copenhagen and a six-pack of Dr Pepper. He'd also been thoughtful enough to snag my carton of Camels, which meant that every man in the Shura Building could now take a tactical pause to crack open a soft drink and grab a smoke. We all agreed that it was an excellent resupply mission, and fully worth the risk of Larson maybe getting shot.

As I opened up a can of warm Dr Pepper and lit my first cigarette of the day, Larson and I huddled up to review what we knew about the locations of the rest of the men who were still missing.

There was no mystery about Gallegos, who was lying on the north side of the latrines. But we weren't so sure about Martin. Larson was pretty confident that he had been heading in the direction of the Shura Building when he disappeared, so our best guess was that he was somewhere between the latrines and the front gate.

As for Hardt, we were stumped. We were both fairly certain he was dead, but we had no clue where his body might be. All we knew for sure was that if we didn't figure out where he was and get to him, the Taliban would snatch his body up and neither we nor his family would ever see him again.

With that, I called an end to the break by pointing to the three windows on the north wall of the building and explaining to Larson how the game of "grenade chicken" worked.

"Keep chucking those grenades through the window while I link up with Bundermann," I said as I headed for the door to make yet another run to the center of camp. "I need to figure out how we're gonna get our guys back."

When I reached the command post, Bundermann pulled Hill and me together so that the three of us could take stock of where things stood.

Keating was now split in half: almost the entire eastern side was on fire, while we had no control over our western sector. Also, we still had one pocket of soldiers who were completely cut off: John Breeding and his two gunners, Daniel Rodriguez and Janpatrick Barroga, remained trapped in the mortar pit, along with the body of Kevin Thomson.

We agreed that we needed to tackle three things at once. While part of Blue Platoon continued to fight the fire that had all but consumed the ANA side of camp, we had to find a way for the other half of Blue Platoon and the surviving members of Red to recover our dead while simultaneously linking up with and rescuing the men in the mortar pit.

The only way to accomplish that was to launch a second assault in which we pushed, under massive cover fire, all the way from the Shura Building up to the mortar pit, searching for and collecting bodies along the way. This called for a maneuver known as a "bounding overwatch," in which two teams—one led by me on the right, the other by Hill on the left—would proceed uphill in separate stages so that whichever team was on the move would be protected with cover fire by the team that was stationary. To ensure that we were clear on this, Bundermann stepped over to the map on the west wall of the command post and used his finger to trace out exactly how the move needed to unfold.

On Bundermann's command, my squad—which would consist of five guys, including me—would leave the protection of the Shura Building and begin bounding uphill toward the first spot where we would have cover and concealment, which would probably be somewhere around the laundry trailer.

When we were in position, I'd key my radio and announce, "Set!" Then Hill's team—which was supposed to number six guys, including him—would make a dash from the toolshed toward the cluster of buildings around the chow hall. They'd bring a medium machine gun with them, and when they reached a place where they felt secure, Hill would call, "Set."

At this point, my squad would scan for Martin's body, and then make another push—with Hill's men providing cover fire—farther uphill toward the latrines, where we'd set up again in order to cover Hill's men as they made a dash for the mechanics' bay.

We'd continue moving in this manner—first Red, then Blue, each side covering the other while everybody kept an eye peeled for Gallegos's and Hardt's bodies—all the way to the mortar pit.

Given how few men we had, there was little chance that we could successfully defend and hold the pit. So when we got there, we'd grab Breeding and his crew, along with the body of Kevin Thomson, and everyone would peel back to the Shura Building.

Thanks to Hill's team, I'd have a solid wall of outgoing fire protecting my exposed right flank from any Taliban gunners trying to take us out from the Putting Green and the village of Urmul. Thanks to my squad,

Hill would have similar coverage on his vulnerable left flank from any enemy fire sweeping down from the Switchbacks, the Waterfall area, and the Diving Board. And for an added measure of comfort, we'd all have an extra boost of suppressive fire coming from Koppes, who had already been hammering away on his Mark 19 for what seemed like eight hours, and who would continue working his gun truck's grenade launcher like a gangster to cover our back end.

In addition to good communication between me and Hill, one of the keys to pulling this off would be to make sure that the separate arms of the maneuver swung smoothly. So Hill and I would both put our best guys in the middle: in my case Larson, who would be on the left end of my squad; and in Hill's case Harder, who would be on the right side of his team. As we pushed toward the mortar pit in stages, Larson and Harder would pass each other continuously, thereby serving as a kind of mobile hinge that would connect my team and Hill's.

In addition to all of that—which was a lot—there was one other thing I would need in order to uphold my side of the deal.

Most of the bodies—certainly Martin and Gallegos, and perhaps Hardt too—would be lying farther toward the west, which meant that they would probably be discovered by my squad. With only five men, it would be impossible for us to fight our way uphill toward the mortar pit while simultaneously hauling those bodies back to the security of the Shura Building.

"I'm gonna need a couple of extra guys that can carry bodies," I said.

Hill pointed out that HQ Platoon had several men who weren't actively involved in the fight but were willing to help. Among these were Grissette and Private Kellen Kahn, a radio operator who suffered from a bad ankle. If Grissette and Kahn hooked up with Avalos, who was still out at the Shura Building, they could form a three-man casualty-collection team and take care of the job.

With that decided, there wasn't much else to say. It was a solid plan. Now the aim was to make it happen as fast as possible.

"We have to get to our fallen guys before they get snatched," I said. "We need to launch now."

"Negative," said Bundermann, shaking his head.

My primary concern was retrieving our dead. But Bundermann was looking at a bigger picture that involved, among many other considerations, not making a bad situation even worse. His concern—and it was legitimate—was that if anything went wrong on this assault and we got cut off or lost more guys, there would be nobody left to pull us out.

"Get back to the Shura Building and get your team ready," he said. "Then sit tight and wait till I give you the word."

I stared down at the floor in frustration, but didn't object, because I knew that he was making the right call.

We were gonna have to wait for the QRF.

A QRF, or quick-reaction force, is a team of soldiers placed on permanent standby to respond to any emergency in their battle sector. They're equipped to provide either reinforcement or rescue, and they're poised to deploy with extraordinary speed, often within ten minutes or less.

Earlier that morning, shortly after six, when our superiors at Bostick had received word that Keating was in danger of being overrun, one of the first things that they'd done—in addition to scrambling all available air support—was to call for a QRF to be air assaulted into Keating to bolster our defenses. Our brigade's quick-reaction force consisted of two rifle companies from the 1-32 Infantry that were led by Captain Justin Sax and two lieutenants, Jake Miraldi and Jake Kerr. That team, which consisted of almost 150 men, was spread between two neighboring outposts—Joyce and Fenty—when they got the call to come to our aid.

By ten a.m., Sax's entire force had been shuttled into Bostick on a series of Black Hawk helicopters and were waiting on the tarmac while Sax, Miraldi, and the rest of his leadership team gathered inside the command post with Colonel Brad Brown and his staff to figure out the best way to insert the rescue group into Keating.

Among the soldiers in that room, no one was more desperate to see the rescue get under way than Captain Stoney Portis, Keating's commander, who had been stranded at Bostick when the Taliban's attack kicked off.

Portis had already tried to reach us by jumping aboard a medevac helicopter that had flown partway to the outpost before getting recalled because our landing zone was too hot. Now Portis was back at Bostick and eager to hitch a ride in with Sax.

At this point, the information available to the commanders at Bostick about the situation on the ground at Keating was sketchy. They knew that we had enemy inside the wire, but there was confusion about which buildings were still under American control and which were not. That confusion was exacerbated by how rapidly things were changing as we fell back to the Alamo Position, then counterassaulted to retake the ammo supply depot and the Shura Building.

The picture was further complicated by the fact that so much of the outpost was either on fire or obscured from above by thick clouds of smoke. As Sax and Miraldi stared at the monitors displaying the live feeds from the surveillance drones, they scratched their heads in frustration. There was too much haze for the cameras to pick up much in the way of meaningful details, although one thing was crystal clear. Keating's landing zone was far too exposed to enemy fire to risk sending helicopters carrying the QRF directly to the outpost.

In addition to those challenges, the planning team found itself confronting some severe weather issues. By now, heavy rain and thunderstorms were rolling through the Kunar Valley, greatly reducing visibility while encasing the mountaintops with dense cloud cover through which the helicopters would not be able to fly. Soon that storm front would be directly above Bostick. Within another half hour, it would be interfering with bomb drops and air strikes over Keating.

Based on these factors, the commanders initially found themselves debating two possible landing zones. One option was to drop Sax and his rescue team somewhere above the Switchbacks. A second possibility was to insert everyone onto the Putting Green directly above Urmul. Everyone was coming around to the notion that the Putting Green seemed like the best option when a pair of Apache pilots walked through the door and blew that idea out of the water.

• • •

IT WAS RIGHT around ten thirty a.m. when Ross Lewallen and Randy Huff brought the two choppers that had been damaged by the Taliban's *dishka* back to Bostick and managed to land both aircraft safely on the tarmac. Neither helicopter would be able to return to the fight until a repair team that was now on its way from Jalalabad airfield was able to wire the machines back together.

Lewallen used this pause well. First, he borrowed a cleaning rod, the long metal dowel that infantrymen use for swabbing their rifles, located the bullet hole underneath the pilot's seat of his Apache, inserted the rod into the hole, and then stepped back. The cleaning rod was now serving as a kind of crude arrow pointing in the direction from which the bullet had come.

After studying the angle of the rod for a few moments and retrieving his mental notes of exactly where his aircraft had been when it was struck, Lewallen nodded to himself, satisfied that he had a fairly good idea of where that *dishka* was positioned. Then he caught up with Huff, and the two men headed over to the command post to see if they could offer any help in strategizing the air assault.

When they walked through the door, the pilots took one look at the diagram that the commanders were working up and declared, in no uncertain terms, that somebody needed to come up with a better idea—unless the goal of this operation was to get everybody killed, in which case, dumping the QRF on the Putting Green would definitely be a kick-ass way to go.

As a new plan was being put together, two additional Apaches arrived at Bostick from Bagram Airfield and proceeded directly to Keating. Within a few minutes of entering the battle space, one of those helicopters was struck by *dishka* fire. The damage, which was severe, forced both birds to break contact and return to Bostick for repairs, confirming Lewallen and Huff's warning about the vulnerabilities of the Putting Green.

AFTER HEARING LEWALLEN and Huff's assessment, the command team switched gears and decided that the helicopters would shuttle as many men as possible into Fritsche, where the rescue force could consolidate and then walk down to Keating. The descent would take about four hours. If necessary, they would fight their way down the entire mountain.

That was acceptable to the pilots. Fritsche's landing zone was large enough to enable three Black Hawks to land simultaneously. Based on the total number of soldiers they needed to insert, they calculated that it would take five separate trips, or "turns," of three Black Hawks, with two Apaches flying in front and behind to provide gun support and hopefully prevent the heavily loaded Black Hawks from getting shot down.

Time was not on their side. By now, the thunderstorms were directly above Bostick and the sky had grown dark. The weather radar indicated that this particular storm system would be followed by a brief window of clear weather, after which there was another line of thunderheads that might force the helicopters out of the mountains and keep them grounded for quite some time. The good news, however, was that the two-man repair team that had been dispatched from Jalalabad to patch Lewallen's and Huff's birds back together was just now arriving—and they had flown themselves up in a pair of undamaged Apaches.

Dashing out to the tarmac, Lewallen and Huff approached the repair team, John Jones and Gary Wingert, before they even had a chance to shut down their engines.

Would it be cool, asked Lewallen, if he and Huff were to borrow these two birds while Jones and Wingert worked on the choppers that had been shot up by the *dishka*?

"Sure," replied Jones.

Next, Lewallen placed a call to his boss back in Jalalabad, Colonel Jimmy Blackmon, and ran the plan past him.

"Okay," said Blackmon when he heard what they had in mind. "Go get it done."

When Lewallen and Huff climbed into the replacement helicopters with their gunners, Chad Bardwell and Chris Wright, the blades were still turning.

The same was true for the three Black Hawks sitting nearby, which were now fully loaded with twenty-one soldiers, including Sax, Miraldi, and Portis.

Now all they needed was a break in the weather.

• • •

SHORTLY AFTER ELEVEN A.M., the sky cleared just enough that the commanders gave Huff, who would be in charge of this sortie, clearance to take off. There was still some doubt about whether the storm system would permit them to fly over Bari Kowt Pass, which they needed to clear in order to enter the Kamdesh Valley, so Huff launched first so that he could survey the weather conditions on the far side. The trio of Black Hawks followed behind him, with Lewallen's Apache bringing up the rear.

Minutes later when Huff punched over the pass, he could see cloud cover with lightning and rain throughout the entire valley. After he and Wright talked things over, however, they agreed that it was possible to complete the mission before the weather rendered flying completely impossible.

With that, the five aircraft headed for Fritsche as fast as possible, ramming through high storm clouds that drenched them with snow and freezing rain. About halfway up the valley, they also started taking enemy fire—at which point the door gunners on the Black Hawks opened up and began shooting everywhere they saw muzzle flashes. Wright and Bardwell followed suit by laying down fire on those same targets with their chain guns.

As they drew near Fritsche, Huff descended first in order to clear the landing zone. Then the first two Black Hawks touched down simultaneously inside an open area at the top of the ridge to drop their passengers off and immediately get back in the air.

As they departed, the third Black Hawk landed briefly, then chased its sisters back in the direction of Bostick to collect another load of soldiers, plus a resupply of ammo and water. Meanwhile, Lewallen wheeled north in the direction of Keating with Huff in tow. They had some unfinished business to take care of with the *dishka* team that had nearly shot them out of the sky.

As soon as the Apaches were back in radio contact with Keating, Bundermann requested that they place a couple of Hellfire missiles into a large rectangular building just down the road on the east side of the outpost. That building normally served as a clinic, but thanks to some communications that had been intercepted by the electronic warfare boys, it was now believed to harbor some of the Taliban commanders who were coordinating the attack.

As Lewallen and Huff shot one Hellfire apiece into the building, Lewallen kept his eyes peeled for any sign of heavy gunfire coming from the ridges to the south of Keating. One of the few benefits of the worsening weather was that the dark skies now rendered muzzle flashes far more visible. Gunfire that would have been impossible to spot from above in direct sunlight now jumped out like neon against the surrounding rocks and vegetation.

Lewallen scrutinized the high ground between the top of the Diving Board and the Switchbacks. Sure enough, right where he suspected, he spotted a telltale orange flash from the barrel of a *dishka*.

I see you, you asshole, he said to himself and immediately turned to attack.

"We've got 'em," he radioed to Huff. "Cover us!"

Lewallen's plan was to destroy the *dishka* team with a salvo of rockets, which could be fired from the backseat where he was sitting. But as he made his approach and prepared to fire to the left, where he'd spotted the gun, Bardwell, who was in the front seat, caught sight of a second muzzle flash.

"I have another one!" Bardwell announced, and opened up with his 30-mm chain gun.

Meanwhile their wingmen, Huff and Wright, had also opened up with their guns, but they weren't aiming at Bardwell's target or Lewallen's. It was then that all four pilots realized that there was not one or even two but three separate *dishkas* emplaced at the top of the ridge.

After saturating the ridgeline with gunfire and making multiple passes over the site to scan for human heat signatures with their sensors, it was clear that they had obliterated all three gun crews. They weren't quite so certain about the weapon systems, however, which appeared as if they might still be operative. If so, and if the Taliban were able to get fresh crews up onto the ridge, those guns could still pose a devastating threat, especially to a medevac attempting to fly into Keating or on its way from the outpost back to Bostick with wounded soldiers on board.

Although the two Apache crews would have preferred to keep hitting the *dishkas* until they were thoroughly destroyed, they were forced to break contact and begin making their way back to Bari Kowt, where the three Black Hawks, having now taken on their second load of soldiers at Bostick, were preparing to reenter the valley and needed an escort into Fritsche.

Just as they were about to turn away from Keating, Wright radioed down to let our command post know that he would be back as soon as possible. He was surprised to learn that whoever he was talking to—it was almost certainly Cason Shrode—still had his sense of humor.

"Oh, so the machine-gun fire stops and now we can't get any love?!"

"Trust me, brother, we are *only* here for you guys," replied Wright, chuckling as the two Apaches made a beeline toward the pass. "But right now we have to help the rest of your relief team get on the ground."

This time the enemy knew they'd be coming, so when the Apaches linked up with the Black Hawks and headed back up the valley on their second approach, they had to weather an even heavier barrage of gunfire from the ground. Nevertheless, they managed to drop their loads safely at Fritsche. But now another problem arose.

As they pulled away, all five pilots could see that the clouds were closing in fast. They had just enough clear weather to make it back to Bostick. But once they arrived, this second wave of thunderheads would slam the door shut behind them and they'd be forced to cool their heels on the tarmac until another window appeared.

The chances of that next window opening up quickly were pretty much zero. Up at Mustang, an observation post that was perched on the ridges high above Bostick, the antennae were getting slammed by lighting. And several thousand feet above that, conditions were getting so bad that one of the surveillance drones, an MQ-1 Predator with the call sign "Kisling," was accumulating so much ice on its wings that its pilot (who was based in Nevada) would soon be forced to crash it into the side of a mountain.

Judging by the weather radar, the soonest anyone could hope for another opening was at least an hour away, maybe even two.

Until then, Justin Sax and his rescue team would be on their own.

IT WAS NOW coming up on one p.m. and Sax was confronting the sort of decision that no field commander relishes.

His superiors had agreed that he needed about 150 men in order to get safely down the mountain and relieve Keating. Right then, he had less than a third of that. The prudent move, therefore, was to wait until the weather cleared and the Black Hawks could deliver the rest of his team.

On the other hand, Sax was acutely aware that Keating's defenders were hanging by a thread and that we badly needed his help. Even more sobering, perhaps, was that Sax held in his hands the lives of Keating's wounded. There was simply no way to secure the outpost's landing zone without the additional manpower provided by Sax's rescue team, and until that landing zone was opened up, there would be no medevac.

Stoney Portis was set on departing immediately—an impulse that was fiercely supported by every member of White Platoon, who were horrified by the radio reports they'd been receiving and were crawling out of their skin with worry about their brothers down below in Red, Blue, and HQ Platoons. But Sax, who had the final call, had to weigh the urge to relieve Keating against the duty to avoid getting in over his head and creating a second crisis on top of the first.

Eventually, Sax and Portis agreed that if the weather didn't improve and the rest of Sax's men didn't arrive by two p.m., they would move ahead without them and hope for the best.

THREE THOUSAND VERTICAL feet below Fritsche, inside the Shura Building on the north side of Keating, me and my team were anxiously awaiting word on when we could launch our next assault toward the mortar pit, and all too aware that each minute of delay lessened our chances of getting our guys back.

We weren't privy to any of the details about the air assault that was taking place on the ridge above us or the challenges that Sax and Portis were up against. All we knew was that it seemed to be taking them forever.

Finally, just after two p.m., Bundermann radioed to let me know that the quick-reaction force had just left the wire at Fritsche and were on their way down the mountain.

"Red Two, QRF is leaving Fritsche," he announced. "Prepare to launch, and tell me when you are ready."

CHAPTER TWENTY-ONE

Mustering the Dead

IF YOU WANTED to select the most likely place for an American soldier to get picked off by an enemy gunner from the ridges surrounding Keating, it would be hard to come up with a better spot than the thirty-yard stretch of bare dirt and loosely scattered pebbles that lay just beyond the south side of the Shura Building. Inside this zone the ground was open, the terrain sloped uphill, and the entire space was exposed to direct fire from virtually every sector. Nobody in his right mind would voluntarily step into that killing ground. Yet that's exactly what was required of the men who would spearhead the push to recover our dead and rescue our team at the mortar pit.

Our right flank would be formed by Stanley and Dulaney, with Dulaney and his SAW on the far end because I wanted the weapon that could inflict the heaviest casualties to shield us, as much as possible, from the Taliban gunners who would be trying to take us down from across the river in Urmul and far up in the Switchbacks. Larson and Raz would take the left flank, while I'd be directly in the center. From there I could serve as command and control, directing our movements while simultaneously communicating with Bundermann back in the command post.

"Redcon One," I radioed to Bundermann, a code that signaled we were ready to launch.

"Roger that," replied Bundermann, who waited until Hill confirmed the same. Then Bundermann called the launch.

"Red—move," he ordered.

"*Go!*" I yelled. And with that, the five of us burst through the west door of the Shura Building and moved out into the killing ground.

THE MOMENT the Taliban realized what we were doing, their gunners opened up and we began taking heavy fire. The first shots came in from Urmul and the Waterfall area. Then all of a sudden, the Switchbacks and the Putting Green kicked in, followed finally by the North Face. Hundreds of bullets ripped up the dirt around our feet while multiple RPGs snaked in, pulling their trails of white smoke behind them and exploding on all sides of us.

The incoming fire was dense and intimidating—but we had the jump on them, and before the enemy gunners could get a solid bead on any of us, we'd sprinted across the open ground and were stacked in a line against the first available cover. Directly to my left was Raz, and beyond him was Larson, who was crouched behind Truck 2 at the far left of our line. Stanley was to my immediate right, and beyond him, Dulaney was butted against the wall of Hescos that made up Keating's outer perimeter. From there, Dulaney was unleashing wicked-sounding bursts from his SAW toward the Switchbacks. Each of us was spaced fifteen meters apart to ensure that an RPG could take out only one of us at a time.

From my position in the center, where I was huddled on the south side of the laundry trailer, I glanced to both sides to confirm that all four of my guys had secured solid cover before keying my radio.

"*Set!*" I yelled—alerting everyone on the combat net we were in position and that Hill's team now had a green light to start their move. Then I glanced directly behind us and spotted something that left me disoriented and confused.

Thirty yards to our rear, Hill was standing in the west door of the Shura Building.

I spun and looked to my left, where a line of six men should have been charging uphill toward the chow hall.

They were nowhere to be seen.

Hill wasn't even remotely close to where he was supposed to be, while the assault that he should have been leading seemed to have disappeared.

What in God's name did he think he was doing?

The moment I raised that question in my mind, I understood that the answer, whatever it might be, simply didn't matter. Perhaps Hill had failed to grasp how this maneuver was supposed to work. Maybe he thought he was doing some good by shooting directly over our heads rather than providing crossfire support, which was what we needed in order to keep moving forward. Or perhaps he was reluctant to order his men into the teeth of the same murderous barrage we had just run through and risk losing all of them now that the Taliban gunners were wise to what we were trying to pull off.

Regardless, it made no difference. The only thing that mattered was that me and my team were on our own with no supporting fire whatsoever, and highly exposed to the enemy's guns from virtually every quadrant.

Right then, the prudent move—indeed, the only option that qualified as a smart play—would have been for us to withdraw. But if we pulled back to the Shura Building, it was unlikely that we could launch out a second time after having telegraphed our move so clearly. Having lost both momentum and surprise, we would have squandered our best chance of retrieving our dead. And that was a price I wasn't willing to pay.

"Hey, we're already committed," I yelled out to the guys on either side of me, while deliberately avoiding any mention of the fact that we had no flank support on our left. "We can't sit here, so we're gonna do this in teams."

Every man knew what this meant: we would split in half and execute the same maneuver that we'd been planning to conduct in tandem with Hill's team, but within a narrower area and without nearly as much protection.

"We gotta push now," I barked, turning back for one last glance at the Shura Building to confirm that Hill and his team weren't moving—and it was then that something caught my eye.

314

Vernon Martin

It was the body of an American soldier, tucked underneath the east side of the laundry trailer.

We'd found our mechanic, Vernon Martin.

DUCKING UNDER THE TRAILER, I could see that Martin was lying on his stomach with his feet facing me. There was no sign of his weapon.

Reaching out with both hands, I grabbed the handle of his body armor, just below the back of his neck, pulled him out, and gave him a once-over. He'd been hit in the leg—probably shrapnel from the RPG that had exploded inside the turret of Gallegos's gun truck—and he had placed a tourniquet over the wound with a strip of olive-colored cloth. That had slowed him down enough to prevent him from covering the final patch of open ground between the laundry trailer and the Shura Building, so he'd crawled underneath the trailer in the hopes of staying hidden. Once there, he'd had nowhere else to go as he succumbed to his wound, dying isolated and alone.

Glancing downhill toward the Shura Building, I keyed my radio, called up Avalos, and told him that he needed to launch out with his body-recovery team to collect Martin.

The job that we'd given Avalos and his helpers, Grissette and Kahn, was both dangerous and exceptionally unpleasant. Thanks to the massive effort that's required to carry a dead body over uneven terrain, they would be forced to leave their weapons behind. What's more, in order to move as fast as possible and hopefully avoid being shot, they also would not be bringing a stretcher with them.

Avalos and Kahn were the first to make the dash up to the laundry trailer. When they arrived, they took hold of Martin and immediately started running downhill as fast as they could, dragging his body through the dirt and rocks. It was an appalling way to treat anyone who had died, much less a person they both had known. But they had no choice—the Taliban gunners fired at them the entire way in the hopes of taking one or both men out.

As they reached the entrance to the Shura Building, they were met by Grissette, who was horrified by what he had just witnessed. As two of the few African-Americans at Keating, Grissette and Martin had been close friends; they'd leaned on each other for support and they'd confided in each other when they needed advice or a sympathetic ear. Now Grissette's buddy was being yanked through the dirt like a tin can tied to the bumper of a car.

"*Man*," he cried out to Avalos in anguish and disgust, "not my *boy*!"

Little did Avalos know that within the next few minutes, he would be treated to the very same horror with a fallen soldier whose friendship and support *he* had known.

WHILE ALL OF THIS was unfolding, I was yelling, "*Go!*" and my five-man squad was making our next push, which would take us uphill another forty yards from the laundry trailer to the latrines, where we would once again have some cover.

Larson and Raz went first, racing madly and followed by Stanley, Dulaney, and me.

When I arrived, Raz was moving toward the door to the latrines while pulling a grenade from his vest pouch.

"Raz," I barked, "please don't frag the shitter!"

He turned around and shot me a look of pure confusion.

"If you throw that grenade in there," I explained, "the explosion's gonna blast through the open space at the bottom of the building and probably kill us all."

"Oh . . . roger that," he said.

"Plus, we're all gonna get covered in shit," I added. "So just enter and clear, okay?"

"Thank God I'm not the one in charge here," he muttered as he stepped up, yanked open the door with his weapon raised—and found himself staring down the barrel and directly into the face of an Afghan man.

It was Ron Jeremy, the interpreter (or "terp," as we called him) who had tried to warn us, just before six a.m., that the Taliban were about to attack. Since then, he had been crouching inside one of the latrine stalls with his legs pulled up to his chest, which is why he could now barely walk.

One way of gauging the intensity of combat—a crude but revealing index of the psychic hold that it can take on those who are swept into its dark energy—is to consider what was going through Raz's head in that instant. A part of his mind, of course, fully recognized Ron: a man whom we all knew and liked, and who had done his best to prevent us from being obliterated. But another part of his mind, the part that was connected to the hand that Raz now had wrapped around the trigger housing of his rifle, registered only one thing: the figure of a man from Afghanistan. And the main thing that Raz wanted to do right then, the *only* thing he wanted to do—was to shoot this fucker in the face and wallpaper the inside of the latrines with his brains.

Part of what made Raz such a superb soldier was that he maintained his violence of action during a firefight by refusing to pause or hesitate. That sort of momentum and focus is essential because sometimes it's the only thing that can propel a man through a set of obstacles and bring him out on the other side. But for reasons that even Raz didn't fully fathom—something that would later leave him puzzled and curious—he *did* hesitate just long enough to allow a mildly disturbing question to break the surface of his thoughts:

This dude standing in front of me is a terp, not a Taliban, so if I shoot him in the head . . . will I get in trouble for that?

Better to ask for permission first.

"Can I shoot him?" he begged me, still glaring down the barrel of the rifle at Ron.

"No, Raz!" I yelled.

"Well, I had to ask." Raz sighed as he lowered his weapon, seized Ron by the shirt, and yanked him outside. "I really, really wanted to."

"We're not allowed to shoot the terp—at least not till we figure out what side he's on," I said, turning to face Ron.

"Where the *fuck* have you come from?!" I demanded.

"I was needing to take a shit at six a.m.," he explained, "and since that time I am hiding inside!"

I paused, thought about that for a second or two, then looked downhill across the open ground toward the Shura Building.

"Well, if you survived this long, I'm pretty sure you can make it back on your own," I told him. "You can't stay here, and you can't come with us. So you know what, Ron? You better start running, and you better *run like hell.*"

Like the porn star who bore his nickname, Ron was short and fat and covered with hair. As he took off at a furious waddle, he looked pretty much exactly like a hedgehog trying to run on its hind legs—a spectacle that caused all of us to start laughing.

We were still cackling, and Ron was still running, when I glanced around me on both sides and realized that we were missing somebody.

"Where the hell's Larson?" I asked.

Everybody shot me a blank look and shook their heads.

"Red Dragon, come in!" I said, keying my radio. "Red Dragon—where are you at?"

No response.

Oh no, I thought to myself, *we just lost our first guy on the assault.*

Furiously scanning the ground around us, I suddenly caught sight of a figure in an American Army uniform crumpled in a ditch about twenty yards away on the south side of the latrines.

He was lying facedown and clearly dead.

"Get your team up here—we've got another body to bring down," I radioed to Avalos. Then I resumed screaming for Larson.

My closest friend was still missing. But we'd found Gallegos.

BACK AT THE SHURA BUILDING, Grissette was still distraught over the savage manner in which Martin's body had been treated. Seeing how upset he was, Avalos didn't think that Grissette was in the right frame of mind to run back through the gunfire and subject Gallegos's body to the same treatment.

"It's just gonna be us," Avalos said, turning to Kahn. "On the count of three, we go. One—two—"

This time, they faced an even longer sprint.

Within the first few yards, Avalos had left Kahn, who was somewhat overweight and out of shape, far behind. By the time Avalos made it to the corner of the latrines, where I pointed him toward Gallegos, he was on his own. (Kahn had been forced to pause and take cover on the north side of the latrines.)

When Avalos reached the body, he realized that Gallegos could not have picked a worse spot to die. Without any assistance, it would be virtually impossible for Avalos to heft the biggest man at Keating to the lip of the ditch. Complicating things still further, one of Gallegos's legs had become wedged between some rocks at the base of the ditch in a manner that would make it even harder to extract him. Finally, the Taliban gunners on the Waterfall area and in the Switchbacks had now caught sight of Avalos and were directing a significant portion of their fire toward him.

Initially, Avalos was so shocked to see Gallegos dead that he barely noted the RPGs and the machine-gun fire because, just like Grissette and Martin, Gallegos and Avalos had some history between them that made

319

this loss personal. As two of the only Hispanic guys at Keating, they shared a powerful bond at the ethnic and cultural level. But their connection went even deeper than that.

Back at Fort Carson when they were first getting to know each other, Gallegos had sort of taken Avalos under his wing in the way that an older brother or a cousin might. In the process, Avalos had seen a different side of the harsh and belligerent badass from Tucson, a side that the rest of us were barely aware of.

The November before we'd deployed to Afghanistan, Gallegos got word that Avalos, who was single, couldn't afford to fly home to California to be with his family during Thanksgiving. So Gallegos had insisted that Avalos join him, his wife, Amanda, and their small son, Mac, at their home in Colorado Springs.

Toward the end of that evening, the family had showed Avalos a Christmas stocking that they'd made for him and were planning to hang above their fireplace. In Avalos's mind, the unspoken message from Gallegos was: *Hey, you don't have to be here for Christmas—but if you don't have anywhere else to go, there's a place for you here, and you will be welcome.*

Since then, they'd been tight enough that Gallegos had shared his feelings about some hard turns that his life had taken, which included a divorce from Amanda and being passed over for a promotion. Avalos had been there to listen, and the trust between the two men had grown even stronger. In fact, only about a week earlier when they were sitting in one of the gun trucks in the middle of the night pulling guard duty, they'd had a conversation about what might happen if Keating was overrun and one of them didn't survive.

For reasons that seemed strange at the time but that now made Avalos wonder if his friend might not have had some sort of weird premonition about what was about to go down, Gallegos had tried to make a joke about how, if he was killed, he'd make absolutely certain that he died in the most difficult place for the rest of the platoon to get to him as a kind of final gesture of defiance. Upon hearing that, Avalos had decided that he didn't find the joke very funny, and he'd resolved to make his friend a promise.

"No matter what happens, I'm gonna be there for you," he pledged. "If I'm alive, regardless of where you're at, I'm going to come get you, and I'm gonna bring you back."

Now, as Avalos recalled those words, he realized that in order to keep his promise he was first going to have to survive by bunkering down and riding things out until the Taliban gunners turned to other targets. Which meant that he was going to have to call upon Gallegos for one last favor—something that neither of them could have anticipated.

Scrunching down on the ground next to his friend, Avalos hoisted Gallegos's body and draped it over himself as a makeshift shield to protect him from the bullets and the jagged pieces of shrapnel that were now caroming off the rocks and drilling into the sides of ditch. It was an ugly thing to do, using your dead friend as body armor. But it was the only option he could think of to stay alive and complete his job.

Several minutes passed before the gunfire seemed to shift away from the ditch. When it did, Avalos shuffled out from beneath Gallegos and cautiously poked his head over the top of the ditch.

About twenty yards to his north he spotted Kahn, and motioned for him to lend a hand. Kahn raced over and jumped into the ditch, and together they were able to hoist Gallegos out. Then both men began dragging Gallegos down toward the Shura Building.

As they disappeared downhill, I was still crouched on the north side of the latrines and continuing, without success, to call out for Larson on the radio.

UNBEKNOWNST TO ME, Larson's final bound had taken him to a point that was just a few yards below the mechanics' bay, where he'd sought cover by ducking inside a connex that we had been planning to use to back-haul equipment to Bostick. As I called for him on my radio, I moved around to the east side of the latrines, which brought this connex into my field of vision and enabled me to look through its doors.

He was crouched inside with his gun in one hand and his radio in the other. From the earnest manner in which he was scanning the North Face while trying to talk into his radio, it was clear that he hadn't considered the possibility that by placing himself inside a steel-sided structure like a connex, he'd cut himself off from all electronic communication.

"Get your ass over here!" I screamed, motioning furiously with my arm.

"What's up?" he asked in confusion when he arrived, still oblivious to fact that his move inside the shipping container had left me convinced that he'd gone off and gotten himself smoked.

"What the *fuck* were you doing over there?" I demanded.

"I was trying to make our linkup with Blue Platoon," he exclaimed. "Where the hell are those guys?"

"Don't worry about them," I replied. "We're kind of on our own right now."

By this point, me, Larson, Raz, Stanley, and Dulaney were tucked behind the north side of the latrines. For the moment, this offered some cover and we felt reasonably secure. But without any support by fire from Blue, we would be horribly exposed—and dangerously far from any assistance—as we tried to cover the final fifty yards of ground leading up to the mortar pit while simultaneously scanning for Hardt. Moreover, if we did find Hardt, it would be impossible for us to provide effective suppressing fire to protect Avalos and his recovery team as they made their way up from the Shura Building for a third time, and then attempted to drag Hardt back.

Knowing that we were stretched too thin and poised on the threshold of overcommitting ourselves, I keyed my radio and called up the mortar pit.

Just before we launched this assault, I'd spoken to Sergeant Breeding for the first time since the attack had kicked off. For the past eight hours, he and his crew had been hunkered down inside their concrete hooch, unable to reach their guns in the pit or even extract the body of Thomson, their slain comrade. During much of that time, they had also been cut off from all communication until Breeding managed to jury-rig an antenna and reestablish a working radio link. When he and I spoke, I'd urged Breeding to hang on because we were on our way, and I'd assured him that when we reached the mortar pit we'd get him, his men, and Thomson's body back down to the center of camp.

Now it was time to have another talk with Big John.

"Look, I got some bad news," I told him. "I'm sorry, brother, but we don't have the manpower to complete this final push. We're not gonna make it to you."

Breeding didn't miss a beat.

"Don't worry about it; you did what you could," he replied evenly. "You do what you gotta do to take care of your team down there, and we'll take care of ourselves up here. We can hang on a bit longer, and if they come for us, we're gonna take a bunch of them out."

Before we signed off, I reminded Breeding that the QRF was already on its way down from Fritsche and that their first stop upon reaching Keating's outer perimeter would be the mortar pit. I also told him that as soon as we got back to the Shura Building, my squad would break a hole in the southwest wall of the building and set up a machine gun to look directly over the top of the pit so that we could waste anyone who even thought about trying to come at him or his guys.

I don't know whether he appreciated those assurances. But as I heard the words coming out of my mouth, I could barely contain my disgust and shame. Earlier that morning, I'd failed to uphold a pledge to a fellow soldier when I'd been forced to retreat from the generator without giving Gallegos the cover fire that I'd promised him. That man's corpse had just been used as a human shield, dragged the length of a football field, and was now lying on the floor of the Shura Building while I fumbled to explain to yet another soldier who needed my help why I was breaking my word.

The whole point of this mission—the thing that had justified the risks we'd taken—was that we were supposed to grab *everybody* and bring them *all* back. Instead, we'd managed to snatch only two bodies while leaving behind a trio of surviving soldiers, plus a third body. On top of that, we still didn't have a clue where the fourth and last body might be.

I suppose I could have laid some of the blame for this on the shoulders of Sergeant Hill. But as I signed off with Breeding and ordered my team to begin displacing back to the Shura Building, the person I was most enraged at was myself.

In war, you play for keeps—and because of that, there are no second chances and no do-overs. The calculus of combat, at its most brutal essence, is binary: you either overcome the hurdles that are flung in front of you and you figure out a way to make things happen, or you don't. It's a zero-sum, win-or-lose game with no middle ground—and no points for trying hard.

The bottom line was that I'd failed. And when me and my team completed our withdrawal and stepped through the Shura Building, the knowledge of that failure added another layer of bitterness to the taste and smell of blood and gunpowder and death that clung to the air within that building.

ONCE WE WERE BACK inside the Shura Building, the first order of business was to break open a portal in the southwest wall and set up a SAW to keep watch over the mortar pit. As soon as that was taken care of, I radioed Breeding to let him know that the gun was in place. Then I made another dash back to the command post to let Bundermann know where things stood.

At this point, my main concern was the lingering question of what had happened to Hardt. After filling in Bundermann on where we'd searched and how much terrain we'd covered before falling back, I laid out what I thought we should do next.

"My guess is that there's an eighty-percent probability that his body is no longer on station, but we need to be sure," I said. "I want to put together one more recon push."

"No way," he replied, shaking his head. "We've pushed our luck out a little bit too far already."

With that, Bundermann ordered me to get back to the Shura Building, make sure that the front gate was fully reinforced with concertina wire, and sit tight until the rescue team arrived from Fritsche. When they got down the mountain, he said, we could resume the search for Hardt.

It was a solid decision and probably the right one. But when I returned to the Shura Building, I wasn't able to shake the feeling that there was something terribly wrong about the fact that we still didn't have everyone accounted for. It was right about then that Larson buttonholed me with a request. He wanted to conduct a solo reconnaissance run to look for Hardt one last time, and he needed me to give the nod.

My first reaction was that this was a lousy idea. I was okay with sending out a squad of men who could support one another. But one guy all by himself? That sounded ludicrous.

Larson, however, had no interest in taking no for an answer. Hardt, he pointed out, was not only one of our own platoon—a compelling reason by itself—but he'd been lost while trying to rescue fellow members of Red, including Larson himself. Plus, there was the fact that Larson had been training up Hardt in the same way that I had once trained up Larson: by taking him under his wing and teaching him not only how to perform, but also how to think. Which meant that Larson had some insight into what was probably going through Hardt's mind during his final moments: where he was trying to get to, how he intended to do that—and therefore, where he might now be.

On and on Larson went, relentlessly trotting out one point after another until finally (and ironically) he'd worn me down in much the same way that Hardt had done a few hours earlier when I'd reluctantly green-lighted the rescue mission that had cost him his life—and thereby set up the argument that Larson and me were having right now.

"All right, you can go," I conceded. "But you need to make sure you get light—and you need to *hustle*."

With that, he started stripping off all of his gear: weapons, ammo, rack, body armor, anything that might slow him down. When he was down to his T-shirt, pants, and boots, he stepped to the side of the door, waited a few seconds for the fire to abate, and broke west.

This wasn't a dash-and-pause sort of venture but a full-on, all-out, heels-on-fire sprint in a massive loop that would take him all the way from the front gate to the laundry trailer, the latrines, and Gallegos's gun truck before he cut east toward the mechanics' bay, then headed back past the shower trailers and the piss tubes to finish of by darting through the east door of the Shura Building.

The assumption behind this planned route was that when Hardt had fled his immobilized gun truck, he was almost certainly headed toward the toolshed and the chow hall. If that was the case—and if Hardt's body hadn't yet been snatched away by the enemy, he was now probably some-where west of the mechanics' bay.

Larson started taking fire the second he hit the ground. But just like in those football games back in Iraq and at Fort Carson, he was unbelievably fast. So fast that the gunners who were trying to hit him never got him locked in their sights and thus never even came close to anticipating the way he cut and swerved and dodged.

He was lost from our sight the moment he passed the shower trailer, and from there we had no idea how he was faring. But three minutes later, he appeared around the defunct Afghan Army mortar pit and whipped back to us as bullets lamely kicked up dust several yards behind him.

When he came through the door, he fell to his knees, gasping for breath, and shook his head in answer to the unspoken question of whether he'd caught sight of Hardt.

Nothing.

Staring out toward the front gate and the river beyond, I shook my head in frustration. It was as if Hardt had vanished into thin air. Or, much more likely, the Taliban had swooped in, scooped him up, and were now spiriting his body into the hills. That prospect was horrifying enough that once he caught his breath, Larson started campaigning for permission to conduct a *second* run and do the whole thing all over again, but cutting an even wider circuit—and exposing himself to even more danger—on the slim chance that maybe Hardt was still out there somewhere.

"No way," I said, and this time there would be no arguing.

Among the many low points we experienced that day, this was surely one of the lowest. After all the effort we'd expended and the risks we'd taken, Hardt was still missing, and Breeding and his team were still trapped at the mortar pit.

Meanwhile, one hundred yards to the east of the Shura Building, a separate struggle was still being fought as Keating's medics desperately battled to save the life of a gravely wounded Stephan Mace before the wild-fire that had already consumed the entire eastern half of the outpost spread to the aid station itself, and burned the thing to the ground.

CHAPTER TWENTY-TWO

Conflagration

NOWADAYS, WHEN I cast my mind back to the Battle for Keating, I find myself increasingly convinced that the drive to save Mace, a campaign that was fought against almost insurmountable odds, amounted to a kind of separate and miniature war of its own—a small battle that unfolded inside the frame of a larger one and, by dint of how hard it was fought and how much Mace meant to all of us, would color the feelings of everyone who was there that day and survived.

More than anything else that took place inside that miserable outpost, the story of what happened to Mace would come to define our understanding of whether we lost, whether we won, or whether the final outcome fell through some weird crack leading to a dark space that partook of both victory and defeat while amounting, in the end, to neither.

Earlier that afternoon when word had first reached the aid station that Mace was still alive, Doc Chris Cordova and his trio of medics—Shane Courville, Cody Floyd, and Jeff Hobbs—were still dealing with multiple casualties, the most urgent of which was the Afghan National Army soldier we called RPG Guy, who had just been brought in with a severe gunshot wound to his left leg that had severed an artery. Floyd was applying a tourniquet to stop the bleeding when the news arrived over the radio that every gun inside Keating needed to go on target so that Mace could be run down to the aid station.

To prepare for Mace's arrival, the medics immediately started moving some of the wounded outside to the protected space in the café area. Then everyone hunkered down and braced themselves as the ordnance from Justin Kulish's B-1 bomber began striking the Putting Green.

To the men inside the aid station, the impact of that air strike was every bit as dramatic as it was within the Shura Building or the mortar pit. As the thunderous concussions reverberated across the battle space, the shock waves shook the walls of the building violently enough to rattle medical supplies off the shelves and even knock down the picture of the Hooters chick—although the Ziploc bag containing the Russian tennis star's perfumed panties remained fixed to the west wall.

Shortly thereafter, Larson and Carter whooshed through the door bearing the stretcher with Mace on board. No sooner were they inside than the medics took over. They placed him on the table and all four of them got to work.

As Floyd started cutting off Mace's clothes and exposing his injuries, they got their first glimpse of what they were up against. The penetrating shrapnel wounds to his abdomen and his right torso had not only torn apart a portion of his bowel and his right adrenal gland but had also shattered his pelvis. He had nine pieces of shrapnel in his lower back, and another nine had lodged themselves in his hip, buttocks, and thigh. Thanks to the gunshot wound in his left leg, he had compound fractures of his tibia and fibula. There were multiple lacerations to his legs and arms, and his right ankle was attached to his leg by only a small piece of tissue. He was barely conscious, and thanks to the amount of blood he'd lost, there was no distal pulse in either his upper or lower extremities.

In short, he was a mess.

When they finished removing his clothes, Floyd put a new tourniquet on his leg while Hobbs replaced the stick that Carter had placed on his ankle with a plastic splint.

Meanwhile, Cordova and Courville were focused on the formidable challenge of getting a line into one of Mace's veins so that they could start pushing fluids and medication into him. Unable to raise a vein in his arms or legs, they tried his hip and then went for his neck. When even that failed, they opted for a FAST1, the same flashlight-shaped, multineedled device that they had used hours earlier on Kirk, and drove it into his sternum.

That line held up long enough for them to run almost an entire bag of Hextend into him, which would help expand the volume of plasma in his bloodstream. But just as the bag ran dry and they were preparing to put in another, the FAST1 line failed, forcing them to resume the search for a vein. Their luck was no better than the first time, so now they switched to a spiral-shaped needle that corkscrews into a patient's bone marrow, inserting it just below the knee on his right leg.

Unfortunately, this second line permitted only a slow drip. If they were to have any hope of stabilizing Mace, they'd need to do more. But just outside the walls of the aid station, another problem had reared its head— one that might force them, at the worst possible time, to move their patient to another location.

The aid station was about to catch fire.

FOR THE PAST several hours, the intensity and danger of the fire that had started on the eastern side of camp inside the Afghan National Army compound had swung back and forth. A midmorning effort to stem the advance of the blaze by several members of Blue Platoon had had little effect. By eleven thirty a.m., the fire was generating enough heat within the ANA compound that the ammunition that the Afghan soldiers had abandoned in their barracks buildings was cooking off and exploding. Soon the flames were spreading into the American sector, first to Headquarters barracks and then to Blue Platoon's barracks. But shortly after noon, as the frontal system that had delayed the rescue helicopters at Bostick reached the skies over Keating, it looked as if a light rain might help extinguish some of the flames.

Within the hour, it was clear that this wasn't going to happen. By two p.m., the flames that were consuming Blue Platoon's barracks were generating so much smoke that Koppes, whose gun truck was stationed just outside the northern wall of the barracks, could barely see or breathe. As Stanley dashed out to the Humvee, started the engine, and moved it twenty feet to the west, the chow hall and the supply room were engulfed in fire and the flames began chewing their way across the camo netting above the alley separating Blue barracks from the command post.

When the command post started filling with smoke, First Sergeant Burton ordered everyone inside to prepare to evacuate. With the electricity still down there was no point in bringing the computers, so the command team simply snatched up all of the maps, along with any radios that were still running on battery power. Then they jumped buildings and set up a new command post in Red Platoon's barracks, where they resumed calling in air strikes and coordinating with the rescue team that was making its way down the mountain from Fritsche.

When word reached the medics that the command post was going up in flames, Courville stepped outside the aid station to gauge how much danger they were in. He was shocked not only by the proximity of the fire but also by the heat that it was giving off. He noted that the flames had leaped onto a new section of camo netting, which connected the command post to the aid station.

"It's gonna spread," he muttered to himself as he pulled out his pocket-knife and slashed at the netting to cut it away. While he was completing that task, Burton approached with some disturbing news.

"If we need to, we're gonna have to push all of you guys up to the mortar pit," said Burton. "Stand by."

This made absolutely no sense to Courville. Why in the world would they try to move their patients to a section of the outpost that was still cut off by enemy gunfire? Moreover, it would be terrible for Mace.

Man, the last thing we need to do right now is to move Mace anywhere, he thought to himself as he dashed back inside.

By this point, Doc Cordova had already ordered a partial evacuation of the aid station. While all the ambulatory Afghan patients were told to start moving toward the Shura Building, litter teams were now on standby to shuttle three gravely injured patients who were unable to move under their own steam. Meanwhile, Floyd was packing supplies they would need to take with them.

In Courville's mind, there had to be a better solution.

Ducking back outside to see if he could come up with a plan, he noticed that the primary threat to the aid station was a tall pine tree adjacent to the command post that was burning furiously. Within a few minutes, it would enable the fire to jump to the aid station.

He also noticed that there was a small orange-and-white chain saw sitting nearby.

"Hey," Courville called out, turning to Ty Carter, who had done some work felling trees before he joined the military. "Can you cut down that tree with this chain saw?"

"Yes," replied Carter.

"Do it," said Courville.

With that, Carter got to work, making a series of wedge-shaped cuts along the base of the trunk in the hope that they would induce the tree to fall toward Blue Platoon's barracks and away from the command post. As the saw chewed through the wood, burning embers from the branches overhead rained down on his head and back, interfering with his concentration. It also didn't help that he was exposed to enemy fire from the North Face.

In the end, Carter miscalculated badly enough that when he finished his final cut and stepped back, the tree toppled in the opposite direction from what he was intending, falling across the alley on the west side of Red barracks and clipping the roof of the abandoned command post. In the process, the branches swept across a trench that ran just outside the southwest corner of Red barracks, nearly killing Justin Gregory and Nicholas Davidson, who were posted inside it with a machine gun.

As Gregory and Davidson stumbled from under the burning branches looking like a pair of pack rats caught in a brush fire, Carter took stock of what he'd done. The tree hadn't landed anywhere close to where it was supposed to. But it was far enough away from the aid station that it could no longer serve as a bridge for the flames.

Mission accomplished, more or less.

By now it was three thirty p.m. and the command team inside Red barracks was letting our superiors at Bostick know that with most of Keating on fire, the entire troop was holed up in the last three hard-walled build-ings in the center of camp.

One of these buildings was the aid station, which Carter's cockeyed lumberjack move had saved, and inside of which Doc Cordova and his team had resumed working on their most critical patient, whose condition wasn't looking good.

During the mad scramble to contain the fire, Mace had taken a sharp turn for the worse.

IT WAS AFTER FOUR P.M. when Cordova noted that, despite everything they'd tried so far, Mace seemed to be sliding downhill. His vitals had not improved, and his mental status was diminishing. All signs pointed toward one fact: if Mace was to have any chance of surviving, he would have to be evacuated to Bostick, where there was an advanced field-trauma center.

With that in mind, Cordova sent Courville over to the new command post to press Bundermann on when he thought a medevac would be able to fly into Keating's landing zone.

"Bro, how long before we can get a bird?" asked Courville.

"It's not gonna happen until after the relief force gets down," replied Bundermann, referring to Justin Sax's rescue unit, which was still making its descent from Fritsche. "Plan on sometime after dark."

Translation: Mace wasn't going anywhere until at least seven p.m.

"How much longer has he got?" asked Bundermann.

"Right now, probably two hours at the most," said Courville as he headed back to the aid station to give Cordova the bad news.

The challenge before Cordova and his team was to figure out how to take the amount of time Mace had left, and double it.

Right then, Cordova knew, Mace's most critical need was blood. He'd already lost a horrific amount of it, and he needed the oxygen-carrying red blood cells, along with their clotting agents, that weren't being supplied by the fluids and the Hextend that they'd injected into his system.

Fresh blood typically is not stored in aid stations at remote combat outposts like Keating, mainly because there's no way to keep it refrigerated without a steady supply of electricity. But Cordova knew that there was one other source he might be able to tap.

Although it's highly unorthodox and less than ideal, direct blood transfusions from one soldier to another have been done on the battlefield since before the Second World War. Cordova had never attempted such a thing himself, but he'd been trained on how to do it. What's more, the unit that had been stationed at Keating prior to our arrival had left behind a "buddy-to-buddy" transfusion kit.

"Say, what'd we do with that blood kit?" Cordova asked Courville.

"We threw it away yesterday when we were cleaning out the aid station," replied Courville—yet another reminder that the preparations to shut down Keating had robbed them of critical supplies precisely when they were most needed.

Cordova swore.

"But wait a second," Courville exclaimed. "Yesterday was Thursday, right?"

"Yup."

"So that means today is Friday!"

"Uh, yeah . . ." replied Cordova, staring in confusion as Courville disappeared out the door.

Because Friday is the Muslim day of prayer, the local laborers at Keating weren't scheduled to collect the trash and take it up to the burn pit for another twenty four hours—which meant that the garbage bag into which the blood kit had been discarded was almost certainly sitting just beyond the door on the west side of the aid station.

A few seconds later, Courville was back inside with the trash bag and dumping it out onto the floor.

No blood kit.

Undeterred, he ran back and grabbed another bag. This time the kit tumbled out.

Now they confronted another hurdle: what the hell was Mace's blood type? His dog tags, which displayed the information, didn't seem to be around his neck.

333

After several anxious moments of rummaging through what was left of Mace's clothing, Floyd managed to find the tags inside one of his pockets.

Type A positive.

A quick survey of the aid station revealed three people with the same blood type: Floyd himself, plus Hobbs and Cordova.

They assembled the transfusion kit while simultaneously drawing a unit of blood from Floyd, and then they attempted to shunt Floyd's blood into Mace using the line that they'd already placed in his right leg with the corkscrew-shaped needle. By this point, however, the flow through that line was far too slow. So they hooked up a power infuser to the blood bag, hoping it would help push the fluid through at a faster rate. When that failed to make a difference, there was yet another problem to solve.

"We need to get a better fucking line into him," said Courville.

Courville looked everywhere for a vein he could tap, finding nothing. Then, by some miracle, he spotted a promising spot in Mace's arm and got a needle in. Ecstatic, he ran some normal saline through the line to ensure that they had good flow. But just as they were switching from the saline bag to the blood bag, Mace, who had been moving in and out of consciousness, jerked his arm and yanked out the IV.

Cursing in frustration, the whole team started looking for a new site for the IV.

After several difficult minutes, Hobbs found the solution by getting a needle directly into Mace's external jugular vein. And with that, Floyd's blood finally began passing into his body.

The effect was remarkable.

Even before the first bag was empty, Mace's vitals were looking better and his mental status had improved. He began making jokes and grousing about the pain in his shattered left leg. He also returned to the subject that he'd been fixated on back when he, Larson, and Carter were trapped in the gun truck.

"Dude," he said to Courville, "can I get a smoke?"

"No worries," replied Courville. "As soon as we get you out of here and you're through surgery, we'll get you set up."

"C'mon, man," Mace pleaded. "Just *one* cigarette . . . *please*?"

There was no way in hell the medics were going to thin his blood with nicotine in the middle of a transfusion. But they were absolutely thrilled that Mace was pestering them—although within a few minutes of the first bag finishing off, he again started to fade.

Time for another bag of blood.

Hobbs sat down and let Cordova take a unit from his arm. Then the same procedure was performed on Cordova, the last man in the aid station with A-positive blood.

With each additional unit that he received, Mace would revive briefly, then start to fade as soon as the bag had drained. He never gave up on his jokes—he declared he was worried about being less of a man after having received blood from Floyd (who was often teased for being skinny and frail-looking). And he badgered anyone who would listen to give him a cigarette. The skin on his face, however, was whiter than a blank sheet of paper.

To the medics it felt like Mace—and they with him—were oscillating back and forth like the pendulum on a slow-moving clock, swinging toward life and then back toward death on a twenty-five-minute cycle. The only thing that seemed certain was that Mace didn't have much time left. They *had* to get him on a chopper and out of Keating soon.

As the third bag was being administered, Courville dashed over to the command post to get a list of all the other soldiers at Keating who had A-positive blood. One of the names on that list was Bundermann's, so Courville immediately sat him down and shoved a needle in his arm.

It was 6:38 p.m. and Bundermann's blood was just starting to draw when some news arrived from the rescue team.

They'd run up against a few delays, but they'd sorted them out and made good time.

They were nearly there.

WHEN CAPTAIN JUSTIN SAX'S quick-reaction force had departed from Fritsche at two p.m., he and his men anticipated that it would take about four hours for them to reach Keating, partly because Sax decided that for the upper part of the journey they would avoid the existing trail and bushwhack. (This would slow them down, but it would also make it harder for the enemy to set up an ambush.)

As they launched out, the big question on everyone's mind was whether they would encounter resistance along the way. If so, their plan was to do whatever was necessary to overcome that opposition and keep moving down the mountain, but it would take even longer for them to reach Keating.

Just before they left, several of the aircraft circling above were called in to conduct air strikes in the hope that saturating the terrain with bombs and gunfire would help clear out any enemy and disrupt whatever plans they might be trying to put in place. The Apaches unloaded a slew of white phosphorus rockets to mark the area, at which point the A-10s conducted multiple gun runs across the southern mountain wall. After that, the Apaches returned to unload a bunch of their high-explosive rockets and flechettes, and then for good measure they took a few passes with their 30-mm chain guns.

As Sax and his team descended the ridge where Fritsche was perched, it wasn't long before they encountered evidence of these air strikes. Trees has been riddled with shrapnel or splintered to pieces by the bombs and the gunfire. There were also large, open areas where the vegetation had either already been reduced to ash by the white phosphorus or was still burning.

Progress was slow because the terrain was so steep. The intermittent rain didn't help either—the ground was rapidly turning slippery. But they pressed on, moving as quickly as possible while keeping a close eye for any signs of an ambush. Shortly after the halfway point, they were skirting around the edge of a piece of open ground when one of Sax's men, Specialist Kyle Barnes, spotted two Taliban crouched behind some rocks.

One of the insurgents, who was holding a radio, had been severely wounded—most of the flesh had been stripped from his right leg—and was in the process of bleeding to death. The second insurgent died when Barnes emptied his 9-mm pistol into the man's chest.

Both of the Taliban were well equipped—between the two of them they had an RPG launcher, two assault rifles, chest racks with magazines, and several grenades. Sax's men gathered up everything they had, and resumed moving.

Within another hour, they'd reached the top of the Switchbacks, where they started encountering dead insurgents in large numbers—pockets of five or six men at a time, eventually totaling somewhere between fifty and a hundred.

Here too they got their first glimpse of Keating, although the lower part of the mountain they were descending was obscured by the smoke and haze from the outpost's still-burning buildings. At this point, Sax split his team in two: one rifle squad was ordered to keep watch at the top while the second proceeded the rest of the way. As the lead squad continued down, the men who were staying behind to perform overwatch were able to pick up the radio traffic inside Keating, including a call from Doc Cordova:

"Anybody else got A-positive blood, I need to know," announced Cordova. "Come to the aid station if you do."

It was shortly after dusk when the lead squad rounded the final switchback and came around the back side of the mortar pit, where Breeding and his men were waiting for them, having wrapped the body of Kevin Thomson in their poncho liners and placed him on a litter. Then everyone descended the ammo-can staircase and stepped into Keating proper.

While Breeding and his team continued on to the aid station with Thompson, Sax's squad gathered by the mechanics' bay to meet with Eric Harder and work out how we would hand over our defensive positions to Sax's team. That's when Harder, in the gathering darkness, tripped over something on the ground and stepped closer to investigate.

It was the body of Josh Hardt, lying facedown in the dirt next to the massive boulder where Truck 1 had sat before he'd climbed into the thing and launched his rescue bid.

He had come full circle and arrived back at almost exactly the same spot from which he'd started his mission to save his comrades who were trapped in LRAS2.

With the discovery of Hardt's body, another circle was also complete. It was just before eight p.m., and for the first time in the fourteen hours that had passed since the attack began, we finally had full accountability on all of Keating's soldiers: who was dead, who was alive, and where everyone was at.

As they gathered up Hardt and prepared to take him down to the aid station to join his six fallen brethren, I found myself wishing that I could head up to the mechanics' bay to pay my final respects.

Unfortunately, that wasn't going to be possible, because I had just been given the order to move out across the concrete bridge spanning the Darreh-ye Kushtāz River and secure the landing zone so that we could get Mace on his way to a proper medical facility before we lost him too.

INSIDE THE AID STATION, Mace, who was lying on the table under a blanket while the transfusion line continued feeding the blood of his comrades into his neck, was showered with so much attention that it seemed as if he'd become something of a celebrity. The medics were monitoring his condition continuously: every five minutes Floyd took his vitals and never left the patient's side unless another medic was standing by. Meanwhile, any soldier whose business took him anywhere near the aid station made a point of popping through the door to say hi, ask how Mace felt, and tell him what a total badass he was.

One of those well-wishers was Raz, who swung by to find out if Doc Cordova was still looking for A-positive blood and, if so, to donate some of his own. Cordova, who was standing right outside, told him they were doing good on blood—they'd just pulled a pint out of Bundermann, and the medevac would be on its way soon.

"How's he doing?" asked Raz.

"He's doing good, man," replied Cordova brightly. "Go in there and talk to him—he wants to hear from you guys."

By now they'd started getting some morphine into him too, so Mace was feeling pretty dopey. He also had an oxygen mask over his face, which made his voice sound hollow and faraway. But despite that, and despite the horrific wounds that Raz knew were underneath the blanket, it was the same old Mace.

"Hey, dude?" Mace said weakly. "Any chance you got a cigarette on you?"

Raz was pretty sure that was the last thing Mace needed right now, so he shook his head and moved on to other topics: the lame bantering that soldiers trade among one another when the air between them is filled with things that are too serious and too heavy for anything else.

Raz knew that as soon as the medevac arrived, Mace would be whisked off on the first leg in a series of flights that would take him through trauma centers and hospitals at Bostick, then Bagram, followed by a stop off in Germany before his final destination, which would almost certainly be Walter Reed in Bethesda, just outside of Washington, DC. Raz also knew that it would be a long time before they saw each other again—assuming, of course, that Raz managed to survive the remaining eight months of the deployment without getting killed. And he knew that, thanks to the extent of Mace's injuries and the many obstacles on the long road of recovery that lay ahead—the pain and the surgeries, the physical therapy and the psychological challenges—Mace might not be quite the same person he had been when they met again.

But one could always hope.

"Hey, good luck, man," said Raz as word arrived that the chopper was inbound. It was time to start getting the patient prepped for his flight and moved out to the landing zone. "Take it easy, and I'll see you down the road."

"All right, dude," replied Mace, clasping his hand. "I'm gonna miss your saggy balls."

Always the jokester, Raz thought to himself as he walked out, shaking his head. *He's sort of right about my balls, though. They do kinda sag more than they should.*

THE HELICOPTER that was tasked to extract Mace was a UH-60 Black Hawk whose pilot, Carlos Hernandez, had served as a tank gunner before earning his wings with army airborne. Hernandez and his crew had been champing at the bit since word of the attack had first reached Jalalabad, where they were based, early that morning just after sunrise. The bird had launched immediately and made a beeline for Bostick, where Hernandez picked up a handful of soldiers including Stoney Portis, our stranded commander, who was desperate to get to Keating. But shortly after getting airborne again, he was denied permission to land at Keating and ordered to return to Bostick, where he and his crew sat on the helipad with the rotors spinning, waiting for clearance.

While they waited they'd anxiously monitored the radio traffic as Doc Cordova called in one casualty report after another and submitted repeated requests for a medevac. Five or six times Hernandez received clearance, only to subsequently be ordered to shut down because the landing zone at Keating was taking too much fire or, later in the morning, because the Apaches were getting hit by *dishka* fire.

Captain Brendan McCriskin, the flight surgeon on the medevac, was so infuriated by these repeated delays that at one point during the day he was on the verge of storming into the command post and pushing for clearance. McCriskin had backed away from that impulse only after speaking with his friend Ross Lewallen and learning that the Apache pilots were fully expecting to be shot out of the air each time they returned to Keating on their next sortie.

Finally, after many hours on edge, the medevac received approval to launch and Hernandez got in the air, flying under night-vision capability, with two Apache gunships escorting them in.

As they raced toward the outpost, McCriskin and his medic scrambled to set up IVs and get their equipment in order. Meanwhile, down on the ground at Keating, me and five other men, including Larson, moved through the front gate, sprinted across the concrete bridge over the river, and secured the landing zone.

Hernandez pushed his Black Hawk as fast it would go, but as he neared the battle space he was ordered to hover at ten thousand feet while the Apaches swept in to confirm that the area was clear. Then Hernandez took them down, corkscrew fashion, while peering through the haze that the smoke from the fires created on his night-vision goggles.

By now, Mace, who had been wrapped up with a hypothermia kit to keep him warm, had been moved on a litter to the Shura Building and then across the bridge to the LZ. The final bag of fresh blood, Bundermann's, rode alongside him on the litter. Directly behind him were two other litters with the most gravely wounded of the Afghan soldiers.

The medevac touched down at 8:07, and Hernandez kept the blades turning while the chopper was loaded. He was on the ground for less than four minutes as the litter teams carried the patients down a steep incline at the edge of the landing zone and placed them on board. Then Hernandez lifted off, put the hammer down, and started hauling ass toward Bostick.

As we watched them go, our sense of relief at seeing Mace finally get on his way was mixed with something else—something that didn't quite feel like victory, but was perhaps the next best thing in line.

We'd lost seven men that day, not one of whom we'd had a prayer of saving. But Mace was different. We'd been allowed a small measure of control over what happened to him, and we'd used that in some extraordinary ways. Out of thin air we'd somehow managed to conjure a series of miracles that had involved plucking Mace from the battlefield, running him through a hail of gunfire, and perhaps most improbable of all, keeping him alive with our own blood using a tool that we'd retrieved from the trash. And despite the horrific odds that had been stacked against him surviving any one of those stages, much less all of them, he was in good hands now, with an excellent chance of making it.

If Mace managed to pull through, his survival wouldn't make up for having lost those seven men whose bodies were now awaiting transport out of Keating on the next set of choppers. But that loss was certainly colored and, to a certain extent, counterweighted by the fact that more than half of those men had perished while trying to save Mace, while the rest of them had given their lives to the larger defense of Keating and their fellow soldiers, Mace included.

It was 8:11 when the Black Hawk lifted into a night sky filled with the smell of burning pine pitch and smoke wafting through the moonlight. Mace's life wasn't worth more than the men who died. But saving Mace helped to anchor their deaths with meaning and context in a way that mattered hugely.

• • •

IT'S ALMOST IMPOSSIBLE to overstate the difficulty of trying to provide trauma care to a gravely wounded soldier from the inside of a roaring Black Hawk when it's pitch-dark. Nine months earlier, when McCriskin had arrived in Afghanistan and started flying missions as a flight surgeon, he'd assumed that this would be the most challenging environment he could imagine in which to practice medicine. What he'd discovered since then was that actually doing it was ten times harder than anything he'd conceived in his mind.

Perhaps the biggest difficulty was simply seeing your patient and trying to figure out what he might need in order for you to keep him from dying before the chopper reached its destination. You were wearing your helmet and your night-vision goggles, plus almost fifty pounds of gear and protective clothing. You were maneuvering within an impossibly cramped space with only inches to spare as the helicopter threw itself through viciously tight turns and banks to avoid fire from the ground. Thanks to all the vibration and noise, it was almost impossible to feel your patient's pulse, you couldn't listen to his lungs, and you could barely hear what he was saying.

McCriskin called this "sensory-deprived medicine," and one of its most important tools, he'd found, was his pen light, which he gripped between his teeth and which provided a dime-sized speck of illumination that offered just enough light to assess Mace.

McCriskin could see that Doc Cordova had done a stellar job of keeping his patient alive, and there wasn't much in the way of additional service which he could now perform. Mace had a good IV line running through his neck, and three good tourniquets in place on his legs. He was getting oxygen, and the wounds in his belly were dressed. All McCriskin could really do as he crouched above Mace's head in the dark was to hook him up to a cardiac monitor, replace his IV bags—which were nearly empty—and check his tourniquets to make sure they were secure.

The one additional thing he was able to do was to talk with his patient. Mace was in the late stages of severe hemorrhagic shock from the amount of blood that he'd lost. While his heart was racing, his blood pressure was as low as McCriskin had ever seen in a person who was still alive. Nevertheless, Mace was conscious throughout the brief flight, and he was alert enough that he was able to pepper McCriskin with questions. He wasn't concerned about himself—his wounds, his prognosis, or what would happen to him when they reached Bostick. The only thing he wanted to know was how we, his friends back at Keating, were doing—and if we were okay.

When McCriskin assured him that we were all fine, Mace looked up at him with relief, and then offered a brief sitrep on himself.

"I'm not in any pain, Doc," he reported. "I'm not in any pain."

At 8:21, barely ten minutes after they'd left Keating, the Black Hawk touched down on the helipad at Bostick and the medical team flipped into overdrive.

The trauma crew who grabbed Mace off the helicopter were so eager to get him into the aid station that they almost dropped his stretcher right there on the tarmac. Within sixty seconds, they had him inside the trauma tent and undergoing an initial evaluation by a nurse and his surgeon, Major Brad Zagol, who made the call to wheel him into surgery immediately.

Within another two minutes McCriskin, who had trundled behind Mace at every stage, was helping to get him intubated and under anesthesia while the surgical team prepared to operate.

Just before Mace went under, he seemed to experience one last period of lucidity and had a brief chat with McCriskin. Again, he wanted to confirm that the guys back at Keating were okay. When McCriskin assured him that we were doing great and mostly just worrying about him, Mace smiled and asked McCriskin to let us all know that he was doing fine.

"I'm almost done over here—my tour's almost over and I'm going home soon," said McCriskin. "You wanna meet up when we get back to the States? I'll buy you a beer."

Mace said that he would.

"What kind of beer do you like?" asked McCriskin.

"Coors Light," replied Mace, somewhat sheepishly, and closed his eyes as the anesthesia pulled him under.

CHAPTER TWENTY-THREE

Farewell to Keating

ODD AS IT MAY SOUND, one of the few members of Red Platoon who hadn't made a specific point of dropping by the aid station before Mace departed from Keating in order to shake his hand and wish him luck was his very best friend. That's the exact opposite of what you might expect. But as it turned out, there was some sound reasoning behind it.

At 7:39 p.m., a solid half hour before Mace's medevac arrived, Zach Koppes was finally relieved of his duty on the Mark 19 grenade launcher. At that point, he'd been standing inside the turret of LRAS1 almost continuously for more than thirteen hours. During that time, he'd been carefully monitoring the reports on Mace through his radio, so when he finally stepped down from his gun truck, he knew that the picture was looking pretty good. Good enough, in fact, that Koppes started having second thoughts about heading over to check in and say farewell.

He wanted to, of course. But the more he thought about it, the more worried he became about the possibility that if he enacted some sort of good-bye ritual, he might wind up jinxing Mace's chances. Plus, they would certainly see each other again—maybe even at Bostick, if Mace's surgery went well enough that they decided to keep him there for a bit before sending him on to Bagram.

So in the end, Koppes decided that the best thing for him to do was to avoid counterweighting Mace's luck and his karma with any action that might suggest, however faintly, that he and his friend wouldn't be meeting up, and soon. Instead, Koppes decided to focus on doing the one thing that, in his estimation, Mace would value more than having yet another dude drop by to ask how he was feeling, which was to gather up the personal effects that meant the most to him—his laptop, his iPod, his uniforms, and his pictures of his family—and make sure that all that stuff got onto the medevac so that it traveled with Mace, wherever he might be headed.

With that in mind, the first place that Koppes headed after he climbed down from his gun truck was over to Red barracks, where he dropped by Mace's hooch, grabbed his backpack, and started stuffing items into it. When he was through, he handed everything off to First Sergeant Burton— and it was then that he discovered that although he'd been relieved of his position on the LRAS1, his duties were far from finished.

"Okay," Burton said to Koppes and Chris Jones, who was standing nearby, "let's get our heroes outta here."

The task that Jones and Koppes were being handed would involve hauling the bodies of the slain Americans out to the landing zone and getting them ready to be loaded onto a series of helicopters that would be arriving to take them to Bostick shortly after Mace's helevac departed.

By this point, Doc Cordova had formally pronounced death on all seven men, and his medics had packaged their bodies for transport by placing five of them in body bags and wrapping the remaining two, Thomson and Hardt, in plastic poncho liners because they didn't have enough bags on hand to accommodate them. The corpses had then been shuttled from the aid station to the Shura Building by members of Blue Platoon. It would be up to Koppes and Jones, together with a few guys from Justin Sax's rescue unit, to carry them the rest of the way out to the landing zone.

When they got to the Shura Building, Koppes and Jones found the bodies piled alongside one wall. There was no way of telling who was who except for Thomson, who was so tall that his boots stuck out from the end the plastic wrapping. They also found something else: a large puddle of blood on the plywood floor, onto which an Afghan soldier was in the process of pouring fistfuls of dirt in an attempt to absorb it. Assuming that the blood belonged to Kirk, Jones suddenly felt himself overcome by a wild and implacable sense of fury.

"Fuck *you!*" he screamed at the bewildered Afghan soldier. "Don't put that dirty fucking *dirt* on that man's fucking blood, you motherfucking *fuck*. Clean that up now or I will fucking *kill* you!"

While the Afghan prudently withdrew, Jones blinked a few times and took a deep breath, stunned by the heat of his own rage.

Then he and Koppes got to work.

Like the men whose bodies they were carrying through this final stage of their time at Keating, each trip from the Shura Building through the front gate and across the bridge over the river was different. Gallegos was so heavy that Jones, whose back was injured, had to strain himself to avoid letting the body bag drag over the rocks. Hardt was wrapped loosely enough that the prop wash from one of the helicopters peeled back the plastic and exposed his face. And Kirk was so cumbersome that one of Sax's soldiers who was trying to lend a hand lost his grip as they were placing him on board and dropped one end—a mistake that so enraged Raz, who was also there to help with the loading, that he threatened to punch the guy in the face.

The helicopters touched down and took off in a line. The first two removed our dead and our walking wounded. Then came the Afghan wounded and the Afghan dead. Each aircraft also dropped off a consignment of supplies—gear, water, ammo, fuel, and batteries—before taking on its load of passengers.

This continuous shuttle of supplies in one direction and bodies—dead and wounded alike—in the other was confusing and exhausting for Jones and Koppes. It also made for some surreal moments, perhaps the strangest of which occurred when they looked out at the landing zone just after one of the helicopters had taken off and realized that there was a body bag sitting in the middle of it. Appalled by the possibility that one of his fellow soldiers had been left behind or, far worse, had somehow fallen out of the sky, Jones tentatively picked up one end of the bag and experienced a sense of horror as he realized that the contents were bending and shifting in a way that no human body should.

When they pulled back the zipper, they discovered that the bag was filled with boxes of ammo. Apparently, the crew at Bostick was unloading the bodies, then repurposing the bags and sending them straight back to Keating without stopping to consider how this might look to someone on the receiving end.

On and on it went, one chopper after another. And throughout the whole process as Koppes and Jones concentrated on their loading, Larson, Grissette, and I stood just beyond the landing zone, performing overwatch to make sure that the area was secured.

As the evening wore on, we lost track of how many sorties came and went. It was draining to still be on duty, but in some ways we were grateful for the assignment. During the intervals between one chopper and the next, the three of us were able to sit there in the darkness, thinking about all that had happened that day and talking quietly about what had gone down and what lay ahead.

The one subject to which we kept returning was revenge. We still had the better part of a year left in our deployment, and each of us seemed to draw comfort from the idea that this might offer enough time for us to pay those bastards back for what they had done to our friends.

AFTER THE LAST of the birds departed, we were finally able to stand down. Sax's two rifle companies had already taken over Keating's defensive positions so that none of us needed to stand guard. This meant that we were free to bed down for the night—although there was initially some confusion about where, exactly, we should do that.

Most of the barracks buildings had been completely destroyed, while a sizable section of Red's quarters were now serving as the new command post. So, with no better plan, each man headed off in whatever direction he thought best. A lot of the guys in Blue Platoon wound up on the café outside the aid station, where they did their best to keep warm by bundling into whatever extra clothing they could scrounge from the soldiers who hadn't lost all of their possessions and gear to the fires. Meanwhile, my guys in Red scattered. Jones racked out on a shelf in the ammo supply room, just above Koppes. Larson leaned against the outer wall of our barracks, not even bothering to remove his body armor. Raz did the same up at the mortar pit, and I ended up crashing inside our barracks on top of the small card table on which we had played countless games of spades and dominoes.

As the night deepened and the outpost settled down, one of the few places that still saw activity was the aid station, where Cordova and his medics, in an effort to prepare for a counterattack first thing in the morning, were doing their best to clean up and restock whatever supplies they might need to tend to a new flood of wounded. Thanks to the damage that had been done to the generators, there was neither electricity nor water, so they worked in the dark with their headlamps, picking up blood-soaked scraps of clothing and stuffing them into trash bags, then swabbing down the floor with Kerlix padding. They ended up smearing streaks of brownish-red blood all over the blue linoleum tiles. Illuminated in the flittering beams of their headlamps, the aid station looked as if a deranged artist had crept inside it to create a ghoulish fresco of death.

Sometime after ten p.m., Cordova, who had now been up for more than thirty-six hours, went off to bed. Soon he was followed by Floyd, Cody, and Hobbs, which left Courville all by himself, sitting in the darkened room cleaning his rifle and listening to Shinedown on his headphones until the door swung open and Bundermann walked in.

Some things never change, thought Courville. Even now, the aid station was the place where a guy came when he needed to get something off his chest.

While Courville ignited two MRE heaters and made each of them a cup of coffee, Bundermann talked about what had happened. He talked about how Blue Platoon had lost two of its members while HQ and the mortar crew had lost one each, but that it was his platoon, Red, with three dead and one still fighting for his life on an operating table in Bostick, that had been hit the hardest. He talked about how his rightful place during the battle—the place where he *always* stood for every engagement, without exception, and where he should have been that day—was out at Gallegos's gun truck in the center of the battlefield, the place with the finest visibility and vantage, where he could have seen what was going down while participating in the actual fight. He talked about how *he* should have led the counterassault to retake the ammo depot and the front gate and the Shura Building. And most of all, he talked about how truly sick he felt about holing up in the most heavily fortified building inside the wire running a bunch of radios, while fifty soldiers stood up and gave everything they had to ensure that, if it came to it, he would have been the last man to perish when what should rightly have happened, what he would have preferred, and what was his duty as the leader of his platoon, was for him to have died first.

After taking all this in, Courville did what he could to remind Bundermann of the other side of the picture: the side that everyone else saw and knew to be true, which was that Bundermann had risen to the role that had been handed to him and that he'd performed with incandescent foresight and skill; that he had done far more good inside the command post than he ever could have out on the periphery of camp, because if it hadn't been for his leadership in the command center, none of us would have made it through and all of Keating—including the room they were sitting in— would have been under the control of the Taliban.

Courville said all of that knowing that the weight of its truth meant little to his lieutenant in comparison to the far greater weight of Bundermann's conviction that he had failed to perform to the fullest measure of his calling as a leader and, in falling short of that mark, had also failed his men—men for whom he was responsible, men who were directly under his care and who were now dead.

They talked far into the night until the magnitude of Bundermann's exhaustion finally overtook his sense of guilt and self-recrimination, and he was forced to head off to get some sleep.

That left Courville once again by himself. But instead of following Bundermann's lead, he decided that he had one last thing to do, which was to pad around camp and make sure that every man in the troop had taken off his socks before going to bed so that his feet could dry out.

Courville was loath to wake anybody up, so he did his best to slip everyone's socks off while they were still asleep. Most of the guys were racked out deeply enough that they never even noticed. Indeed, a handful of them were so still that Courville found himself checking their breathing and their pulses to confirm that they were alive. But one or two sat bolt upright as soon as they realized that someone was messing with their feet.

"What the fuck are you doing?" demanded Jones.

"Just taking your socks off, Jonesie," said Courville softly. "You can't sleep with them on."

As Jones lay back, muttering to himself in confusion, it occurred to Courville how absurd it must seem to these men, after everything else that had happened since the attack broke out, for a medic to be obsessing about such a trivial detail. Courville himself wasn't truly sure why he was performing this task—except, perhaps, as part of an effort to impose a tiny return to something resembling normalcy in what had otherwise been a day of virtually uninterrupted horror.

Regardless of the reason, he kept at it, moving through the darkness and carefully placing the socks he removed next to each sleeping figure. As he worked his way through camp, he was vaguely aware that far above him, somewhere up there in the moonlit sky, there were aircraft moving about. He could hear the dull roar of jets, the sharp-edged clatter of helicopter rotors, and occasionally, the sound of something else: a metallic whir from the gun systems on Spooky, an AC-130H that was pinning down the coordinates of any handheld Taliban radio in the surrounding mountains and unleashing a burst from its 30-mm auto cannon with a chilling moan that sounded like *waaaaahhhhhhhhhh*.

Unbeknownst to Courville or anyone else on the ground at Keating, something else was afoot too.

Around one a.m., a sortie of four Chinooks loaded with 130 special forces soldiers—a combined unit of Americans and Afghans—headed from Bostick to Fritsche. There the commando team disembarked and melted into the hillsides, where they would spend the rest of that night and the next several days engaged in a cave-by-cave and village-to-village sweep looking for the men who were responsible for the attacks at Keating and Fritsche, and systematically eliminating them.

Meanwhile, the four Chinooks returned to Bostick, where a pair of them were tasked with the final mission of the battle.

When they lifted off the helipad at Bostick, they were carrying Keating's dead to Bagram, the first in a series of journeys that would eventually take Josh Kirk and Justin Gallegos, Kevin Thomson and Michael Scusa, Vernon Martin and Chris Griffin and Josh Hardt all the way to Dover Air Force Base in Delaware, where their bodies would be autopsied before being sent off to reunite with their families across the United States.

But in addition to those Chinooks, there was another helicopter that was carrying one other body—although most of the guys at Keating, including me, wouldn't hear about that until we awoke from our collective stupor.

ON THE MORNING of October 4, the sun rose at 5:51, just a few minutes later than it had come up on October 3, and for Zach Koppes, this event— the fact that the sun had actually decided to rise—was perhaps the only thing that those two mornings had in common with each other.

At the combat outpost where Koppes awoke, there was no possibility of a hot breakfast, because the chow hall was now a crumbling pile of still-glowing ash and embers. There was no anticipation that he might be able to skim through the pages of a magazine—or do anything else, for that matter—from the turret of his gun truck, because his armored Humvee had been shot to pieces. And there would be no hot shower for himself or anybody else, because there was no water in camp and because the showers, along with the latrines and the command post and the gym and pretty much everything else, had all been destroyed.

Nevertheless, Koppes did his best to rally his mood and brace for the day as he gathered his gear and prepared to head out to perform whatever duties the First Sergeant or anyone else might think up for him. And it was then that Armando Avalos, who was passing by on some task of his own, turned and remarked in the most casual way one could imagine:

"Hey, I don't know if you heard yet, but Mace didn't make it last night."

And then, as if this were just any other piece of news, Avalos kept on walking and headed outside, leaving Koppes to stand there and stare at his boots and blink hard while trying to square this information up with everything else that he'd heard about Mace prior to that very second. About how things were looking good and how the medics were feeling so positive about his chances. About how, once Mace got into the operating room, everything was going to be good because it's there, in the OR, where they can fix all your problems—and how it was the job of keeping him alive until he actually got there that was supposed to have been the hardest part. And most of all, he thought about how all of this information had enabled him, Koppes, to put his worries about Mace to rest and get some sleep in the knowledge that everything was going to be cool—and that all of this had underscored that Koppes had made absolutely the right call in opting not to say good-bye to the closest friend he'd ever had.

A moment later, Jones walked in.

"Hey, man, are you good?" he asked guardedly.

Somehow, Koppes managed to stammer out that Mace had died.

"Yeah," Jones replied gently, "I know."

Then he walked out too.

I am not going to tell you what happened to Koppes after that, not specifically, except to say that the information he was struggling to take in drove him to his knees—and that when he buckled to the floor, he stayed there for a very long time.

In some ways, Koppes still hasn't gotten up off that floor—and neither have the rest of us, because that's what Mace meant, and continues to mean, to the guys who were his friends and who had tried harder and given more to save his life than we'd ever tried or given at anything in our own lives.

Instead, I will tell you how things ended with Stephan Mace.

IT WAS JUST after nine thirty p.m. when the med team at Bostick carried Mace into surgery and put him under anesthesia. By this point, more than twelve hours had passed since he'd received his first wounds, and the effects of that delay were evident the moment that his surgeon, Major Brad Zagol, opened him up.

Zagol, who had graduated from West Point and trained at Walter Reed, could see that much of the tissue in his bowel appeared to be dead—too much time had passed without a supply of oxygen-rich blood for the cells to survive. The left side of his colon and most of his small bowel were perforated with holes, and he was bleeding internally near his right kidney.

Zagol got to work, doing his best to stop the bleeding and repair the damaged abdomen. But thirty minutes into the operation, Mace's heart stopped beating.

Zagol immediately performed CPR, which got his heart started again. But the beat was irregular and unsustained. So about forty-five minutes later, Zagol opened up the left side of Mace's chest to try and confirm that there had been no damage to the heart muscle itself. Then he gently took Mace's heart between the palms of his hands and tried to massage it back to life, a technique that rarely works but is used when there are no other options.

Not long after that, Brendan McCriskin, the flight surgeon who had helped get Mace out of Keating—and who had since been called away to a different firebase on yet another evacuation—landed back at Bostick and immediately dashed toward the aid station.

Like everyone else, McCriskin had high hopes that the surgery had gone well. In fact, he was fully expecting to pick up Mace, get him back on board his Black Hawk, and transport him straight to Bagram for advanced postop treatment. But as he pushed through the doors, McCriskin spotted an anguished and exhausted-looking Zagol leaning in a doorway across the room. His face was streaked with tears.

Choking with sorrow, Zagol told McCriskin that Mace had coded during surgery, and that once they'd lost him they couldn't get him back.

According to his official medical report, Mace died from massive blood loss resulting from multiple ballistic injuries to his torso, bowel, and adrenal gland. But those of us who fought with him at Keating know that the truth is somewhat different.

We know that Mace had willed himself to stay alive for so long—so

Stephan Mace

much longer than any ordinary person ever could have—because he wanted to be with his friends. And we knew that when he finally left Keating—when he was no longer with us, but had been told that we were okay—that he had stopped fighting and decided it was time to let go.

When Mace was pronounced dead at 10:35 that night, he brought the total number on our roster of the dead from seven to eight.

That was the butcher's bill for the defense of Combat Outpost Keating.

THE REST OF that day was pretty much a blur for all of us.

As we awoke and took in the news about Mace, we found ourselves confronting a scene of devastation and ruin that mirrored similar feelings inside each of us. Everywhere we turned lay the wreckage and the detritus of battle: burned-out skeletons of armored vehicles; heaps of charred wood and rubble where our buildings had stood; trees that had been cut down

Keating after the battle

by automatic gunfire; small, curled piles of human turds and dark, gluti-nous puddles of human blood. And in every direction, glittering layers of brass shell casings, interspersed with the bodies of dead Taliban soldiers.

There were dozens of them, the Taliban dead. One was sprawled in the middle of the open area between the Shura Building and the showers. Another was splayed out behind the latrines, and a third, who was wedged inside of a ditch just south of the mechanics' bay, must have taken a direct hit with a grenade, judging by the way his legs had been folded up over his head.

We felt no pity for these men whatsoever, and if we demonstrated any respect for them at all, it was only to take stock of how well equipped they were—the ammo in their chest racks, the tennis shoes on their feet—and to acknowledge that what they had pulled off was impressive. To stage simultaneous attacks against two fortified outposts, each of them heavily defended with American firepower and backed up by American airpower, required organization, planning, and boldness. They had clearly demonstrated all three—although they had also paid a tremendous price.

The army would later estimate that Black Knight Troop and the aircraft that supported us killed somewhere between 100 and 150 militants in the process of repulsing their assault, a casualty rate somewhere between 25 and 35 percent.

On our side of the ledger, the toll was no less gruesome. Among the fifty Americans at Keating, twenty-seven had been wounded and eight were dead. That was bad, but when you took a closer look at the numbers, it was even worse, because only about thirty of our soldiers had been actually fighting. Among those who actively participated in the defense of the outpost, our casualty rate was directly comparable to what the Taliban had suffered.

And then there were our Afghan allies. Eight of the forty-eight soldiers were wounded, three soldiers and two security guards were killed, and fifteen soldiers had simply disappeared.

We had no idea what befell those missing men, but the ones who remained inside the wire became the targets of our disgust and outright hatred. It was bad enough that most of these men had abandoned their posts and spent the entirety of the battle hiding from the fight. What made things even worse was a discovery that took place later that morning as the Afghans were preparing to board a series of helicopters that would take them to Bostick.

When they were forced to empty out their bags because of weight restrictions, a trove of energy drinks, magazines, headphones, candy bars, and digital cameras came tumbling out. Recognizing that those items belonged to us, we realized that while we were busy defending the outpost, the Afghans had been looting our barracks and stealing our belongings.

To say that we were glad to see them go would be an understatement.

While the helicopters shuttled the Afghans to safety, we turned to the first order of business, which was to secure the village of Urmul.

WHILE I TOOK a small team of guys from Red Platoon up to the Switchbacks to find a spot where we could look down on the village and perform overwatch, a five-man squad from Blue Platoon headed out the front gate, across the bridge, and directly into Urmul. When they arrived, they encountered a level of devastation that rivaled the scene inside Keating.

The place was a shambles. Most of the buildings had been completely destroyed, and those that remained standing were so pockmarked with holes that it seemed only a matter of days before they too came tumbling down. The patrol saw only four living people—a woman who was working in her field and an old man with two young boys—but the dead were everywhere.

From the evidence, it was clear that the tiny police station in the village had been attacked first off, and that the officers who survived the initial strike had been herded together and executed by the fighters who occupied the place. There were plenty of bodies clad in the brown robes of the Taliban too, many of which lay where they had died.

While the team picked through the wreckage searching for anything that might offer useful intelligence—radios, photographs, written documents—a similar assessment was unfolding back inside Keating. There, Colonel Brown and Captain Portis were methodically pacing from one end of the outpost to the other in an effort to piece together what had happened: how our defenses had collapsed, where the enemy had breached the perimeter, how much damage there was, and whether anything that remained—supplies, ammunition, gear, or armor—could be hauled away and salvaged.

As the two officers moved about camp making their assessment and debating whether what was left of the outpost should be destroyed or simply abandoned, they were shadowed by a delegation of women from the surrounding villages who had come to retrieve the bodies of the Taliban soldiers for burial.

These women were clad in *burkas*, the indigo robes that cover the female figure from head to toe, and they seemed to float above the ground like blue ghosts, silent and wraithlike as they went about the business of gathering up the dead. Meanwhile, the members of Black Knight Troop who were still in camp were conducting their own desultory effort to sift through the debris and pull out anything that seemed like it might be worth saving.

It was sometime in the early afternoon when Ryan Schulz, the sergeant with HQ Platoon who was part of our intelligence unit, emerged from the wreckage of John Deere's Haji Shop holding several of the Afghan commando T-shirts that the Afghan Army soldiers were so fond of.

"Hey," he said, walking up to Jones and offering him a shirt. "Make sure that Mace gets this, okay?"

Clearly, word about what had happened had yet to spread through the entire camp.

"Mace isn't ever gonna wear that shirt," Jones said, and walked away.

And so it went for the rest of that afternoon, all through the next day, and well into the third: extracting things from the wreckage and packing up what we could for transport until our superiors finally passed down word that it was time to get the fuck out of Keating.

FITTINGLY, WE LEFT AT NIGHT, and with every intention of blowing the place sky-high as we departed.

By the evening of October 6, a team of combat engineers that had been flown in from Bostick had packed the entire camp with explosives and wired everything together with detonation chord connected to a triggering device that could be operated from the front gate. By this point, we had salvaged whatever equipment we could and sent it out by helicopter. All that remained was us.

The Chinooks were scheduled to arrive in waves, starting well after nightfall. Captain Sax's relief force would be on the first flight out. Fifteen or twenty minutes later, the Chinooks would return to collect the members of Blue and Headquarters platoons, along with most of the medics. This would require several trips, and when it was done, the birds would come back one more time.

As usual, Red would be the last to leave.

The shuttles went like clockwork, each Chinook coming in, taking off for Bostick, and then coming back for its next load until the next-to-last flight ripped out and left about twenty of us standing together on the landing zone with just our weapons, radios, and a small supply of water.

We had stacked ourselves in a crescent formation along the west side of the landing zone, which would enable us to collapse back toward our helicopter in an orderly formation. Now that everyone else was gone, there was nothing left for us to do but sit there in silence, staring out toward the dark river in front of us and the even darker ridgelines above, and wait for our ride.

We waited for fifteen minutes, and then waited some more as we slid past twenty. It was around the twenty-five-minute mark that the doubts we'd all been wrestling with started to take hold and form words.

"They're out there," exclaimed Justin Gregory, who, as always, was the most jittery guy in the platoon—and who was now convinced that he was seeing enemy movement in the distance. "They're coming to get us, I know it."

"Dude, if you don't shut the hell up, I'm gonna knock you out right now," said Avalos, who was right next to him. "Let's just wait for the Chinook to get back and get on it, and then we'll be gone."

Avalos was right—we all knew that. But we also knew that Gregory had given voice to fears that each man was wrestling with, all of which boiled down to a question:

Are they not coming back for us?

Finally, at well past the thirty-minute mark, we heard the sound of rotors and rose to our feet with weapons raised in case the Chinook started to take incoming fire.

When the bird landed, our line began folding toward the ramp at the rear of the chopper. Nick Davidson boarded first, followed by Koppes and everyone else.

As the loading neared completion, Colonel Brown, who had remained behind with us, paused to activate the timing device, which would trigger the explosive charges in twenty minutes. Then he stepped on deck. He was followed by First Sergeant Burton, who had been waiting for Brown to board so that he could claim bragging rights as the last to leave Keating. But Burton had failed to notice the two men who had been charged with rear security—and who were still on the ground standing in the shadows at either side of the ramp.

When Burton had boarded, Brad Larson and I locked eyes to make sure that we were in sync. And then, just as we had planned it, our boots left the ground at the exact same instant so that neither of us could claim the honor of being the last man out.

We both had cigars in our pockets, which we now stuck in our mouths and chewed on.

As the Chinook lurched into the air and started on its way toward Bostick, applause broke out, punctuated by a few yells of *"Woo-hoo!"* Then everyone turned to face the back hatch in the hopes of catching sight of the final explosions. But for whatever reason—either the timing device or the explosives had malfunctioned—the blast never came. Which, in a way, was kind of a symbolically perfect fuck-you from Keating.

WE SORT of had the last word anyhow.

Later that same night, a B-1 bomber made a pass over Nuristan, opened up its doors, and dropped several tons of smart bombs on a dozen grid coordinates inside Keating. The following morning, for good measure, a second B-1 came by and dropped another load.

Those air strikes should have been enough to level the entire outpost. But the next day, when a Predator drone was sent over to survey the damage, the images revealed that several structures were still standing, and that fourteen Taliban were strolling around the camp. So two more drones were dispatched, each of which loosed a pair of Hellfire missiles.

According to army records that were later released, the insurgents who were obliterated in that final blast included Abdul Rahman Mustaghni, the commander who had led the attack on Keating.

CHAPTER TWENTY-FOUR

Trailing Fires

OUR ARRIVAL AT BOSTICK was a surreal experience not only for us but also for the soldiers who watched us emerge from the Chinook. Most of us were covered in dried blood, and aside from the weapons we toted and the clothes we wore, almost all of our possessions were gone. But each of us carried an odor on our skin and on our breath that was redolent of Keating and everything that place stood for: a stink that was composed in equal parts of rage and fear and death.

By now the Battle for Keating had made national news back in the States and it was widely reported that a bunch of us had been killed, so it was important to let our families know that we were alive. After the phone calls to our loved ones were complete, we spent the next couple of days trying to get ourselves squared away by requisitioning new uniforms and tending to our wounds.

While we went about that business, we wrestled with the memories of the men whose bodies were being autopsied inside the army's mortuary at Dover Air Force Base in Delaware. And no one felt the burden of those memories more than our platoon leader, who was still convinced that he had somehow failed us.

Needless to say, the rest of us didn't see things that way, and we did our best to drive home the message that if not for our lieutenant, it was almost certain that none of us would have made it through. With him, we'd lost eight men. Without him, we would have lost everyone.

After the battle

Despite our best efforts, none of this ever seemed to sink in to the level where Bundermann was willing to let himself off the hook. He simply didn't believe us. But when the army finally concluded its analysis of what had gone wrong and released the results during the first week of February 2010, the official report buttressed the message that we'd been trying to get across.

THE INVESTIGATION into the assault on Keating was led by Army Major General Guy Swan, who conducted interviews with 140 American soldiers and Afghan nationals who were either at the outpost or had information about the attack. Swan's report offered conclusive proof that what had gone wrong at Keating had nothing to do with anyone who fought there that day.

According to the report, after repeatedly attacking the outpost in order to gather intelligence on our battle drills, the enemy had analyzed our response patterns, then used this information to create a detailed assault plan that would exploit the weaknesses they were able to observe. They had started by targeting our generators, our mortar pit, and our gun trucks with large numbers of RPGs, and they did not begin their ground assault until they achieved decisive fire superiority. The insurgents had also positioned snipers and machine guns to cover the doors in buildings and living quarters where they had observed reinforcements exit during previous attacks.

All of this, Swann's analysis made clear, was made possible by the fact that the Taliban occupied the high ground and could see everything we did.

The investigation concluded that as the commander and senior officer at Keating from Black Knight's arrival until the September 20 change of command, Captain Melvin Porter bore the greatest responsibility for what went wrong. Among the faults for which Porter was cited, he had "rejected recommendations from senior noncommissioned officers to execute additional protective measures, including the proposed emplacement of sniper teams and other small kill teams outside the perimeter to deny the enemy key terrain." In addition, Porter had also "failed to adequately construct or reinforce defensive positions, though excess lumber and sandbags left by the previous units were available," and he had repeatedly denied requests to check, reposition, or change out claymore mines that had been emplaced by the previous unit around the perimeter of the outpost.

Finally, the report stated that Porter had neglected to close and secure "a well-known gap in the perimeter at the ANA portion of the COP—an avenue of approach that was used by AAF forces to penetrate the COP on Oct. 3."

AS WE MOVED through the days that immediately followed the battle, each of us grappled with his private feelings of loss in his own way, but we were united by one thing. Like it or not, we still had the better part of a year left in our deployment, and our jobs would not afford us the luxury of dwelling on grief or mourning the men who were no longer with us.

Aside from the handful of guys in Black Knight who were on their first deployment, we all knew the drill. Bottle your feelings inside, bury them deep, and if any of those emotions refuse to stay down, harness that energy and channel it into doing your job well until the deployment is complete and it's time to head home. Then when you're back in the States you can unlock the door to the room where all that pain has been stored and try to take stock of what it all means.

Or not.

We spent the next eight months providing security for the big military convoys that were responsible for pushing supplies north out of Jalalabad into the network of American outposts that were scattered through the valleys and ridgelines of Kunar Province. We also spent a lot of our time meeting with local Afghans in nearby villages to help provide them with roads and bridges, schools and water projects, until we received word, late in the spring of 2010, that it was time to wrap things up.

In the process of completing those duties, we suffered two more casualties. Kent Johnson, one of Red Platoon's replacement soldiers, was shot in the ass during a firefight that took place in December. Later the following spring, another replacement soldier in White Platoon was badly wounded when he was riding inside an armored vehicle that was hit by an IED. He would later wind up losing one of his legs.

Other than those two incidents, everybody made it through safely until May, when we were finally sent home.

IN APRIL OF 2011, almost a year after arriving back in the States, I ended my military career, moved my family from Colorado to North Dakota, and tried to put the army behind me by taking a job as a safety supervisor in the oil fields just outside the town of Minot. It was there, in the autumn of 2012, that I found myself sitting in the cab of a pickup truck next to an oil rig when a call arrived from a colonel who was stationed at the Pentagon. He was phoning to ask if I'd be willing to hop on a plane to DC and drop by his office.

I had no idea what this might be about, but I'd already used up my vacation time for the year, so it was another month before I could comply with the request. When I was finally able to make the trip, I was brought into a conference room and invited to join a group of colonels and generals who were sitting at a long table. It was at this point that I requested an explanation for why I was there.

"You don't know?" someone asked.

When I shook my head, they explained that after conducting an extensive review of my actions during the Battle for Keating, I was slated to receive the Medal of Honor, the highest military award the country can bestow.

It would be an understatement to say that I found this news confusing. In fact, it made no sense whatsoever. Singling me out for such a superlative commendation struck me as both inappropriate and wrong. In my view, nothing that I'd done that day was any different from what my comrades had accomplished. What's more, I could easily have picked half a dozen men—especially Gallegos, Kirk, Hardt, Mace, and Griffin—who truly deserved selection because they had given their lives in an effort to save others.

But me? No way. The idea seemed to violate my sense of what was most important—and what deserved to be commemorated—about that day.

Although I didn't know it at the time, it turns out that most Medal of Honor recipients feel exactly the same way. It also turns out that this fact has had little impact on the way that I feel about the honor that I was selected to receive—and everything else that would later unfold from it.

They picked the wrong guy.

IT WAS ANOTHER seven months before the ceremony could be scheduled, and when it finally took place at the White House on the morning of February 11, 2013, the event served as a reunion of sorts. Larson was there, along with six other surviving members of Red Platoon: Bundermann, Raz, Koppes, Jones, Avalos, and Knight.

They all found the White House a strange experience. None among them felt comfortable greeting the president, so the rest of the guys forced Jonesie to go first.

"First in, last out, dude," said Koppes, reminding Jones of his place in the hierarchy as he pushed him toward the podium.

"Nothing changes," Jones muttered, shaking his head. "When the shit hits the fan, *send in Jonesie*."

Having no idea how to address the president, Jones found himself at a loss for words as he shook hands with Barack Obama. But later that night, he'd returned to his normal state of volubility.

"The man had soft hands," he reported, which was apparently his main impression from his brief encounter with the commander in chief. "I mean, *real* soft. In fact, I don't think there's any part of my body that's that soft."

The other thing that struck Jones, along with a number of the other guys, was an unusual scent that was wafting off a woman in the audience. They all agreed that the aroma, which was heady and unmistakable, transported them directly back to Nuristan and the little Ziploc bag that once hung on the wall of Keating's aid station.

When Courville approached the woman and politely inquired what type of perfume she was wearing, we finally learned that before Maria Kirilenko, the Russian tennis star, had mailed her panties off to Afghanistan, she'd misted them with a spritz of Obsession.

AS FOR ME, most of my memories from that event are a blur, except for the things that I found truly important, and there were really only two of those.

First, I was overwhelmed by the chance to see the guys—men I hadn't connected with since we'd left Afghanistan. They are, all of them, the closest friends I will ever have. And because of that, the bond I share with them—and will always share—is bedrock: a thing that is as immutable as the Hindu Kush.

In addition to that, I was deeply moved by a group of relatives who represented seven of the eight men we had lost that day at Keating. This was my first opportunity to meet these Gold Star families and bear witness to the pain they carry—a sentiment that was expressed with perhaps the greatest force and eloquence by Vanessa Adelson, Mace's mother, in a letter she had written to the president, from which he quoted just before he presented the medal:

"'Mr. President,'" Obama said, reading from what she had written, "'you wrote me a letter telling me my son was a hero. I just wanted you to know what kind of hero he was. My son was a great soldier. As far back as I can remember, Stephan wanted to serve his country.'"

The letter, Obama explained, went on to speak of how deeply Mace had cared about us, his brothers in Black Knight Troop: how much we meant to him; how proud he was to serve alongside of us; and how he would do anything for us, including sacrificing his own life.

"'That sacrifice,'" the president concluded—still quoting from the letter—"'was driven by pure love.'"

Thirty minutes later as the ceremony wrapped up, I worked my way down the line of representatives from the Gold Star families, greeting each and giving them all hugs. At the end of the line stood Gallegos's widow, Amanda, and his young son, Mac, who I scooped up in a huge embrace.

He was just seven years old, and he and his mother had come all the way from Alaska.

ACCORDING TO the official citation that was read that day, I was directly responsible for killing more than ten enemy fighters with my machine gun and the Dragunov sniper rifle that I'd plucked from the hands of the wounded Afghan soldier who was awaiting treatment in the aid station. The report also stated that I was indirectly responsible for the elimination of more than thirty Taliban who were killed by Apache gunships and fighter jets using coordinates that I provided during the battle—and that the men I'd led in retaking the base had killed, at minimum, another five enemy soldiers.

I don't know about any of that. Such estimates are notoriously inaccurate, but the real reason I place little stock in them is that official accounts tend to possess a cleanness, a sense of order, that could not be more at odds with the reality of what unfolds during combat.

In the end, only one set of numbers means anything to me: the lives that

Medal of Honor ceremony, Washington, DC

were lost, and that might have been saved if we—if I—had acted differently. It's true that I did the best I could. What's also true is that I could have done more. In the space between those two facts reside eight graves, the memories of the men whose names are etched on the stones that mark those graves, and my own deeply mixed feelings about receiving the highest medal this country can bestow.

As for the medal itself, when I got back home, a question arose for which I didn't really have an answer:

What exactly do I do with this thing?

I don't know what most of the other recipients do, although I've asked a handful of them. A few have ordered up replacements so that they have something to wear and to show folks when they ask to see it, while they store the original in a safe-deposit box. Others keep the medal in a sock drawer or on their nightstand. As for me, I never bothered to get a duplicate and I eventually took to carrying the original around in my front pocket. As a result, it's taken several accidental trips through the washing machine, so the gilded surface is a bit tarnished, and the blue ribbon has begun to fade. But that doesn't bother me a bit. In fact, I kind of like it that way, perhaps—in part—because I don't truly regard it as mine.

Like it or not, there are eight other guys with whom I served to whom that medal rightly belongs, because heroes—true heroes, the men whose spirit the medal embodies—don't ever come home. By that definition, I'm not a true hero. Instead, I'm a custodian and a caretaker. I hold the medal, and everything it represents, on behalf of those who are its rightful owners.

That, more than anything, is the truth that now sustains me—along with one other thing too, which is a belief I hold in my heart.

I know, without a shred of doubt, that I would instantly trade that medal and everything attached to it if it would bring back even one of my missing comrades in arms.

Epilogue

IF THERE ARE SOLDIERS who miss the fury of combat, who find themselves tortured by the desire to return to its flames, I cannot number myself in their company. I have no wish ever to return to Keating or to Afghanistan, and most of my men feel the same. However, the bond that kept us together as a unit, a team, is something that I long for and continue to cherish.

It is also something that is very much alive.

Shortly after our return from Afghanistan, Zach Koppes transitioned out of the army, moved into the basement of the house in which Mace's mother lives, and put himself through college. He recently graduated and is hoping to get into local politics in Virginia.

Chris Jones followed a similar path after he left the army, although he opted to pursue a hands-on trade and is intending to become a machinist. He prefers to keep his location under wraps, but we stay in touch.

That's also the case with Thom Rasmussen, who remains one of my closest friends and companions. Upon entering civilian life, he found work in the oil fields along Colorado's Front Range, and he spends as much of his free time as possible working with a veterans' outreach group that offers a waterfowl-hunting program. He also moonlights as a duck-hunting guide around our old stomping grounds outside of Fort Carson.

Before leaving the army, Andrew Bundermann was placed in charge of a Military Entrance Processing Station in Minneapolis, where he handled new recruits. He is currently living in the Twin Cities and working for a company that manufactures some of the bombs that were dropped on the Taliban during the Battle for Keating.

As for Brad Larson, at the urging of Captain Stoney Portis, he was given a "direct-select" opportunity by General Curtis Scaparrotti to leapfrog over the normal vetting process and attend Officer Candidate School—an honor that is reserved for only the finest and most gifted rank-and-file soldiers. As a result, Larson has transitioned to the "dark side" on two counts.

As a member of the aviation branch of the Nebraska National Guard, he is no longer an enlisted soldier, and his boots aren't on the ground anymore. Instead, First Lieutenant Larson is currently completing yet another overseas deployment as the pilot of a Chinook helicopter.

Me and the rest of the guys worry about him staying safe. But we're even more concerned that he doesn't lose his perspective and forget where he came from—which is why we're toying with the notion of logging on to PoopSenders.com and ordering a consignment of elephant dung to be delivered to the base where he's stationed.

For the moment, we're holding off on placing that order, because the signals we've been getting from Larson are reassuring. Just before he deployed, he told me that he's refusing to follow the model of a West Point ring-knocker. Instead, he wants to be a leader just like Bundermann.

As for the men of Black Knight who served in Blue and White Platoons, they are a bit more distant and I hear from most of them only occasionally—although much of the news is good.

Eric Harder and Shane Courville are still in the army and continuing to serve. Jonathan Hill got out, but has been doing some tremendous work helping veterans deal with PTSD and integrate back into the workforce. And Daniel Rodriguez fulfilled a promise he made to Kevin Thomson, his closest friend at Keating, that he would try his best to fulfill a dream he had of one day playing professional football. He made it to Clemson, then was drafted by the Redskins and eventually traded to the Saint Louis Rams.

And so it goes. We all do our best to stay in touch because we are welded together, and will remain so for the rest of our lives. We are united by the memory of battle, but our lives are also joined and consecrated by the knowledge that the eight men who lost their lives are with us still, because we carry them in our hearts.

They will never leave us.

In Memoriam

Sergeant Justin Gallegos, Team Leader

Specialist Chris Griffin, Scout

Sergeant Josh Hardt, Team Leader

Sergeant Josh Kirk, Team Leader

Specialist Stephan Mace, Scout

Sergeant Vernon Martin, Chief Mechanic

Specialist Michael Scusa, Scout

Private First Class Kevin Thomson, Mortarman

Notes on Sources

AT SOME POINT long after the shooting is over, almost every soldier who has survived combat feels himself caught between two conflicting impulses.

On the one hand, there is the instinct to remain silent. Language is an imperfect tool, and anyone who has been through combat understands that words are incapable of conveying the real horror of battle. This is why the deepest truths of war can never be spoken, only understood, by men who have touched it and been touched by it.

On the other hand, there remains the uneasy awareness that without language, without words, the experience of war and everything it entails—including the sacrifices made by both the living and the dead—can neither be preserved nor communicated to others.

Somewhere between those two opposing truths lies a special zone, a kind of DMZ in which soldiers do what we have always done. In the absence of anything better, we tell one another stories, and we do so with the knowledge that while our stories may not be perfect, they are the closest we will ever come to transmitting a sense, and preserving the memory, of what we endured.

The Battle for COP Keating was covered extensively by the American press, both in print and on television, in the days and weeks that followed the attack. Three years later, the journalist Jake Tapper published *The Outpost*, a book that investigated both the decision to establish Keating and the reasons why the army continued to maintain the firebase in the face of such immense tactical and strategic challenges.

Tapper's research was conducted with painstaking care. But the one thing that he could not do was to produce a chronicle of what unfolded during that final battle—an hour-by-hour account of the actions of the living, as well as roll call of the dead—in the words of someone who was there at the time and who participated directly in the fight. That is a thing that could come only from one of our own. And although I'm often described as a man of few words, this description is a thing whose importance and urgency has only seemed to grow with the passage of time.

During the past two years, I conducted multiple trips across the United States in order to meet directly with key members of Black Knight Troop with whom I served at Keating, record their recollections of the battle, and then juxtapose those recollections against my own notes and memories of what unfolded that day. I also combed through hundreds of pages of eyewitness testimony, radio transcripts, and other materials that were amassed by General Swan in his official report.

This book is the result of that labor, and while it is not intended to serve as an absolutely definitive account of the battle, I have done my best to accurately represent the events that I and the people I was closest to—the men of Red Platoon—either participated in or witnessed.

I would like to make it clear that this is a work of nonfiction. Everything in quotation marks was said to me or by me, is part of an official transcript, or was later recounted to me directly by the person who is quoted. In instances where a man's thoughts are laid out, those thoughts were shared with me by the soldier himself, and the text is set forth in italics.

Although I entered into this project with some reluctance and hesitation, my sense of conviction burgeoned with each passing month. Eventually, I came to believe that telling this story—*our* story—was the only way to properly honor what we had done. Odd as it may sound, I also came to believe that this might enable me to fulfill the final part of my duty to those of my comrades from Keating who did not survive.

It was the only way for me to bring them home.

Acknowledgments

I OWE A DEBT OF THANKS that can never fully be repaid to each and every member of Red Platoon, as well as to the men with whom I fought most closely during the Battle for COP Keating: Andrew Bundermann, Brad Larson, Shane Courville, Matthew Miller, Mark Dulaney, Christopher Jones, Zachary Koppes, and James Stanley. I am also deeply grateful to Armando Avalos, Damien Grissette, and Kellen Kahn, along with the rest of the men in Black Knight Troop, especially those who served in Blue, White, Headquarters, and Mortar Platoons.

To the helicopter pilots of the 7th Squadron, 17th Cavalry Regiment of the 101st Airborne Division, including Ross Lewallen, Chad Bardwell, Randy Huff, and Chris Wright, and to the pilots of the fighter jets and other aircraft who supported Keating—especially Michal Polidor, Aaron Dove, and Justin Kulish—those of us on the ground never even knew most of your names, but we are alive today because of your skills and your courage. Thank you.

I am grateful to the men of Chosin Company, 1-32 Infantry, who were led by Justin Sax and who formed the QRF that relieved COP Keating. I would also like to thank our brigade's medical staff, including Chris Cordova, Cody Floyd, Jeffery Hobbs, and the entire medical team at Bostick.

During the course of putting this book together, many people were kind enough to sit down for extensive interviews in which they shared their insights and memories. I appreciate everyone who was part of this group, including Vanessa Adelson, Jimmy Blackmon, James Clark, Eric Harder, Brendan McCriskin, Jake Miraldi, and Stoney Portis.

I would like to thank everyone at Dutton and Penguin Random House, especially Ben Sevier, Christine Ball, Amanda Walker, Carrie Swetonic, and Paul Deykerhoff. I am indebted to my agent, Jennifer Joel, as well as Madeleine Osborn, Sharon Green, Josie Freedman, and the rest of the team at ICM. And I'm grateful to the writer Kevin Fedarko for helping me find a way to tell this story.

Finally, I would like to express my deepest thanks and extend my most profound condolences to the families of Justin Gallegos, Chris Griffin, Josh Hardt, Josh Kirk, Stephan Mace, Vernon Martin, Michael Scusa, and Kevin Thomson. You bear the heaviest burden of all.

About the Author

Former Staff Sergeant Clinton L. Romesha enlisted in the army in 1999. He deployed twice to Iraq in support of Operation Iraqi Freedom, and once to Afghanistan in support of Operation Enduring Freedom. At the time of the attack on Combat Outpost (COP) Keating on October 3, 2009, Staff Sergeant Romesha was assigned as a section leader for Bravo Troop, 3-61st Cavalry, 4th Brigade Combat Team, 4th Infantry Division. He is the recipient of numerous awards and decorations, including the Medal of Honor. Romesha separated from the army in 2011. He lives with his family in North Dakota.